WINNING THE NATIONAL SECURITY AI COMPETITION

A PRACTICAL GUIDE FOR GOVERNMENT AND INDUSTRY LEADERS

Chris Whitlock
Frank Strickland

Foreword by the Honorable Robert Work

Apress®

Winning the National Security AI Competition: A Practical Guide for Government and Industry Leaders

Chris Whitlock
Colorado Springs, CO, USA

Frank Strickland
Centreville, VA, USA

ISBN-13 (pbk): 978-1-4842-8813-9
https://doi.org/10.1007/978-1-4842-8814-6

ISBN-13 (electronic): 978-1-4842-8814-6

Managing Director, Apress Media LLC: Welmoed Spahr
Acquisitions Editor: Susan McDermott
Development Editor: James Markham
Coordinating Editor: Jessica Vakili
Copy Editor: Kezia Endsley

Distributed to the book trade worldwide by Springer Science+Business Media New York, 1 New York Plaza, New York, NY 100043. Phone 1-800-SPRINGER, fax (201) 348-4505, e-mail orders-ny@springer-sbm.com, or visit www.springeronline.com. Apress Media, LLC is a California LLC and the sole member (owner) is Springer Science + Business Media Finance Inc (SSBM Finance Inc). SSBM Finance Inc is a **Delaware** corporation.

For information on translations, please e-mail booktranslations@springernature.com; for reprint, paperback, or audio rights, please e-mail bookpermissions@springernature.com.

Apress titles may be purchased in bulk for academic, corporate, or promotional use. eBook versions and licenses are also available for most titles. For more information, reference our Print and eBook Bulk Sales web page at http://www.apress.com/bulk-sales.

Printed on acid-free paper

Contents

About the Authors

Chris Whitlock is the co-founder of aiLeaders LLC, a firm dedicated to equipping national security leaders to win the global AI competition. He spent the majority of his 40-year career providing advanced analytics, AI, and management consulting services primarily to national security clients in the Department of Defense, Intelligence Community, and Department of State. Chris helped pioneer the rapid prototyping and integration of advanced algorithms with software applications starting in the early 1990s. In the past 10 years, Chris' work has focused on machine learning and artificial intelligence applications. He led a large market offering in Deloitte Consulting focused on Mission Analytics and AI in addition to leading large programs for cabinet-level departments and agencies.

Chris co-founded an analytics company, Edge Consulting, personally leading the development of algorithmic approaches to quantify the value of intelligence. After an acquisition by IBM, he served as a partner in IBM. Chris also was a leader in Booz Allen Hamilton, focusing on analytics and strategic change. Prior to consulting, Chris served as a military analyst with the Central Intelligence Agency and as an Army infantry officer.

Frank Strickland is the co-founder of aiLeaders LLC, a firm dedicated to equipping national security leaders to win the global AI competition. During 22 years of government service, Frank helped lead innovations including evaluating and transitioning to production the nation's first long-endurance unmanned aerial system, delivering intelligence to the tactical edge using narrow- and wide-band technologies, and agile prototyping of big data analytics. The Director of Central Intelligence awarded Frank the National Intelligence Medal of Achievement in recognition of these accomplishments. Frank was also the National Reconnaissance Office's (NRO) Legislative Director and a member of CIA's Senior Intelligence Service, where he received the NRO's Medals of Distinguished and Superior Service.

In the private sector, Frank co-founded Edge Consulting and helped lead Edge's growth resulting in an acquisition by IBM. As a partner in IBM and subsequently Deloitte, Frank led large practices providing AI and analytics solutions and services to national security clients, including innovations in massive-scale property graphs and agent-based simulation. Frank began his career as a US Marine.

Advance Praise

"America and liberal democracy are under attack from enemies foreign and domestic. AI can give American intelligence and all instruments of national security a winning edge. Chris and Frank—who are exceptionally well qualified in this field—have given leaders throughout the national security enterprise the principles and practices necessary to realize that edge."

—General (retired) Michael Hayden, former Director of CIA and Director of NSA

"The National Security Commission on AI highlights the critical importance of fully integrating AI throughout the U.S. Department of Defense. The scope and scale of this mission-critical challenge requires qualified leaders who can drive systemic action throughout the national security enterprise. I have been fortunate to personally observe Chris and Frank leading AI programs and projects, and know of their excellence in equipping diverse leaders in both government and industry so they can bring the best of AI to the fight. This book is a timely and practical guide to meeting this nationally significant opportunity."

—Heather Reilly, Principal,
Deloitte Consulting LLP

"An essential primer on the all-important domain of artificial intelligence—and an intensely practical handbook on how to understand and implement it. The authors leverage their peerless, and hard-earned, experience and expertise to provide insights and advice invaluable to both AI novices and data professionals in business or government."

—General (retired) Stan McChrystal,
former Commander Joint Special Operations Command

"Effectively using data for delegated decision making by humans and machines at scale is an imperative for mission success. Leaders must reform recalcitrant bureaucracies so they can embrace an AI-enabled future. The authors' scar tissue of experience establishes a practical framework to accelerate breakthrough change in the humans and systems we manage."

—Honorable Jeffrey K. Harris,
former Director National Reconnaissance Office

"Winning the National Security AI Competition provides an intelligent framework and foundation for realizing the urgently needed benefits of Artificial Intelligence. Future operational successes will be achievable because dedicated leaders applied the principles found in this book."

—Doug Wolfe, former CIA CIO and
Associate Deputy Director for Science and Technology

"Vladmir Putin may have been right when he said that whoever becomes the leader in AI will be the ruler of the world. The authors fully grasp the power of AI, but they provide something far more valuable—a practitioner's guide to harvesting this power. Chris and Frank mine their extensive experience in program acquisition and resource management to shepherd AI technical experts through the bureaucratic labyrinth they will face in implementing their programs."

—Bryan Smith, former Budget Director,
House Permanent Select Committee on Intelligence

"Leaders across the Special Operations community readily acknowledge that data-centric approaches and artificial intelligence will play increasingly significant, perhaps even dominant, operational roles in the future security environment. The challenge for many leaders is moving from a general level of understanding to a practical, execution level. Drawing from their decades of experience in the field, Frank and Chris have written the definitive AI leader's guide for those in the national security community. In Army parlance, this is the Ranger Handbook for AI implementation!"

—LTG (retired) Ken Tovo, former Commanding General,
US Army Special Operations

"This book does yeoman's work in breaking down the key challenges that leaders looking to move beyond the proof of concept and achieve real outcomes must face. Bringing many of the concepts of the data-centric AI movement into the national security paradigm establishes an effective framework for both AI practitioners and organizational leaders to build a common understanding."

—Jim Robesco, PhD, Co-founder and CEO Striveworks

Acknowledgments

While this work is our own and responsibility for any errors is ours alone, we are thankful for the many national security leaders and clients who have poured into our lives and careers—too many to mention by name. Our careers also benefited from working with hundreds of advanced analytics and AI practitioners and leaders from whom we have learned much. You know who you are. We appreciate you.

We especially thank several long-term colleagues for giving us the benefit of their insights on the first draft of this book. Mike Greene and Steve Hardy are executive AI leaders in Deloitte Consulting. Both have a unique level of not only data science mastery, but also complex AI solutions development and delivery that has improved the entire book. Keith McCarron, a senior leader with IBM, and Vaden Ball, a senior leader in Deloitte Consulting, are expert data scientists with years of experience in the practical application of technology. Dave Thomas, a Principal in Deloitte Consulting, lent his expertise as a computer engineer and architect of several successful big distributed systems to ensure that we correctly highlighted key technology points. Chris Grubb, a data science leader in Systems Planning and Analysis, is tremendously thoughtful and experienced in the application of advanced quantitative methods to a range of problems. These four sharpened the more technical elements of the book. Tom Fox, a co-founder of Augr, LLC, brought excellent domain knowledge in defense and intelligence and the perspectives of the readers who are not data scientists. Todd Johnston, an executive leader with Deloitte Consulting, has a remarkable blend of experience in several national security missions and leadership of hundreds of advanced analytics and AI projects. His strategic insight helped us make a major structural improvement to the book.

We thank these and many other advanced analytics and AI leaders for helping us learn and grow over the years.

Foreword

by the
Honorable Robert O. Work

When I first reviewed this book, I told Chris and Frank that in my view the book's content addresses a strategic need—the development of AI leaders across the national security enterprise—at just the right time. Let me explain why.

Years before military forces meet in battle, there is a period in which those militaries develop capabilities. Military capabilities encompass not just weapons and support systems, but also the mental preparation—the thinking and learning that goes into operational concepts of employing the force to win and tactics for engaging and defeating an adversary in battle. For the United States and other liberal democracies around the world, these periods of preparation for war are foremost designed to deter adversaries so that war never begins. When an adversary refuses to be deterred, however, the U.S. military must be prepared to fight and win.

Beyond the immutable characteristics of war—such as the friction and uncertainty that always accompanies war—global military powers try to anticipate the changing nature of future conflicts and develop forces and capabilities most aligned with it. In doing so, these powers observe what other militaries are doing—especially those of their adversaries—and factor an adversary's development of capabilities into the design and development of their own. Like war itself, these periods involve a series of moves and countermoves between the developing forces. I will illustrate this with the most prominent example since the advent of nuclear weapons that has created the current imperative for artificial intelligence (AI) in U.S. national security capabilities.

In January 1991, during Operation Desert Storm—"the first Gulf War," a U.S. led coalition force defeated the fourth largest army in the world at that time in just 100 hours of ground combat. There were necessarily several significant contributing factors to such a stunning victory: a broad-based coalition of 35 countries including several Arab nations; superior logistics supplying a massive naval, air, and land force; and the soldiers and other warriors who magnificently executed the campaign and supporting battles. However, one principal contributing reason for the coalition's decisive victory the formation of a "battle network" that could sense the entire theater of operations and promptly apply precision effects against Iraqi targets whenever and wherever they were found.

Less than a decade before Operation Desert Storm, and after watching the United States demonstrate the ability to "look deep, shoot deep, and kill deep" in a large-scale exercise, Soviet military thinkers concluded that "reconnaissance strike complexes" employing conventional guided munitions could achieve battlefield effects similar to those of tactical nuclear weapons. These complexes were an integration of three capabilities: sensors that could "see" not only the front but deep into an enemy's rear area; long-range guided munitions that could accurately destroy targets throughout the battlespace; and a command and control network that could link the two together.

The U.S. military operationalized and demonstrated the power of guided munition-battle network warfare (e.g., reconnaissance strike complexes) in Desert Storm. Even though guided munitions made up less than ten percent of all munitions expended during the campaign, other nations' military forces took note of this transformation in warfare, especially the military arm of the Chinese Communist Party (CCP), the People's Liberation Army (PLA).

By 1999, the PLA began a series of capability developments to counter the United States' first mover advantage in guided munition-battle network warfare. Some of these came in the form of advanced munitions capable of hypersonic speeds. Additionally, by developing a chain of maritime bases on artificial islands, as well as islands they have annexed, the PLA has created favorable positioning for its forces well into international waters. A third development—one squarely targeting U.S. strength—is expressed in this statement: "The PLA now characterizes and understands modern warfare as a confrontation between opposing operational systems [作战体系] rather than merely opposing armies." Elements of what the PLA defines as its concept for "systems destruction warfare" are also being pursued by other hostile nations' investments in capabilities such as electronic warfare, counter-space, and cyber weapons.

Over the course of the last two decades, as the United States was focused on waging a global war on terrorism, the PLA and other competitors like the Russian military began to close the gap in guided munition-battle network warfare, to the point they were coming uncomfortably close to achieving rough military-technical parity with the U.S. military. Accordingly, in 2014, the Secretary of Defense tasked the Defense Science Board (DSB) to study how the U.S. military could restore and expand the Joint force's conventional military advantage in light of adversaries' capability developments.

The DSB concluded that DoD "must take immediate action to accelerate its exploitation of autonomy [fueled by AI], while also preparing to counter autonomy deployed by adversaries." The DSB believed AI-enabled autonomous systems' would:

- Reduce the number of warfighters in harm's way
- Increase the quality and speed of decisions in time-critical operations

- Enable new missions that would otherwise be impossible

- Help to restore conventional overmatch and thereby strengthen conventional deterrence

With some AI and autonomous initiatives already underway, DoD focused additional attention on AI with the creation of a Joint AI Center (JAIC), a Chief Data Officer (CDO), investment in cloud computing, and other priorities driven at the SECDEF/Deputy Secretary of Defense (DSD) level. Congress magnified the focus and urgency by creating a National Security Commission on AI in 2018. Former Google CEO, Eric Schmidt, and I co-chaired the NSCAI, working with 13 outstanding commissioners with relevant backgrounds in industry, government, and academe. Our full report is found at www.nscai.gov. Congress has already begun implementing many of the report's recommendations in legislation.

Upon her swearing in as the DSD, the Honorable Kathleen "Kath" Hicks, saw the need to leverage these initial activities while increasing the scale and pace of DoD's use of AI and related technologies. She rationalized several disparate organizations under a new Chief Digital and AI Officer (CDAO) position, hiring an industry executive with substantial AI experience as the first CDAO.

Now is the time for DoD and all national security departments and agencies to advance the development of AI-enabled operational concepts and solutions at enterprise scale. The complexity and uncertainty of the global security environment, compounded by the capability developments autocratic regimes have driven over the past two decades, demand urgent action at global scale by U.S. national security leaders and our allies. Thanks to billions of dollars in commercial investment across all industries, AI and related technologies are well beyond research and are now in the engineering and production realms.

In my judgment, the United States is ahead of China and other competitors in AI and autonomous systems research. However, the lead is fragile and the U.S. government lags in putting these technologies into production systems. DoD and other U.S. national security players must now focus on integrating and deploying solutions into operations. If Congress and the Administration continue to provide the resources and support—as they are doing at this time—then I believe that rapidly increasing the number of qualified AI leaders may be the key factor in driving production at the scale and pace required.

Thus, this book addresses a strategic need in that it is a practical guide for leading AI programs and projects. From what I have read and seen as the NSCAI Co-Chairman, this book uniquely equips government and industry leaders to drive improved mission results using AI. Within DoD and other elements of the national security enterprise, we have large numbers of technically qualified leaders and staff. I believe these personnel need insights and best practices on how to specifically apply AI to large-scale solutions. As a career operator and leader in national security—specifically defense—I cannot say for certain, but I believe the content of this book will help leaders in all government sectors successfully apply AI to their missions.

My thoughts here reflect what I believe is the relevance of this book's content to a national imperative. I am also motivated by my personal knowledge of Chris' and Frank's experience. I first met these two shortly after Operation Desert Storm in the National Reconnaissance Office (NRO), where they had been helping drive the development of advanced algorithms and analytics solutions for some time. I have observed their impact over the years, such as their quantification of full motion video's impact on counterinsurgency and counterterrorism and have always been impressed with their implementation and leadership of advanced analytics and AI.

Chris and Frank are not newcomers to this field. They have been leading advanced analytics and AI at the project, program, and senior executive levels for 30 years. What they share in this book is a result of their hard-earned practical experience.

This book is not the last word on leading AI in the national security enterprise, but I believe it is an essential starting point. I commend it to all government and industry leaders—especially those in national security—who seek to drive improved mission and business results using AI.

Introduction

We first met in early 1991 while working in a highly secure yet non-descript World War II era facility at the Naval Research Laboratory. The building's bland façade was appropriate as it contained a covert or "black" intelligence program. The System Program Office (SPO) that occupied the building was responsible for the research, development, and operation of a satellite reconnaissance system. After a short stint as an enlisted Marine, Frank joined the program as a government civilian in 1984. Chris came to the program in 1991 as a Booz Allen Hamilton contractor, having served as an imagery and all source analyst at CIA and as an infantry officer in the Army Reserve.

Code named "Classic Wizard" within the Navy, the satellites collected, processed, and reported what was then large volumes of data every day on the location and characteristics of radars and some communications emitters around the world. "Processed"—the term we used back in the day—meant applying algorithms to the raw sensor data. The U.S. military, especially the Navy, relied on the data for everything from characterizing Soviet military capabilities to warning of an attack. So reliant was the U.S. Navy—and so good was the program's cover story for a time—that when asked about his need for space systems, a fleet commander said: "I don't need space; I have Classic Wizard."

If you have seen the movie, The Hunt for Red October—based on Tom Clancy's book by the same title—you have a sense for the Intelligence Community's mission to warn of attacks. Red October, a Soviet nuclear ballistic missile submarine, was equipped with a first-of-its-kind technology—a propulsion system that enabled the submarine to elude detection by running virtually silent underwater. As Soviet Captain Ramius explains to CIA analyst Jack Ryan in the movie, "Well, there are those who believe that we should attack the United States first. Settle everything in one moment. Red October was built for that purpose."

Red October was fictional, but the Soviet Union's ability to deploy its nuclear naval forces while evading detection by U.S. intelligence capabilities was quite real. In the 1980s, the Soviet navy did just that. They put most of their naval forces to sea—unreported by U.S. intelligence—and thus were able to potentially deliver a devastating first strike on the United States without prior warning to the President and U.S. military.

James E. "Jim" Morgan was, at the time, the SPO division chief responsible for the solutions (algorithms, processing, communications) that turned what the satellites sensed into intelligence reports. Morgan began his career as an enlisted Marine, then became a Navy officer in the early days of Classic Wizard. At the time of the Soviet force generation exercise, Morgan had retired from the Navy officer corps and was a senior Department of the Navy civilian. He brought the passion of a Marine and the experience of someone who had been deploying algorithms for over two decades.

Morgan was incensed by the SPO's failure to warn of the Soviet exercise. In ways that probably would not be acceptable in today's workplace, Morgan made it clear to his team that such a failure would never happen again. Decades before agile software development, data science methods, and technologies prevalent today, Morgan created a center combining experts in data, algorithms, software, intelligence, and naval operations. This Product Development and Exploitation Center (PDEC) created dozens of breakthroughs in intelligence reporting from raw data and deployed hundreds of advanced analytics systems worldwide.

This effort to systematically derive insights from data collected by reconnaissance satellites became part of a larger national effort, instantiated in law by Congress, called the "Tactical Exploitation of National Capabilities" (TENCAP) Program. TENCAP programs funded the creation of communications systems to distribute the data down to the tactical level and software applications to exploit the data for tactical missions as well as the associated training, education, and exercise support to help tactical commanders and operators "train the way they will fight."

We grew up in this environment over the 1980s and 1990s. The national space capabilities were exciting, highly capable against multiple intelligence requirements, and novel for most in the military and the national security enterprise. These systems also produced what, at that time, were massive volumes of diverse types of data: multiple types of image data, structured text and parametric data, and semi-structured to unstructured text data.

This mission and culture taught us the work required to create insights from large volumes of data by applying advanced algorithms and software to the data, and integrating those insights into commanders' and operators' decisions and actions. We learned firsthand how to drive results from these programs and projects by working alongside amazing quantitative analysts, software engineers, and operators with deep mission experience. We also learned by observing some the best leaders in the field—Morgan chief among them.

In 2004, we took a loan from Frank's father-in-law, LTG (retired) Julius Becton, Jr., and co-founded an analytics start-up, Edge Consulting. Edge, as the company was fondly known by its clients and employees, would pioneer the use of data, algorithms, and software to quantitatively assess the performance and impact of intelligence capabilities. After selling Edge Consulting and becoming part of IBM, we led analytics and AI work for IBM's national security clients. Then, we joined Deloitte Consulting, where we formed a business unit focused on applying AI and analytics to national security missions and select agencies in the civilian government. We experienced and led a wide range of AI-related projects across a variety of mission tasks working day-to-day with government leaders to craft solutions and answer critical questions. These successes as entrepreneurs and executives in large global analytics and AI businesses added depth and breadth to our experience in Jim Morgan's PDEC.

Consequently, we bring a very practical perspective to generating results with AI-related solutions. We focus on how to get work done and deliver results. We are neither extravagant promoters nor excessive detractors of AI. We are—like most of you reading this book—passionately interested in improving the performance and impact of government missions by leveraging AI, especially in national security. From over three decades of experience in the field—having successfully led the delivery of hundreds of programs and projects as well as the development of several break-through capabilities—we know firsthand that advanced analytics and AI can be used for strategic effects in mission performance and impact.

The Three Imperatives to Develop AI Leaders

"*[Artificial Intelligence] will literally affect every operation, mission that we do. And it's going to require a different way of training and educating our commanders and our people.*"

—Former Deputy Secretary of Defense, Robert Work, 2021

© Chris Whitlock, Frank Strickland 2023
C. Whitlock and F. Strickland, *Winning the National Security AI Competition*,
https://doi.org/10.1007/978-1-4842-8814-6_1

"Senior leaders championing AI adoption and workforce development are essential, yet their understanding and appreciation of AI is highly inconsistent and support often ends when that leader rotates out."

Georgetown University's Center for Security and Emerging Technology & MITRE, 2021

"Field grade officers need to learn how Artificial Intelligence and Machine Learning (AI/ML) work in order to use, advise, and lead AI/ML development and procurement efforts."

—Kurt Degerlund, The Field Grade Leader, 2020

Summary

Major technological innovations initially create tension between wild-eyed enthusiasts and hard-nosed skeptics. Roughly 15 years after the NRO and U.S. military began innovations to apply space-based intelligence data to military operations through the TENCAP program, the U.S. military executed Operation Desert Storm in Iraq. After the war, government studies evaluated the performance of many systems, including satellite reconnaissance systems. A theme emerged: *military users' expectations often far exceeded what they experienced in operations.* We took a two-fold lesson that has heavily shaped how we lead advanced analytics and AI: 1) Capabilities that are poorly contextualized to actual mission tasks are prone to conceptual hype and over-inflated expectations; and 2) Conversely, lack of imagination impedes the development of breakthrough applications using advanced technology.

We believe AI presents a similar challenge to today's government and industry leaders. Those who let enthusiasm get ahead of practice can unintentionally whip up frothy concepts of a wonderful new world that is well over the horizon. Some of these idealists can ignore the hard choices as well as the time and effort it takes to bring about major results through AI. Those who are overly skeptical—if not outright cynical—about what they see as "AI hype" can mistakenly prevent breakthrough concepts from being developed. Thus, they can delay the potentially transformative power of AI at the scale and pace required.

We believe that developing qualified AI leaders throughout the enterprise is the key to managing this tension and, more importantly, winning the national security AI competition. Before asking you, the reader, to consider seven chapters of best practices for leading AI, we the authors should make the case for why we wrote the book and why we encourage you to read and apply it. We believe that three imperatives make that case: the mission needs imperative; the AI imperative; and the AI leader imperative.

Imperative #1: Mission Needs

When a new development seeming to hold tremendous potential emerges onto the scene, it is natural for some to hype the potential. Buzzwords and phrases bubble up to communicate lofty concepts about the thing. AI certainly fits this pattern. Statements like "data is the new oil" become ingredients in a conceptual casserole that causes many serious leaders to feel a bit nauseous or discreetly roll their eyes. Having spent our careers in high-tech systems, we are no friends of Luddites[1]; technology haters. However, we can understand how some leaders can become jaded amid the hype.

Without data, there is no AI. Data is the essential ingredient for AI solutions and much of the serious discussion about AI centers on problems with data. This is logical, as the field of AI is technically about the application of math, software, and computing to data. Moreover, as every AI practitioner and most leaders know, data is problematic. In the wild, the problem with data manifests in five "Ns". Data is often: N-accessible; N-correct; N-complete; N-consistent; and in the world of cyber warfare, can be N-authentic.

The mission task must be the starting point, despite all the necessary discussion of data and AI solutions. Data problems and other elements of creating a deployable AI solution are major problems to be solved, which we address in this book. However, the first and foremost imperative for AI solutions is not data nor any other component of the AI solution stack. Mission need is the first imperative. AI is an important means, but it is a means not an end. Mission impact is the end.

By "mission," we mean the reasons for a government department's existence. The U.S. national security enterprise—which we define as the Departments of State, Defense, Homeland Security, Justice (portions thereof), and the Intelligence Community—exists to create the capabilities and conduct the operations that protect Americans and advance American interests around the world. The diligence of these departments and agencies in executing their missions can deter major conflicts and effectively respond when crises emerge. Each department and agency depends on a set of mission-enabling functions, including human capital, finance, facilities, and other "back office" functions.

---

[1] In the 19th Century, *Luddites* were textile workers in England who expressed their opposition to the increasing use of machines in textile factories by acts of sabotage.

The missions within this enterprise are staggering in scope. As you are reading this book, consider that the following subset of national security missions are underway:

- Federal Bureau of Investigation (FBI) agents are trying to identify and arrest a few thousand spies—hidden in plain sight among 330 million people in the United States—spies who are stealing American companies' intellectual property among other things.

- Customs and Border Protection agents are responsible for 3,500 miles of U.S. land border plus 328 sea and airports of entry, inspecting and allowing approved cargo and people to cross into the United States while identifying and detaining illicit cargo and people.

- The Department of Defense (DoD) is conducting operations and preparations to deal with a revanchist Russia, hegemonic China, nuclear armed North Korea, violent extremists supported by Iran and other terrorism sponsors, and regional instabilities in every corner of the world, among other global missions.

- Foreign service professionals from the Department of State are on the ground in nearly 200 countries seeking to advance American interests in each country, its region, and the world overall through diplomacy.

- The U.S. Intelligence Community is charged with providing the President and all customers in the national security enterprise with knowledge and insights on the world as well as conducting covert operations by direction of the President.

In supporting these missions with AI, every mission customer and AI leader must address questions such as:

- What question(s) does the customer need answered for this mission?

- How does the answer(s) integrate into the customer's decision cycle and action flow?

- How much of an effect might the answer(s) have on mission performance and impact?

- What is the cost of getting the answer(s)?

In parallel with conducting operations around the world, national security departments and agencies are also investing in and developing the capabilities they believe are necessary for future operations. This macro problem invokes questions such as:

- What is the customer's operational shortfall or risk in this scenario?

- What type of AI solution might address the shortfall, mitigate the risk, and/or create an advantage for the customer?

- How much gain in mission impact might be achieved by the AI solution?

- What is the cost of realizing the potential gain?

AI algorithms and autonomous systems have the potential to deliver gains in sense-making (making sense of data), decision-making, and action-taking in national security missions. Secretary Work outlined this in the Foreword, and the NSCAI report provides 800-pages of detail. Other global powers are working to leverage AI for policies contrary to a liberal democratic order. However, hard choices are required to isolate where and what type of AI will benefit a given mission over others, and hard work is required to deliver the AI solutions and realize mission results.

▥ **The National Security Commission on AI (NSCAI)**   The Fiscal Year 2019 National Defense Authorization Act commissioned the NSCAI with creating a "strategy for winning the AI era." The commission iteratively issued its recommendations, helping Congress instantiate approved recommendations into ongoing legislation.

Imperative #2: AI and Autonomous Systems

History records a long progression of people using data, math, and devices to better understand their world and its activities. Monks and other learned people of the 14th century used a machine—albeit a mechanical one—plus data and math to make predictions, such as the times of planetary movements. In WWII, U.S. Navy vessels introduced automated fire control systems to direct gunfire in naval engagements. Over the past 40 years, combinations of advanced sensors with algorithms running on fast computers, leveraging temporal and spatial positioning data provided by systems such as the Global Positioning System, have enabled U.S. forces to rapidly identify and target hostile combatants. Throughout this history, a fundamental combination of data + math + machines is apparent.

While AI is simply adding another chapter in this progression, we believe that six areas of technical innovation demonstrate that an AI era is much more than hype. At the highest end, the AI era opens pathways to fully autonomous systems; that is, machines capable of sense-making, decision-making, and action-taking independent of human interaction. However, these six areas of innovation combine to create a wide range of opportunities to improve the national security enterprise other than fully autonomous systems.

Data. The operations cycles for every national security mission begin by making sense of data; this may be for surveillance, to operate an exquisite supply chain, to orchestrate complex movements, or operate combat capabilities. People do not draw inferences from a vacuum; they need data. And the current era is fundamentally different in terms of the types and volumes of data available. Rather than cite some estimate of how many bytes of data are being created per unit time in a given geography, let's drop below the clouds a bit to consider an operational factor that characterizes the world's data.

- Ubiquitous technical surveillance (UTS): UTS is a term within the Intelligence Community (IC) to state the ubiquity of technical sensors—phones, camera, satellites, others—around the world, all of which are producing data on human and machine behaviors as well as the environments in which those behaviors occur.

- This is in stark contrast to a time not that long ago when most technical sensing systems were in tight vertically integrated stacks and belonged primarily to governments and select large non-governmental organizations.

- Today, there is so much data being created around the world by phones, cameras, and other sensing systems—including much of the world's people—that former acting Director of the CIA Mike Morell called UTS an "existential threat" to the CIA's clandestine human intelligence operations.

Algorithms that create insights for mission depend on data, and there is more data than ever and the amount and types of data will continue to grow as more sensors are deployed and people create new ways of generating data, for example, massive-scale simulations of digital twins. The explosion of data is by itself a sufficient distinction for the AI era.

Computing. We presume readers are at least roughly familiar with the transformation in computing being brought about by cloud. Anyone with ten or more years of work experience who has stood around waiting for compute resources personally knows the benefits of cloud. Those even older, who have stood in line to have their punch cards loaded into the mainframe, are especially thankful to work in the current era. However, beyond the availability and increased affordability the cloud has brought to computing, there is another innovation relevant to AI:

- There are important advances in high-powered computing "edge devices"; that is, the devices that can go with operators to the tactical edge of operations. As we will discuss later, this is an essential innovation, as not all AI algorithms can operate in a centralized architecture. High-powered edge computing enables timely processing of data at the tactical edge, and presents the potential—and the challenge—for an architecture that brings coherence to AI solutions and operations from the edge to the enterprise.

Software. Major innovations in software—including and especially software for deploying, orchestrating, and maintaining algorithms in production—are relevant to this era in that they enable AI solutions to operate at enterprise scale. In August 2011, tech pioneer and venture capitalist Marc Andreessen wrote a seminal op-ed in the *Wall Street Journal:* "Why Software is Eating the World." Andreessen hypothesized that "we are in the middle of a dramatic and broad technological and economic shift in which software companies are poised to take over large swathes of the economy." This has proven correct in the decade since it was written. This revolution in software has and is driving products for the entire AI lifecycle.

Robotics. Both software and physical robotics solutions are platforms for AI solutions. Every pilot does not have an R2 unit (yet), but innovations are well along in robotic sensing, movement, manipulation (grabbing, turning, cutting, etc.) and other areas that enable machines to perform human and human-like tasks. These technologies are being deployed in a wide range of form factors, from automobiles to molecular sized medical instruments. Robotic process automation (RPA)—software that performs routinized tasks, such as opening a submitted form, copying select content, and posting that content to a database—is in such widespread use that no human should be sitting at a computer performing routinized tasks. When considered with algorithms that can accomplish sense-making much faster than humans, the integration of algorithms with robotics makes some autonomous systems a matter of engineering not scientific research.

Networks. Increases in network capacity and latency open new opportunities for data access and AI enablement. In the United States, high bandwidth Internet and wireless networks are so ubiquitous that we can take their impact for granted. Networking technology—including the emergence of 5G—provides the central nervous system for a range of implementations from smarter, more sustainable, cities to highly distributed military operations by smaller units. Networking technologies—and advances in systems/computer/software engineering processes—provide the means by which large numbers of smart digital devices can be interconnected and work together for common ends (a stark operational difference from the days of tightly integrated vertical stacks). These improvements are not without limits and certain tactical situations will no doubt continue to present challenges, but network improvements enable continued AI progress.

Capital. Investment capital is the resource that enables entrepreneurs to turn ideas into technology innovations. Unlike previous decades in which government investment has been the primary driver of national security capabilities, global commercial investments are driving the development of intelligent machines capable of autonomous action. AI and autonomous systems have the potential to transform every industry, from fast food restaurants, to farming, and beyond. Recognizing these opportunities, capital investors poured $77.5B globally into AI companies during 2021 alone.[2] Investment itself obviously isn't distinctive, but the amount of investment in AI is a clear signal of the market's belief in the benefits of AI. It has driven and will continue to drive product innovations that the national security enterprise can leverage without investing in the up-front engineering and development.

AI models have the potential to deliver benefits that every national security leader and operator craves, namely a more complete and accurate description of the situation; a greater ability to diagnose why things are happening; an ability to probabilistically estimate what might happen next; and an ability to simulate "what if" actions and effects in an at-scale digital replica of the operating environment. AI models integrated into autonomous systems have the potential to replace humans in some roles and extend human capacity in other roles.

AI will likely continue changing major swaths of global industries in the second quarter of this century, much the same way that software changed entire industries and economies in the first quarter. And while we are likely further from AI changing the world than some enthusiasts predict, initial deployments of AI and billions invested in AI technology development indicate that we are closer than the skeptics proclaim. Machines are advancing toward the goal of thinking and acting in ways similar to—and in some case better than—humans. AI and robotics have the potential therefore to bring about a new era of national security capabilities.

---

[2] According to VentureBeat's analysis of a 2021 report by Tortoise Intelligence / Crunchbase.

Imperative #3: AI Leaders

A number of studies and individual experts like those quoted at the opening of this chapter have observed that the national security community needs to educate and equip many more leaders to drive results using AI. While strong general leadership skills are essential to delivering results on any major change strategy, the national security enterprise is not well served by merely equipping leaders with broad conceptual awareness of AI. An AI leader must have leadership, knowledge, and skills contextualized to practical applications of AI to mission. Consider as an analogy the U.S. military's officer corps, which creates tens of thousands of leaders with strong general leadership skills. It does not then assign any general leader to command any military unit. It provides specialized leader training contextualized to disciplines, for example, logistics, infantry, air, subsurface, and many other operations, each with its own systems, doctrine, and tactics.

Likewise, national security departments cannot assume that any general leader will be an effective AI leader any more than we can assume a competent logistics officer would immediately be a competent commander of armored formations or complex air operations. Nor can we assume any leader with a STEM background will immediately be an effective AI leader. In the early 2000s, the DoD recognized that software is essential to all modern weapons systems and that program management for large software-intensive systems was deficient in both DoD and its industry partners. DoD had decades of experience educating and training major system program managers, whom almost always had strong STEM backgrounds. After several notable struggles in large software-driven programs, however, DoD recognized that specialized training in leading major software programs was required. This is an applicable analogue to the challenge of leading AI programs and projects. Smart technical leaders can still fail if they lack the specialized knowledge and skills for leading AI programs and projects.

These studies and lessons learned align with our 30 years of experience leading advanced analytics and AI as entrepreneurs and as executives in large global firms. In every phase of our careers, we observed that the number of qualified leaders was the primary limiting factor to at scale impact. The AI industry is producing excellent technical education and training but has not produced much in the way of a comprehensive guide to leading AI. It seems impossible to be anywhere close to "AI ready by 2025" unless a broad-based and aggressive program is undertaken to train AI leaders at the multiple levels required for enterprise-scale solutions and mission results:

- Senior department/agency leaders (and the staffs that serve the leaders)

- Program Executive Office (PEO) leadership (PEO oversee multiple programs)

- Program leadership (those who oversee multiple projects)

- AI project leadership

- Cross-departmental AI leaders (potentially multiple departments, PEOs, programs)

We wrote this book as a practical guide for leaders in these multiple roles. The book reflects not only our experience leading hundreds of projects and thousands of practitioners, but also what we have learned from working with some of the best advanced analytics and AI practitioners and leaders in the public and private sectors. Given our background, we are especially focused on leaders in national security. That said, we believe much of the book's content can help AI leaders across other government sectors. As Secretary Work noted in the Foreword, this book is certainly not the last word on leading AI, but we believe it is a helpful beginning.

Outline of the Book

This book is organized into eight chapters. Chapter 1 summarizes the need for AI leader training and development. Chapter 2 addresses the sometimes messy question of what AI is and provides a practical way for AI leaders and their customers to think and communicate about AI.

The remaining six chapters are grouped around three complementary sets of content:

- Chapters 3 and 4—Leading the integration of AI into major programs and secure multi-year funding - focus on what senior leaders must do to prioritize and resource AI programs.

- Chapters 5 and 6—Leading the data science process and AI projects - focus on what project leaders must do to deliver quality results.

- Chapters 7 and 8—Leading the people and the technology—equip leaders to develop the people and leverage the technologies for AI solutions.

We believe these six chapters cover the major dimensions of leading AI in the national security enterprise. Each chapter begins with a short summary, after which we provide axioms and best practices, illustrated with case examples, for leading AI in the dimension of that chapter. We encourage senior executives, program managers, and project managers to read and reflect on all of the content. Senior executives and program managers will benefit from the chapter on data science, for example, as it is the foundational discipline enabling AI solutions development. Similarly, project managers can best contribute to AI strategy formulation if they understand structuring and resourcing AI programs. Leaders at all levels will benefit from improving their skills in leading AI practitioners and making technology choices.

Leaders Are Essential

Two recent Gartner reports paint a dismal picture of AI actually delivering results. According to these reports, projects within perhaps the best understood and practiced form of AI modeling—machine learning—only deliver results 15 percent of the time. Gartner reports that only half of these projects make it out of the prototyping phase. Steve Nunez of *InfoWorld* writes, "The success or failure of AI initiatives has more to do with people than technology." We believe that is roughly right. Qualified practitioners in multiple technical disciplines are vital to driving results with AI. However, leaders are *essential* to driving results with AI on a global scale at a brisk pace. We hope the following chapters make a difference in your leadership of AI.

How Leaders Should Think and Talk About AI

"*Thirty years ago, a math whiz told me that AI is when you ask a machine a question and it responds: 'You asked the wrong question.' Then it tells you the answer to the right question. Everything else is just fancy processing, meaning math and algorithms.*"

—Rich Haver
Former senior official in U.S. intelligence and industry senior executive

© Chris Whitlock, Frank Strickland 2023
C. Whitlock and F. Strickland, *Winning the National Security AI Competition*,
https://doi.org/10.1007/978-1-4842-8814-6_2

"Let's be real. A lot of this talk about AI is just bull****"

—Matt Carroll
Founder and CEO, Immuta

"You've got to start with the customer experience and work backward to the technology—not the other way around."

—Steve Jobs
Co-founder and former CEO, Apple

Summary

When you consider the tremendous range of national security missions, the existing systems in operation, and the global footprint of America's national security interests, AI leaders will need to make wise choices about the problems on which they will focus resources. This requires a dialogue between AI leaders and their customers. This dialogue should not begin with or revolve around AI models or some framework that seeks to explain AI in a single conceptual graphic. These conversations need to focus on customers' mission problems and the potential impact of AI. From this central focus, the four types of AI projects—all of which share the same technical DNA—will keep the dialogue practical and accessible to all. AI technology has transformational potential, but only if it is used to fundamentally change and improve the operations that drive mission outcomes. That is the central focus—not algorithms, not tech, but mission outcomes.

This chapter is organized around four axioms that will help AI leaders and customers have a mission-focused discussion about the value and type of AI for a given problem. After a brief introduction to the chapter, we explain each axiom and describe how the axiom is relevant to clarifying the needs for AI solutions and services. The section on each axiom ends with a bulleted summary of the salient points, giving AI leaders an easily accessible refresher when applying the axiom in conversations with customers.

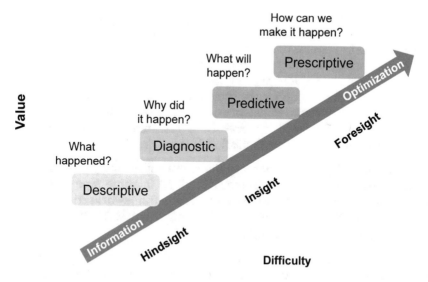

Figure 2-1. Gartner's Analytics Ascendency Model (2012)

If you want to start a nerd bar fight, serve up some beers to a group of AI practitioners and then ask: "What is AI, really?" We have not witnessed such a bar fight, but we have observed several passionate debates on the definitions of analytics, data science, AI, and related terms. There are times when AI practitioners and leaders require a clear, common understanding of a term. If an AI leader says, "Let's first attack this problem with the regression family of models," then they do not expect a practitioner to reach for unsupervised machine learning (ML). Then, why does it become difficult to define terms when we discuss the entire discipline of AI as a whole?

For starters, national security professionals have used math and machines to extract insights from data since the advent of sonar and radar over a century ago. While some of these professionals used the term "algorithm"—a term with roots that go back centuries—practitioners have used many other terms, some as bland as "data processing." In the intelligence program where we started over 30 years ago, the intelligence data was called "product" and the application of algorithms was called "exploitation." While the availability and capability of computing has radically improved over time, much of the math we use today—even that in advanced AI models—has been around for centuries. Haver's comment is illustrative; those who have used math and machines over past decades to generate insights from data have not used the same terms. Many of them probably find an element of contemporary conversations about AI to be "new paint on an old barn."

AI practitioners come from multiple disciplines, also contributing to debate and confusion over the "correct" definitions. Most of today's AI practitioners got their start in operations research, systems engineering, other engineering disciplines, math, statistics, or computer science. Pick people from two of these disciplines and you might hear one say "variable" and another say "feature" when talking about the same thing. A 20-something, fresh out of a data science boot camp, thinks of AI as primarily machine learning models. Meanwhile, someone with an operations research or systems engineering background would also have simulation in their view of AI.

Insert a consulting practitioner into the conversation and you are guaranteed to encounter an attempt to summarize all AI in some type of framework (consultants are genetically wired to create frameworks that summarize complex topics). We suggest that Gartner's framework (Figure 2-1) is a sufficient conceptual framework.

We have seen AI leaders and practitioners stumble when starting conversations with customers based on a conceptual AI framework. We doubt many customers of AI care how AI practitioners conceptually define the details of our discipline. Our experience is that productive conversations with leaders and operators are anchored in what they care about: *insights from data that enable the decisions and actions to affect a desired mission or business outcome.*

Therefore, we are decidedly averse to creating a new slogan or offering a conceptual framework that seeks to provide a unified definition of AI. That runs counter to the practical focus of this book. Frankly, it also runs contrary to our deeply held focus on national security mission impact. Instead, this chapter is a way to think and communicate about AI in terms that should be meaningful to those who make decisions and do the work of national security. In doing so, we will help AI practitioners effectively communicate with the customers they serve as well as helping those customers communicate with their AI providers.

We fully understand the differences between analytics and AI. However, we also know that there is a natural progression from one to the other in practice. Indeed, every AI project begins with a task called "exploratory data analysis," a task that begins with analytics used to describe the data. Rather than create a new term or acronym that encompasses analytics and AI, we simply use the term, AI. When doing this, we imply both analytics and AI. Later in this chapter, we further elaborate on the relationship between analytics and AI in the project portfolio we suggest for every AI program.

We suggest that the most productive thinking and conversations about AI will emerge from the application of these four axioms:

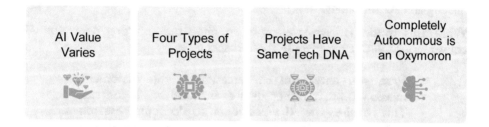

| AI Value Varies | Four Types of Projects | Projects Have Same Tech DNA | Completely Autonomous is an Oxymoron |

AI Value Varies

Leaders and managers who make big decisions for their enterprises as well as the operators or workers who do the work of the enterprise only care about AI indirectly. In other words, they care about AI only to the degree that it accomplishes something they directly care about. Figure 2-2 provides a high-level starting point for what the customers of AI care about.

Figure 2-2. Basic operations cycle

Those familiar with the military will recognize this cycle as a version of Colonel (retired) John Boyd's "OODA loop" (Observe-Orient-Decide-Act), just with terms we hope are more descriptive across all of national security. (Engineers and scientists will recognize this cycle from control theory.) The customers of

AI directly care about how AI can improve the mission results they seek; the actions in pursuit of those outcomes; the decisions that drive those actions; and the sense-making process that generates insights from data for decision-making and action-taking.

While this model is high-level, it is an important starting point for AI conversations with customers in three respects:

- First, you enter the conversation in the customer's mission context rather than a technical or AI context. This requires the AI practitioner to do some research and analyze the customer's mission. This benefits the customer because the conversation is in terms meaningful to them. Additionally, it benefits the AI practitioners because their minds are starting to focus on the customer's mission.

- Second, national security enterprises have instantiated this model in well-established systems and processes—some of these have existed for decades. Since the AI will most often need to work with these existing systems, it is helpful for the AI practitioner to begin the conversation with some understanding of the existing systems and its data.

- Third, this focus will help mission and AI leaders begin to attack the hardest strategic problem for AI in national security: where to focus resources to drive the greatest impact.

To illustrate this strategic challenge, consider that U.S. intelligence officers are primarily concerned with sense-making; there are thousands of systems in place to enable the intelligence mission. Similarly, military decision-making is enabled by an equal number of command and control (C2) systems spanning the fires of an individual weapon system to the campaign operations of a large, deployed force. Border Patrol officers, FBI agents, and other national security leaders and operators also have existing systems spanning this sense-making, decision-making, and action-taking cycle. Thus, thousands of operational systems in national security execute this cycle.

Both individually and collectively, these systems have a baseline performance. This operational baseline presents a practical, meaningful starting point for discussions about AI: Can AI potentially improve performance in this cycle for a given mission and, if so, by how much?

As one example, consider that an imaging satellite platform has an integrated set of sensors and image-processing algorithms for sense-making. These systems have evolved over six decades with government and contractor teams still working today to improve some parameters in the process, for example, image quality, timeliness of the process, and so on. Questions or hypotheses regarding the value of AI need to look something like the following:

- How might road mobile missiles operating out of their garrison be detected, tracked, and engaged at greater rates than today's strike operations by automating the detection and tracking of these objects in an image scene using AI algorithms?

The national security community has a vast number of questions and operations focused on dozens of mission areas such as countering the proliferation of weapons of mass destruction, disrupting international drug smuggling, stopping human trafficking, conducting raids against terrorists, conducting diplomatic operations, and preparing for conflicts with major powers. Picture a table with these and many other national security missions in rows and roughly 200 countries in columns. Now, imagine the cycle (Figure 2-2) operating in each of the intersections. Millions of opportunities for AI exist at these intersections.

Most readers will notice that the examples used in this chapter are from just one segment of national security: the Intelligence Community (IC). As we demonstrate in subsequent examples, all segments of national security face the challenge of identifying where AI investment is worth it. This includes defense, homeland security, diplomacy, intelligence, and those elements of law enforcement engaged in national security operations.

As seen in the image processing example, AI might improve upon existing rule-based or algorithmic approaches that have been deployed in national security systems. In other cases, AI might provide a new capability altogether, such as automatically warning of threatening events by quantifying the probability of that event occurring based on machine learning models running against a variety of data. The AI models might integrate with applications or code that automates work across multiple systems—work that was previously performed by humans.

As seen in case example that follows, the value and type of AI is not uniform across the vast array of opportunities in national security. AI is not an "easy button" that delivers magical improvements whenever and wherever it is applied. It takes work to define where the "juice is worth the squeeze" from AI, and to practically apply AI in a way that produces the expected result. Identifying where AI is worth the investment among the vast array of potential opportunities is the primary challenge for leaders and AI practitioners.

Case Example: Exploring the Limits of AI's Value

Locating radio frequency devices and other objects in time and space is a common task for national security systems. The National Ocean and Atmospheric Agency published a study in 1984 entitled "Algorithms for Confidence Circles and Ellipses." It states, "In many hydrographic surveying, navigation, and position location systems the observed position is defined as the intersection of two lines of position each of which may be in error."

Error ellipse probable

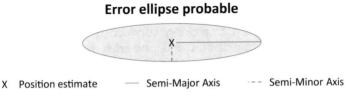

X   Position estimate   —— Semi-Major Axis   --- Semi-Minor Axis

Figure 2-3. Error ellipse probable illustration

In plain language, all sensors measure with some degree of uncertainty or error. Some sense-making systems estimate the position of an object by bounding the error or uncertainty within an ellipse or circle. The size of the ellipse is driven by the probability that the object is within it. Consider one example widely used in national security systems: error ellipse probable (EEP).

Assume that the EEP seen here calculates a 95 percent probability that the emitter is contained somewhere within the ellipse. The estimated position of the object is at the center. The sense-making system has calculated an ellipse with semi-major and semi-minor axes to capture the object's actual location with 95 percent confidence.

How might AI improve the calculation and/or reporting of EEPs? To illustrate the challenge and the opportunity, we frame several possible approaches in Table 2-1.

Table 2-1. Potential AI Applications to Signal Geolocation

Potential AI Application	Description	Issues
Reduce the size of the EEP while holding the containment probability steady	Reducing the EEP's size can increase the accuracy and timeliness of actions toward the emitter. Can AI help calculate a smaller-sized ellipse at the same confidence level using the same sensor inputs?	Substantial variation in sensors' input data and types of objects confound AI model development. What gain, if any, is possible over baseline techniques?
Automate anomaly resolution	Some EEP reports have issues such as locating an emitter in an implausible location. Such reports are flagged for human review. Can AI help automate these reviews, reducing the time required to release the report?	Could elements of this process be automated by integrating software robotics and AI for matching or scoring risk? Doing so would likely require the use of additional data beyond the sensors' input to create the risk scoring models.
Limit the area inside the EEP using other information	Given the earth's many features, emitters are not always likely to be anywhere within the EEP. Data on the terrain can help exclude portions of the EEP as low probability locations for the emitter. Can AI automatically classify these low probability spaces such that the report conveys a more accurate location?	First, classification models must be used to characterize blocks of the environment. Then, this information must be integrated into EEP calculation to exclude portions of the EEP, as appropriate. Finally, a new reporting format would be required to communicate the excluded area.

This is only one practical example that illustrates the challenge in constructing AI programs and projects. This case illustrates a generalizable principle: AI is not uniformly applicable and not equally easy to implement for various tasks. As national security leaders operate in a resource-constrained environment, it is essential to focus not only on priority mission problems, but also on those that realistically hold potential for gain by applying AI. Understanding baseline performance and setting realistic program- and project-level expectations are crucial to driving the desired gains.

◾ Summary: The Value of AI Is Not Uniform

- Conceptual AI frameworks tend to fall flat with customers because they are impractical abstractions focused on the means of AI rather than the mission ends for which customers exist.

- AI leaders and practitioners should think and communicate with their customers in terms of how AI might drive mission results. Then, they should reach for the AI to deliver the desired impact.

- There are millions of potential applications of AI to national security missions; these may integrate into existing systems or be developed as a new system.

- Mission/business leaders should focus on a quantitative understanding of baseline performance to prioritize where AI might have the most impact.

- This axiom is not suggesting a Luddite approach to "defining all the requirements" before doing anything with AI tech. As we explain in the next axiom, the value of AI can be explored through experimentation.

Four Types of Projects

The AI field is understandably rich in technologies for data management, mathematical modeling, computing, and user experience design as well as other functions for creating, deploying, and maintaining AI models. Even when you begin thinking about AI by seeking to understand mission-AI fit, you can fall into the trap of reaching for a technological product or set of products too soon. Before doing so, we suggest you stop and think about this question: what type of AI project is most appropriate given the desired mission result and the contextual circumstances?

The highest aim of AI could be characterized as machines that learn, decide, and act on behalf of and in collaboration with humans for the purpose of human flourishing. This level of AI is called "general AI." This assumes that the AI will be integrated into a fully autonomous system. The AI performs the sense-making and decision-making with some type of robotics performing the action-taking, creating a fully autonomous system (i.e., a system that performs the entire cycle in Figure 2-2).

If you have any experience with AI as a practitioner or customer, you know that national security enterprises will not make one giant leap from where they are today to fully autonomous systems. The paranoia regarding killer robots is not where our minds should go first. There are many opportunities for AI to improve mission performance in the near-term. There is a natural progression of AI capabilities with some projects being more complex than others depending on the objective and circumstances.

From our experience executing hundreds of projects, we summarize the progression of AI in two dimensions: understanding performance to driving improvement, and studies to operational capabilities. These dimensions frame the four types of projects any enterprise will need in an AI program (Figure 2-4). There is nothing canonical about the terms we use for the four project types, but there are important differences in the substance of each type. We explain the purpose of each project type using the primary dimension, understanding performance to driving improvement, as our guide.

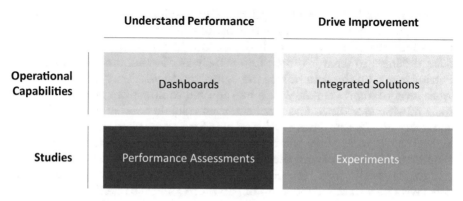

	Understand Performance	Drive Improvement
Operational Capabilities	Dashboards	Integrated Solutions
Studies	Performance Assessments	Experiments

Figure 2-4. Four types of AI projects

Understanding Performance

Understanding baseline performance is not just important to an AI program and project, it is essential. Earlier in this chapter, we established that there are thousands of potential applications for AI in any national security enterprise. Leaders will have some intuition as to where AI might have the most impact. However, as a leader, you want to test your intuition with hard data before committing the resources required for a successful AI deployment. Leaders who operate solely on their intuition can create a lot of chatter about AI but fail to create any sustained impact on the enterprise.

A multi-billion-dollar national security enterprise was unaware of the fact that the volume of its flagship product had decreased by 5x while its operational personnel had doubled. Upon seeing this performance data, the senior executive over production began a set of knee-jerk assertions of the causes ranging from, "Our analyst population is less experienced" to "I'm glad production is down 2x; it means we are spending more time in the room talking with decision-makers."

The average experience of the analyst population had increased slightly over the same period. Further analysis revealed that the enterprise's operational personnel had created a major new product, produced by the thousands, which was completely outside any quality or other review by the agency.

Leaders, you must exhibit humility and tempered judgment if you are going to encourage and equip a bureaucracy to identify and characterize opportunities for improving performance with AI.

At the project level, the effort to quantify baseline performance produces substantial returns. Quantifying performance helps the AI team as practitioners come into practical contact with the perceived problem and its associated data, drilling into what is most often initially an abstract problem statement. Putting hands on the data refines the conversation with your customer about what level of improvement would be required to affect the next horizon for their mission workflow. The team can then think in specific terms about the suitability of different types of AI modeling for the problem and available data, as well as the technology and other elements of the AI lifecycle (subsequent chapters address this cycle, the AI team, and technology in detail). The team can create an informed plan of toll gate progress reviews along what would otherwise be a murky continuum of "do more and do better."

A data-driven quantitative grasp of baseline performance equips the AI leader and key customers/stakeholders to think together about constraints: "We could achieve that level of performance improvement boost if…". Now, the team has a reasonably detailed definition of resource investment, expected return, schedule, and deliverables. This also gives the leader a factual basis to advocate for resources and rationally set a quantitative target for improvement.

As seen in Figure 2-4, projects to understand performance are either studies or operational capabilities. Performance assessments are generally one-off studies in that a team conducts a quantitative assessment of a problem and reports the results in writing. Given the size of the national security enterprise, there are multiple staffs across DoD, DHS, DoJ, and the IC that conduct performance assessments, measures of effectiveness analyses, and so on. These staffs are part of the Executive Branch's oversight process. (In Chapter 7, we discuss the relationship of these staff elements to the programming and budgeting process.)

A dashboard is an operational visualization of performance data in software, normally focused on highlighting some number of key performance indicators to decision-makers or operators/workers. As an operational capability, the dashboard receives updated data on a recurring schedule. While anyone can read and understand a performance assessment well after it is published, the content is static. Dashboards provide a dynamic, current view of performance.

A Look at Quantitative Performance Assessments in the Wild

The term "studies" can have a negative connotation in national security; the traditional study approach has often been a "bunch of guys and gals sitting around a table" talking—"BOGSAT," as people derisively call it. Performance assessments are a fundamentally different approach to studies in that they use sufficient volumes of hard data to quantitatively assess a problem. A company we co-founded, Edge Consulting, pioneered this type of study for a number of national security problems. The "High Value Individual (HVI) Study," as it became known in the Department of Defense, is one example.

An Exemplar Performance Assessment: High Value Individual (HVI) Study

The Mission Problem

Following the U.S. invasion of Iraq in 2003, Iraq slid into a sectarian civil war. According to the U.S. military, daily homicides in Baghdad alone rose from 11 to 33 during 2006. To put that threefold increase in deaths into context, the year 2021 was the deadliest in a quarter of a century for the city of Chicago with an average of a little over two homicides daily—less than 10 percent of the daily homicides experienced by Baghdad's citizens in 2006. It was a dark time in Iraq and growing darker by the day.

Special operations force (SOF) commanders and operators engaged in Iraq were using a long-endurance drone, known as "Predator," to surveil targets using full motion video (FMV) sensors on the drone. The Predator could surveil a target or area for well over ten hours, sending FMV to a ground station in real time. The drone's crew, a pilot and an FMV sensor operator, sat side by side in the ground station. Connected with operational forces via voice and chat communications, the crew could fly the aircraft and steer its FMV camera in response to real-time events on the ground—a revolutionary new capability.

The commander and operators in a Joint Special Operations Task Force (JSOTF) were especially desirous of much more FMV capability. The JSOTF was engaged in a campaign to collapse the violent networks in Iraq by capturing or killing HVIs in the networks. These individuals were leading bad actors who were killing or enabling the killing of Iraqis and U.S. and coalition forces. The JSOTF submitted a formal request to the Department of Defense for a four-fold increase in FMV. Within the Pentagon, where planners needed to decide how much FMV budget was enough, there was vigorous debate about the operational value of FMV. There were as many or more skeptics as believers regarding the need for so much more FMV.

Quantitative Assessment of Mission Value

Chris and Frank had formed an analytics startup, Edge Consulting, in 2004. The Pentagon contracted with the company to quantitatively study the value of FMV. Chris and a team of data scientists created an approach that tested the temporal, spatial, and relational connections between 13 major types of intelligence data and the outcomes of 2,500 SOF raids against HVIs. The JSOTF commander, LTG Stan McChrystal, and his operators enabled the study by providing access to raw data. They also allowed Chris to directly observe operations, and key commanders and operators made time for Chris to interview them. This qualitative data provided the necessary context to the team's analysis of the primary empirical data extracted by the team from operations and intelligence systems. The team began work in January 2007 and presented its initial findings five months later in May.

Impact

The HVI study conclusively demonstrated that (a) FMV was highly correlated with SOF mission success, (b) FMV was the most valuable intelligence capability across all phases of the SOF's operational cycle ("Find-Fix-Finish-Exploit-Analyze"), and (c) much to everyone's surprise, FMV was the primary intelligence contributor to the Find phase of the cycle. Results from initial study report, which spawned a body of studies over the next few years, contributed to the DoD directing roughly a billion dollars of investment to intelligence systems. It also helped both special and some conventional forces better deploy FMV assets to operations.

Senior leaders, including LTG McChrystal and the Under Secretary of Defense for Intelligence, Dr. Steve Cambone, embraced the study results. However, the study generated some intense conflicts with advocates of other intelligence systems and, eventually, with other senior commanders in Iraq. At one point, a senior executive in the Pentagon sought to have the company's contract cancelled in response to complaints from the senior commander in Iraq. In the end, the Under Secretary of Defense for Intelligence at the time, Jim Clapper, shut down any notion of contract cancellation by stating, "We go with the data."[1]

As the HVI study illustrates, a performance assessment study can impact major programmatic and operational decisions. When performed properly, a performance assessment can also be a diagnostic tool for the AI program leader. With it, the leader can gain a clear, concrete understanding of baseline

---

[1] For more details and lessons learned on the HVI and related studies, see "Assessing the Value of Intelligence: Lessons for Leaders" (Whitlock, Strickland; IBM Center for the Business of Government). https://www.businessofgovernment.org/report/assessing-value-intelligence-lessons-leaders

performance that informs AI program advocacy, resource allocation, and preparation for related AI work that may follow the assessment. With a qualified team, most performance assessments can start returning results in as little as 30 to 60 days and finish in months (we discuss team qualifications in Chapters 6 and 7). These are fast, affordable projects that deliver important insights for investments, operations, and the AI program.

Performance assessment studies can often be performed with available open-source technologies such as Python (more on these technologies in Chapter 5). Perhaps because these studies do not deliver in some fancy tech product, leaders typically underappreciate the performance assessment as one type of project in an AI portfolio. As the HVI study and many others demonstrate, performance assessments are a powerful component of a portfolio of AI projects.

A Look at Dashboards in the Wild

All automobile drivers are accustomed to looking at the car's dashboard to monitor basic measures such as speed and automated alerts, such as the indicator light for an overheating engine. In the late 20th Century, IT researchers and product developers brought the concept of a business performance dashboard to life with the introduction of three technologies: data warehouses, online analytic processing (OLAP), and a dashboard. The data warehouse combined operational data from multiple enterprise systems. OLAP enabled responsive extraction of select data from a data warehouse. Lastly, a dashboard enabled users to query the warehouse and visualize the data.

Business analytics or business intelligence dashboards have proliferated since the early 2000s. Unlike a one-off performance assessment study, the dashboard provides a recurring, up-to-date view of key performance indicators (KPIs), the metrics a decision-maker deems essential to regular monitoring of performance. Dashboards provide leaders with KPI trends over time, views of whether a KPI is within an acceptable range, alerts if a KPI falls out of range, and many other performance metrics.

During Michael Morrell's podcast, Intelligence Matters, Maja Lehnus and Norm Roule, former Intelligence Community (IC) senior leaders for weapons of mass destruction and Iran, respectively, stated their expectation that the IC will compare intelligence over time to assess whether or not intelligence judgments and confidence are improving, remaining static, or declining on specific questions in these two vital mission areas.

Dashboards are well suited to the initial levels of this type of performance assessment, enabling leaders to quickly spot major changes such as the aforementioned case of a 5x decrease in flagship production despite a 2x increase in resources. Senior leaders must understand that dashboards, or any of the AI projects, are a means to complement the leader's intuition from experience, not replace it.

An Exemplar Dashboard: Naval Fuel Analytics and Characterization Tool (NFACT)

The Mission Problem

The U.S. Navy operates over 2,600 fixed and rotary wing aircraft around the world that require a steady supply of reliable fuels suited to the various aircraft propulsion systems. The Naval Air Systems Command's Propulsion and Power Engineering Department's (AIR-4.4) missions include testing fuel samples for compliance with the technical specifications for a particular fuel type. For example, AIR-4.4 experts test a fuel sample's viscosity. Fuel sample tests look at dozens of parameters beyond viscosity across multiple fuel types. These tests are technically complex, examining a sample at the molecular level and drawing upon data from historical tests dating back to previous decades.

AIR-4.4 fuel chemistry experts analyze fuel sample data in response to requests from operational naval air forces as well as ongoing research into the effects of fuel properties. Historically, AIR-4.4 experts would gather test data through a laborious, weeks-long process of manual query and response of Defense Logistics Agency (DLA) databases. If you have analyzed data for a complex problem by querying a database, you know the challenges created when the response to your query has a time lag. Compounding the challenge, experts would spend substantial amounts of time "cleaning" the data (correcting errors and inconsistencies, formatting, etc.) before analytical work could begin. This legacy process was inefficient, introduced too many opportunities for error, and inhibited the experts' research and analysis.

Standardizing Data Cleaning and Visualization

Working with AIR-4.4 customers and leaders, a data science team quickly prototyped an automated data pipeline and visualization using open-source tools in Python and JavaScript, respectively. This rapid prototype gave the users hands-on experience with their data and dashboard features, enabling them to provide refined input on their needs to the data science team. The team hardened the data pipeline from DLA to the dashboard so that it would continuously operate. Then, they coded the operational dashboard into a more production-quality JavaScript toolkit, Svelte. While iterations continued over time, a small team of two data scientists provided an initial capability in less than a year.

Impact

For both operational and research fuel chemistry analyses, the dashboard immediately accelerated experts' ability to query and explore data that was already "cleaned" for analysis. The responsiveness of executing a query and immediately seeing results was necessary for hypothesis testing and exploratory analysis. Researchers with ideas on exploring the effects of individual molecules or sets of molecules across potentially hundreds of features from a lab test now had a tool that supported their thinking. Over time, this has the potential to help experts explore new areas such as the relationships of fuel chemistry with different propulsion systems—analytical questions that were largely impractical with the legacy system. Additionally, AIR-4.4 now has a capability that can scale to various types and greater amounts of fuel chemistry analyses, providing the potential to serve others in DoD as well as the Navy.

Like all quantitative methods, dashboards can disappoint customers if there is simply counting and visualization without any regard for the decision-maker's questions and decision-making workflow (thus the first axiom's focus on defining the mission problem and its relative priority). Counting things, or "volumetrics," are not inherently bad, as some leaders think. However, you must count and visualize with some relevant decision-problems and KPIs in focus.

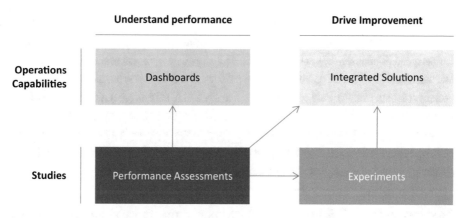

Figure 2-5. Relationships between AI project types

Here also, performance assessment studies can contribute to refining leaders' key questions, identifying KPIs, preparing or "cleaning" the data, and even testing select visualizations with customers in a static report. As shown in

Figure 2-5, performance assessments are an important feeder system to the other three project types. At some level, every useful dashboard development has a performance assessment at is core; the performance assessment is essential to refining the KPIs for the dashboard.

Gartner's Magic Quad for Business Intelligence and Analytics platforms assesses 20 dashboard products on "completeness of vision" and "ability to execute." This assessment illustrates the tremendous variety of dashboard products. There are commercial products, or commercial off-the-shelf (COTS) software, such as Tableau and Qlik. There are COTS products closely aligned to other technologies such as the integration options Microsoft offers for PowerBI and other Microsoft products like Office365 and Excel. There are cloud-native dashboards like Google's increasingly popular Looker visualization tool, which runs on the Google Cloud Platform (GCP). There are also open-source visualization libraries in JavaScript, Python, R, and other AI software.

Driving Improvement

While understanding baseline performance is an essential first step, AI aims to drive improvement in the mission and mission-enabling areas. This requires putting AI models into production at the scale required by the problem. While the technologies and processes to deploy models are maturing and proliferating across enterprises, there is a substantial gap between the expected benefits of AI and the results national security enterprises have achieved to date. This gap, as you will see, is felt across commercial industry, not just national security.

In surveys from 2017 through early 2022 by Rexler Analytics, MIT Sloan, McKinsey, NewVantage Partners, and KDnuggets, data scientists indicated that models were successfully deployed into operations less than 25 percent of the time. We suspect that most AI leaders in national security resonate with this data point. This is not to say that AI models are not being successfully deployed. However, it does indicate that we still have a lot of work to do in closing the gap between the expectations of AI and the realized impact. While deploying a model is a step toward realizing impact, a deployed model does not guarantee the expected return. AI leaders must constantly remind themselves that AI is a means, the mission result is the end.

As shown in Figure 2-5, projects to drive improvements are either experiments or deployed models. Experiments are another form of studying a problem and its solution. Like the benefits of performance assessments, experiments are another means to test and learn quickly so that you make good technology choices, select the right modeling approach for the problem, fine tune a model's performance to a problem, and a host of other lessons. Deployed models have automated connections to required data as well as some type of ongoing output. The AI team can deploy the model within an existing system or create a new capability built around the AI model. The most sophisticated AI implementation is the integration of AI models into a fully autonomous system. We discuss fully autonomous systems later in this chapter.

A Look at Experiments in the Wild

By "experiments," we are not referring to the production testing of AI models. All AI models and their associated software undergo production testing during development and before deployment. AI experiments—like the classic use of the term—are designed to test the value and viability of a potential AI solution. As implied by the arrow from experiment to production in Figure 2-5, experiments can be an important means to test the potential return on an investment in production AI models. That said, we are not implying that an experiment must precede every production AI project.

Similar to performance assessments, experiments are also a practical means to assess the availability of relevant data and test the gap between available data and a modeling approach. Experiments are a means to test and refine cutting edge approaches, such as current newsworthy examples, for example, AI that can paint a painting or write a children's story.

Experiments can be especially useful as part of an AI program's portfolio of projects under circumstances such as the following:

- Mission and/or resource sponsors need to be shown— not told—that the prospective project is worth the investment required for production.

- There are major questions among AI professionals on the approach and/or technologies to use against a decision problem, thus multiple aspects should be explored.

- The risk or sponsor's risk tolerance for the problem is such that a controlled step is required to demonstrate that the project can mitigate these risks.

- The current fiscal environment will only support a limited first step.

- The team is breaking new ground in terms of the AI model(s) or another aspect of the technical approach.

- Security considerations make it necessary to study an approach with unclassified data before moving to a classified environment working on operational mission data.

An Exemplar AI Experiment Releasing Official Government Records to the Public

The Mission Problem

Democratic governments, such as that of the United States, operate in the open. So much so that the U.S. Congress and President have enacted laws governing the storage and release of government information. The Federal Records Act of 1950, its amendments, and federal regulations set the standards by which U.S. government organizations will store and maintain the records documenting the government's operations in accordance with the law. There is a government entity dedicated to the act's implementation: the National Archives and Records Administration (NARA). Additionally, a leader is charged with its implementation: the Archivist of the United States.

The U.S. government publishes an abundance of information such as census data, economic data, and many other types of data. Since 1967, the Freedom of Information Act (FOIA) has enabled citizens to request the release of unpublished government records. Understandably, there are exemptions to what the government will release to whom (e.g., someone cannot write to the IRS and ask for your tax return, as one example). Certain national security and law enforcement records are also exempted from a FOIA release. However, many records inside national security departments and agencies are available to the public through FOIA requests. With billions and billions of records in storage and large numbers of FOIA requests, imagine the number of people required to review and appropriately release information in a timely manner.

Experimenting with Machine Review of Documents

Traditionally, national security departments used manpower to search for, review, and release documents in response to FOIA requests. This is a classic case for AI. Natural language processing (NLP) is a type of AI model in which the computer reviews and evaluates text in the way a human would, but much faster (NLP is further explained in Chapter 5).

Imagine that you have received a FOIA request and the tool at your disposal is a keyword search of a data store with billions of records. Even if you are great at forming Boolean search queries, the returns from your search will keep you quite busy. Meanwhile, the citizen who made the FOIA request waits. Now, imagine an AI model has been trained to return only those records with a high probability of responding to the FOIA request. The AI has greatly decreased the workload on the humans and accelerated the speed at which the FOIA request is satisfied. A data science team tackled this problem for a cabinet department in national security. Human experts took a body of test records—say, email—and coded a portion of them as official or personal (in general, personal records are exempted from FOIA requests). The trained model was then tested against the portion of the data the humans did not code. Data scientists and experts in the data contents then assessed the AI model's performance.

The model initially made correct and incorrect decisions about documents. Data scientists used these results to tune the model's parameters, such as "stop words"—words that the machine model should never use in a query— or "boost terms"—the weight a term receives in context of the document where the term appears. This is not entirely a manual process. As just one technique, the data scientists used simulation to create 100 random combinations of parameters, then statistically assessed each combination's performance. This identified the parameters with the highest probability of "true positive" and "true negative" responses (i.e., responses that correctly identified records aligned to the FOIA request or not aligned to the FOIA request).

Impact

Experimentation was helpful in this case for multiple reasons. Accurately responding to FOIA requests is a matter of complying with U.S. law. Therefore, national security departments take the responsibility very seriously. The department was not ready to immediately jump into development and deployment of an operational NLP capability. They needed to see how much a machine model would help this process. The experiment helped make a technical, foreign concept, NLP by a machine, explainable to government staff and their leaders.

The experiment also helped the FOIA staff and data science team assess various technologies. Could adequate performance be achieved with existing technology or was investment required? If the latter, how much investment and for how much gain? The experiment answered these questions with hard data. The experiment gave the government staff and leaders the hard evidence that enabled them to move the experiment into a production phase.

Experiments enable leaders to test and learn where AI is most impactful to mission. The progression from basic research to applied R&D to a system program of record is well known—but not always well valued—in national security. In most cases, AI experiments can be accomplished with modest investments and initial results gathered in weeks to months. As incremental results are seen, it is easier for leaders to terminate an experiment in any phase if performance expectations are falling short. Contrast that with the difficulty in terminating a program of record or a major project on which leaders have invested political and fiscal capital. Consequently, a mature AI program should have a robust, ongoing set of experiments.

A Look at Deployed Models in the Wild

A model is an abstraction of reality. Thus, you can better understand the adage: "All models are wrong, but some are useful." Data scientists—the AI practitioners who model data—do not seek to create a perfect representation of reality from the available data. They seek to create a useful representation of reality from the data—a representation that is mathematically faithful to the data and, importantly, produces an insight that informs decision-making and action-taking (Figure 2-2). Data scientists refer to this process as "fitting the data to a model."

As Figure 2-5 implies, the term "integrated" means something different than what happens in a dashboard. Dashboards—often called "business intelligence and analytics platforms"—typically use foundational statistics to describe data through visualizations. In the AI industry, the term "integrated" connotes a more mathematically complex approach to the data. A dashboard might show you the range of scores and the average score of Army soldiers' performance on the Combat Physical Fitness Test (CPFT). An AI model might seek to predict which soldiers will benefit from more training on a given CPFT exercise as well as how that training might improve the soldiers' CPFT scores (we provide a practical introduction to various types of AI models in Chapter 5).

Data is modeled to some degree in all four project types: performance assessments, dashboards, experiments, and integrated solutions. However, the national security community's desire for AI to substantially improve the operations cycle in Figure 2-2 means that large numbers of models must be integrated into operational systems, thus the "integrated solutions" project type. Integrated solutions will create a speed of machine to machine, and machine to human, operations that requires special attention to certain details during model deployment as well as ongoing maintenance of the model after deployment.

An Exemplar Deployed Model Project Maven

The Mission Problem

Beginning in the early 2000s as wars unfolded in Afghanistan and Iraq along with counter-terrorism operations elsewhere around the world, full motion video coverage of a variety of targets and regions grew exponentially. Hundreds of thousands of hours of video were collected, but the military and IC struggled at times to even perform basic exploitation tasks, constrained by manual exploitation processes. Young military analysts monitored screens to isolate activity of potential importance to operational units, posting some of this in relatively rudimentary data bases to track priority activity. Frustration grew as exploitation and dissemination of intelligence from the data streams lagged operational needs.

By Fiscal Year 2017, Central Command reported that unmanned aerial systems and other platforms collected the equivalent of 325,000 feature films in terms of full motion video. The volume outpaced the ability to meaningfully analyze and report. Exploitation needed to occur both at forward locations as well as select bases in the continental United States. Some practical means was needed to automate major elements of this video exploitation process.

Deployed AI Solution

The Office of the Under Secretary of Defense for Intelligence (USDI) led the response to this challenge, drawing on industry experts like Eric Schmidt to craft a path forward, experiment, then build operational capabilities. The Automation Working Group first assessed options for approaching the challenge and recommended leveraging Silicon Valley work in image processing, computer vision, and scene understanding. The commercial need to process massive social media volumes among other image and video sources drove these technologies. The Office of Secretary of Defense acknowledged these recommendations and advocated for a new start, the Algorithmic Warfare Task Force, to Congress, ultimately receiving funds to support this new program with Project Maven as the cornerstone.

Project Maven immediately tackled a range of tasks necessary to automate and accelerate creation of decision-support insights from video using AI. A significant effort focused on creating "labeled data" necessary to train the video models. This effort engaged a range of experts and junior military members, including military analysts who had completed initial entry training but were awaiting their security clearances. This mimics Tesla's effort in using high school educated staff to perform data labeling—a crucial task supporting AI modeling. Other parts of the Project Maven effort addressed data access and algorithm development, including user interfaces so front-line intelligence and operations personnel could set acceptable risk or accuracy thresholds on the models.

Impact

Project Maven created a set of deployed solutions and capabilities now ready for transition to the National Geospatial Intelligence Agency for longer-term development as well as operations and maintenance support. The USDI took an acquisition action in summer 2021 to support the transition to NGA and in doing so provided the following summary of Maven's four-year progress:

> "Elements of Project Maven include new frameworks and tools for the creation of algorithms; tailored algorithms to perform discrete tasks, particularly in the fields of computer vision; innovative artificial intelligence (AI) and machine learning (ML) computational environments; new labeling techniques to generate massive scale annotated data for supervised deep learning techniques; new methods of edge computation to bring deep learning algorithms to constrained computational environments; methods to evaluate and determine the effectiveness of algorithmic approaches; interfaces for the display, search, and interaction with algorithmically derived metadata and tabular structured algorithmic output; new techniques, hardware, software, and tools for the training, testing, and validating of algorithms; and storage and indexing capabilities for local algorithmically-produced data. Cumulatively, technologies supporting the Project comprise the AI Pipeline."

Congress is following this transition closely with language in the FY 22 Intelligence Appropriation Act requiring reporting from USDI and NGA on the progress.

Every data scientist wants their models to be mathematically sound and operationally useful, regardless of the project type. However, the deployed models project type will not generally have the benefits of a data scientist readily at hand to contextualize the model's output as is the case with performance assessments and experiments. Consequently, projects to deploy models must pay special attention to details in the model lifecycle, ensuring that the model meets the following standards:

- Development: Performs to quality standards under realistic operational conditions

- Deployment: Is properly packaged such that key features are not damaged in deployment and the model successfully integrates into the users' workflows

- Deployment: Is monitored over time for "drift" (changes in the model's performance based on changes in the data or other operational realities; we provide best practices for quality model deployment in Chapter 6)

▪ Summary: There are Four Types of AI Projects

- A mature AI program consists of four types of projects, helping organizations systematically understand performance and drive improvement across the enterprise.

- Performance assessment studies provide a quantitative understanding of performance and impact in weeks to months; they are an underleveraged means of prioritizing AI investments.

- Automated dashboards are a means to assess performance on an ongoing basis. Isolating a select set of key performance indicators (KPIs) is essential to the dashboard's value.

- Experiments are another form of AI study, testing a hypothesis as to how AI might affect mission performance under realistic operational conditions without substantial resource commitments.

- Integrated solutions are the ultimate objective of AI. Successful deployment may depend more on a coherent use of the four project types to define mission value and AI approach than DevSecOps, data science, and other important technical processes.

Projects Have Same Technical DNA

Throughout this chapter, we seek to help mission leaders and leaders in AI think and communicate about AI in practical, mission-relevant terms (not necessarily the terms of reference that we AI practitioners use among our own tribe). Doing so is especially difficult when thinking about AI technology choices. Many mission leaders are not steeped in technology, but AI spans a number of technology areas. The hundreds of open-source and commercial software products in the AI space only increase this challenge. One senior executive in national security said to Chris in an exasperated tone: "I have product vendors calling and emailing me every day. I could spend most of every day taking demonstrations from vendors."

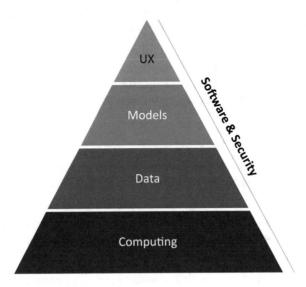

Figure 2-6. DNA of AI solutions

Government technology leaders, product vendors, and technology researchers all have vital roles to play in making AI effective for national security. Government CIOs, CTOs, and program managers generally are the leaders who acquire and deploy technologies for the mission. Product vendors have seen a need in the AI market and are trying to meet that needs in ways that are superior to competitors, delivering superior value to government buyers. Researchers will naturally focus on advancing the technical state of the art. For example, they may research how quantum computing can be applied to AI modeling.

To give AI and mission leaders an accessible framework for communicating about AI solutions, every AI project has the same four building blocks in its technical DNA: computing, data, models, and user experience (Figure 2-6). The order logically flows from the user experience (UX) to the computing. The UX abstracts the underlying tech from the user much like your phone's operating system abstracts all the underlying tech within your phone, cellular network, and application services. All four layers are essential to every AI solution, and these layers are interdependent in every AI solution.

As seen alongside the stack, you must keep software and security at the top of your mind. The instructions by which the four building blocks are created, deployed, operated, and maintained are codified in software. Since national security operates against determined and cunning adversaries, security is essential. If AI is to be woven into most national security systems, then leaders and operators must trust that adversaries have not compromised the data or other components of the AI stack.

The Organization for Economic Cooperation and Development (OECD) reported in 2020 that AI startups received over 21 percent of total global venture capital. The massive investment in AI tech and the equally impressive advances in open-source AI tech present a rich array of product and technology choices when assembling the AI stack for a problem or set of problems. On the other hand, there is tremendous volatility in the AI product market from one year to the next, as a glance at the year-to-year changes in Gartner's ranking of AI products will show.

In light of this volatility, we believe there are two keys to making operationally and fiscally responsible tech choices. First, ensure your AI leaders have considered tech from all of the major types: open-source, COTS, and cloud. Next, demand that your AI architects and engineers build a stack based on exposed open APIs. Such APIs will give you an architecture that is componentized, meaning changes to it work like changes to LEGO™ blocks versus trying to change out concrete blocks.

As the mission and business leader, awareness of this stack will help you ask AI practitioners why they chose a given technology. You will also be able to spot the occasional practitioner who has their "go-to" technology for every problem. For the AI leader, your intent is practical: How do you select technologies and assemble this stack to drive a mission result within the technical, fiscal, and other constraints of your environment? AI leaders and practitioners should reach for those technologies that best support the mission/business problem and operational context, such as time and money available. For AI architects, you must ensure that individual choices are made with an eye to product volatility and the unpredictable global problem landscape so that you create a future-resilient architecture. Otherwise, you end up in a never-ending cycle of big "rip and replace" costs to modernize your IT systems.

This high-level stack can also help leaders think and act strategically, such as policies and systems within the data layer and processes such as ML Ops and DevSecOps across all of the layers. In Chapters 5 and 8, we explore AI technology in further detail. For the purpose of helping you think and communicate about the AI technology stack, Figure 2-7 provides salient points on each of the four building blocks.

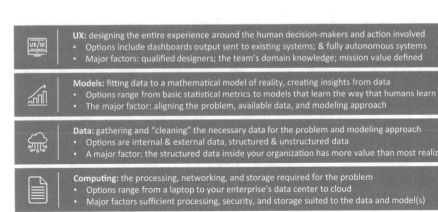

Figure 2-7. Summary of AI solution DNA

We encourage leaders to pay special attention to the most important component of the stack: data. We have established that mission leaders care most about insights that inform the decisions and actions required for operational results. Insights do not emerge from a vacuum; they require data. The proverbial long pole in the AI solution stack is data.

Leaders and AI practitioners can sometimes be attracted to the shiny objects of data types such as the images, video, and unstructured text prevalent in social media. All data sources are relevant to an AI program; some problems and models require specific types of data. As Figure 2-7 suggests, we encourage leaders to pay particular attention to an underleveraged source of data—their internal structured data as this data is relatively easy to access and model. As the principal deputy director for analysis in one of the military services lamented to us, "Heck, we can't count the stuff we have." In addition to its relative availability, the structured data internal to your enterprise is an essential source for that foundational step of quantifying baseline performance.

When it comes to data and the AI solution stack, more than a few leaders fall victim to a desire to "purify all the water before having a single drink." If they aren't careful, chief data officers and other roles over a part of the stack can contribute to this problem. When leaders look at the stack, they should think of vertical lines running top to bottom through the stack. These lines represent the mission threads that you will attack first. Drive development of the stack for the benefit of these mission threads in accordance with a strategic architecture. You must hold both ends of this rope—mission results now and future architecture—in tension. An over fixation on one or the other creates disparate solutions or a feckless architecture.

▥ Summary: All AI Projects Have the Same Core Technical DNA

- AI is technically complex and will become more so in the future, driven by further innovations in AI technology, the challenges of producing, deploying, and maintaining large numbers of models across an enterprise, and adversaries' attempts to counter the value of AI to U.S. national security.

- Mission leaders and AI leaders need a practical framework to think and communicate about AI technology challenges and choices—a framework that is accessible to mission leaders who are not always steeped in technology.

- All AI projects have the same four technical DNA building blocks: computing, data, models, and user experience (UX).

- Leaders should pay special attention to fully leveraging structured data internal to their organizations as it is relatively easy to access and model. Additionally, it is essential to quantifying baseline performance.

- When thinking about this four-part solution stack, leaders must be mindful that the stack is instantiated in software. The solution must also be secure from adversaries' attacks.

Completely Autonomous is an Oxymoron

The cycle in Figure 2-8 is a straightforward definition of a fully autonomous system; it is a system that performs all three phases of the cycle without human involvement. Such systems combine AI, which enables machines to learn and decide in ways similar to humans, with some form of robotics for taking action. Chuck Price, chief product officer TuSimple, a company creating autonomous trucks for depot-to-depot transportation of goods, expresses the sentiments of commercial leaders in every industry regarding AI: "This is no longer a science project. It is not research. It's engineering."

Figure 2-8. Basic operations cycle

In national security missions—especially warfare—fully autonomous systems portend greater speed and less uncertainty, among other potential benefits. Some believe that fully autonomous systems will bring about revolutionary performance gains in the principles of war; these include mass, maneuver, and economy of force. Physical and digital experiments are underway in the U.S. military to test these hypotheses.

In thinking about and experimenting with autonomous systems, leaders should continue applying the two-fold lesson we provided in Chapter 1; that is, contextualize applications to specific mission tasks while not allowing lack of imagination to eliminate potential breakthroughs. Visions of "killer robots" are highly conceptual and prone to ignore that lesson. The Defense Science Board's (DSB) 2014 study of American military power is instructive on this point:

> *Whether mediated by man or machine, all acts, but especially acts related to warfighting, must be executed in accordance with policy and so, in some sense, there is no completely autonomous behavior.* **Any use of autonomy must conform to a substantive command and control regime** *laying out objectives, methods and express limitations to ensure that autonomous behavior meets mission objectives while conforming to policy, [the laws of armed conflict and International Humanitarian Law] (emphasis added).*

The DSB is highlighting two facts about the development and operational deployment of autonomous systems. First, any autonomous system will be the result of tremendous amounts of human engineering and programming. Second, autonomous systems will be deployed in ways that conform to U.S. military command and control doctrine and tactics—techniques—and procedures. As a practical matter, completely autonomous is oxymoronic.

The DSB emphasized the development and use of autonomous systems as the most promising path to offset the PLA's increasing military strength and their doctrine of systems destruction warfare. Having observed the U.S. military's overwhelming conventional force power in Operation Desert Storm, the PLA concluded that defeating the U.S. military required the destruction of the intelligence and command and control systems on which the U.S. military depends—"systems destruction warfare." The PLA's development of capabilities to achieve this doctrine, as well as their deployment of advanced weapons and annexing a series of islands in international waters for the purpose of establishing forward military bases, drove the DSB on behalf of DoD to consider a strategy to offset the PLA's growing advantages.

Not surprisingly, the CCP and PLA have also recognized the import of AI to warfare, economics, and their form of governance. In 2017, the CCP released its plan for AI entitled, "New Generation Artificial Intelligence Development

Plan." The plan is driven by the CCP's stated goal to lead the world in AI by 2030. As a communist dictatorship, the CCP does not face constraints such as concern for Chinese citizens' civil liberties, which gives the CCP's supporting AI activities—government and commercial—a tremendous advantage in terms of accessing the data essential to AI model development. Former U.S. Deputy Secretary of Defense, Robert "Bob" Work, characterizes China as the leader in the ability to deploy AI models while the United States currently leads the development of AI models.

Former Google CEO, Eric Schmidt, and Robert Work co-chaired a commission chartered by the U.S. Congress—the National Security Commission on AI (NSCAI)—to define a "strategy for winning the artificial intelligence era." The NSCAI is a very different congressional commission in that recommendations were incrementally released to Congress in time to impact the annual National Defense Authorization Act. Moreover, the NSCAI commissioners and staff submitted draft legislation and policies for their recommendations with the aim of helping implementation.

An Exemplar Fully Autonomous System in the Making: Self-Driving Vehicles

The fully autonomous system is the pinnacle of AI applications. These are systems in which sensing, sense-making, decision-making, and action-taking are all accomplished by an integrated AI and automated system. These machines will do work that has thus far only been done by humans. Tesla, Inc. is one of the most advanced and well-known examples of this type, demonstrating that this type of AI application is no longer confined to the realm of science fiction.

A Tesla automobile comes with a set of sensors—including optical cameras, ultrasonic sensors, and radar—which give the vehicle input on stationary and moving objects 360 degrees around the vehicle. A computer within the car that uses a type of AI model called "deep learning" creates meaning from these sensors' data. Based on that meaning, the computer makes decisions and issues commands to the car, such as "slow to 35 mph on this stretch of road," "brake to avoid the car that has entered the intersection," and countless other actions that a driver would take.

Although each individual component of Tesla's cars, including the sensors, models, computer, and mechanical devices, are important, Tesla has advanced the state of autonomous vehicles not through these parts, but through the whole system. By "whole system," we are not simply referring to the parts integrated into a working vehicle, as essential as that is.

In fact, Tesla has mastered a much larger system in which cars send data back to a central location where the AI models are constantly being improved by data scientists. Then, these improvements are pushed back out to each car—AI at the edge in operations—through over-the-Internet software updates. Solving the problem of whether AI model development and operation is centralized, decentralized, or both is an essential challenge for driving results with AI. We address this in detail in subsequent chapters.

Leaders should also note that Tesla's implementation required much more than models. It required multiple sensors, an evolving UX, and integration into a platform. We suspect that fully autonomous systems in national security will face many of the same challenges.

With the commercial advances underway in the integration of AI and robotics, some national security leaders are calling for accelerated development and much greater reliance on autonomous systems. In the DoD's Third Offset Strategy, then Deputy Secretary of Defense, Robert Work, advanced a vision of two major categories of autonomous capabilities, which he called "human-machine collaborative battle networks" and "human-machine combat teams." The former brings more autonomous systems to military command and control, while the latter brings more autonomous systems to operational forces and their combat support forces.

The maturation of autonomous technology and operational concepts in commercial industries most likely means a continuing evolution of autonomous systems using AI in national security missions and functions. The key question is not *whether* fully autonomous systems can become operational in national security. Deciding *where* investments in fully autonomous systems will yield the most operational or business impact in a given time period is the key question for national security leaders. This requires much experimentation with different operational concepts and technologies. A deliberate portfolio of AI experimentation is a pass/fail check for leaders at the major enterprise level.

Summary: Completely Autonomous Is Oxymoronic

- Fully autonomous systems integrate AI for automated sense-making and decision-making with some type of robotics to execute actions. The self-driving car is the best-known example.

- Machines that can learn, decide, and act in ways similar to humans can potentially provide a revolution in national security operations.

- Any autonomous system is a product of tremendous engineering and programming by humans, and will be deployed in command and control regimes designed by humans.

- The vision is not for machines to completely replace humans in national security operations, but rather for human-machine collaboration.

- Discovering where and how fully autonomous systems will create the most mission impact is a problem naturally suited to a robust program of experimentation.

Leading the Program

"The Department of Defense (DoD) must set an ambitious goal. By 2025, the foundations for widespread integration of AI across DoD must be in place."

—National Security Commission on AI, 2020

"In consumer software, you can build one monolithic AI system to serve a hundred million or a billion users, and truly get a lot of value in that way. But in manufacturing, every plant makes something different. So, every manufacturing plant needs a custom AI system that is trained on their data."

—Andrew Ng, Renowned AI innovator, Venture Beat, March 2022

"A just-released Gartner Inc. report found that in the last two years, companies with artificial-intelligence experience moved just 53% of their AI proof of concepts into production."

—John McCormick, Wall Street Journal, August 2020

© Chris Whitlock, Frank Strickland 2023
C. Whitlock and F. Strickland, *Winning the National Security AI Competition*,
https://doi.org/10.1007/978-1-4842-8814-6_3

Summary

AI for national security is implemented in the context of government programs—funded by Congress and executed by departments and agencies. Some of these are technology-focused programs of record while others are programs providing services that deliver performance assessments and experiments. The majority of AI implementations will need to be highly decentralized, so leaders must be thoughtful when deciding to pursue centralized efforts. Existing programs like the Army Field Artillery Tactical Data System, Navy Ship Self-Defense System, Air Force Distributed Ground Control System, and many others may implement AI to improve mission performance. Initiatives like the new AI Data Accelerator Program create opportunities for innovation and experimentation. Effective leadership to integrate AI into a broad range of programs is critical to impact America's national security at scale and at pace.

We open this chapter by putting some boundaries on "programs" and follow with a foundational discussion of four axioms or realities that leaders must grapple with in designing, operating, and adapting (or modernizing) programs. After this foundation comes content regarding:

- Illustrations of AI program contexts

- Lean Six Sigma to illustrate centralized/decentralized execution

- Smartphone face ID to illustrate program challenges

- Best practices and key issues in program design, operations, and adaptation

Federal government programs initiate AI projects, integrate AI into enduring solutions, and identify and action substantial gaps requiring new funding or potentially justifying significant new programs. If the U.S. national security community is to achieve anything close to the performance improvements envisioned by the NSCAI, most of the work will take place within the context of formal government programs or "programs of record." The Office of Management and Budget, which is responsible for managing the entirety of the Federal Budget process, takes a broad view when defining "programs." No matter what definition is chosen, the reality is that people and systems constitute the muscle mass of government programs; this is made possible via funding appropriated by the U.S. Congress for specific authorized purposes.

The U.S. Constitution and subordinate statutes give Congress the power to appropriate and authorize all the funding departments and agencies expend on their missions. While there is some latitude in expending these funds, anyone experienced in government knows there is not an unfettered ability to repurpose funds outside the intent of Congress. Congress sets staffing levels for each agency or department (e.g., the number of marines in the Marine Corps). Legislators approve major systems and the programs to build them (e.g., the Aegis Weapon System, the Army Vantage Program). Performance expectations come with the funding; Congress provides oversight to ensure the nation gets what was directed. Consistent with legislative expectations, government program offices procure development solutions as well as services to accomplish desired outcomes. They do so by issuing contracts to vendors—contracts that specify requirements, deliverables, schedules, and funding.

For national security programs, the NSCAI advocated an ambitious objective of ensuring the DoD is AI-ready by 2025. In parallel with the NSCAI's work, departments and agencies have begun emphasizing AI capabilities. For example, the Navy declared AI as one of its top three technology areas for the entire department. Creating AI capabilities across the national security enterprise is a major challenge; the work will continue for decades. In Chapter 2, we defined the broad, varied mission challenges, but mobilizing work across a wide range of government programs is essential to achieve the NSCAI's aspiration for the United States to win the global AI competition in this century.

Four Program Types. The simplest framework to consider programs is to split them into two categories—1) system programs and 2) those focused on providing various services. Major system programs (over one thousand) represent discrete opportunities and challenges with regard to AI integration and application. The service-oriented programs (and associated contract support) can be further subdivided. Together we present four program types national security leaders may experience in driving AI implementations:

- **Major system programs:** These are large programs of record wherein an agency is acquiring a major mission or business system, which can include AI components. These acquisition efforts are managed by Program Executive Officers, Program Offices, System Program Offices. In DoD alone, over 1,000 formal programs across four acquisition categories (mainly based on size) are in development or operation at this writing. The Intelligence Community, Department of Homeland Security, and other national security organizations all have major programs for acquiring mission and business systems.

- **Departmental AI centers:** These are centers and offices performing analysis and developing AI solutions within cabinet-level departments. Examples include the Army's AI Integration Center, the Department of State's Center for Analytics, and the Customs and Border Protection's AI Center of Excellence. These centers can output AI functionality to programs of record or create prototype capabilities emerging from experiments.

- **Cross-departmental AI centers:** These are centers and offices providing analysis and engineering support and even developing AI solutions across multiple departments and agencies, such as the DoD's Joint AI Center (JAIC) and the Government Services Administration AI Center of Excellence. These centers can output AI functionality to programs of record or create prototype capabilities emerging from experiments representing new candidate systems of record.

- **Functional or mission-oriented services organizations/contracts:** Military service staffs, the Joint Staff, elements within the Office of the Secretary of Defense or counterparts in Intelligence and Homeland Security have these efforts. Beyond these a range of components within national security organizations can and do address AI-related needs and opportunities. These can cut across personnel, finance, facilities/installation, supply chain/logistics, intelligence, operations, and other functions. In these environments, small teams may leverage AI-capabilities to perform assessments, enable dashboards, and conduct AI-related experiments.

Four Big Questions. Leaders at the program level must continuously address and monitor four questions if they are to deliver significant mission impact through AI solutions:

1. Are AI efforts focused in priority areas? Programs initiate AI projects and it is crucial given limited resources that these cover priority mission areas. Answering the prioritization question requires some clear sense of strategy. Depending on whether the AI concept implicates a new versus existing program and whether or not the context is an autonomous system will drive many of the options. Each service, agency, organization will have many potential areas for AI-related innovation. Each will also be governed by budget constraints. Leaders, even at the top of the organization and then cascading down, must engage to ensure AI is being explored and developed in priority mission areas. Common frameworks for these organizations whether task lists or enterprise architectures can provide a basis for more comprehensive evaluations of potential and need.

2. Are sufficient resources focused on AI implementation? Programs integrate AI into enduring solutions; this costs money. Among the thousands of potential mission applications of AI in a department or agency, how is AI spending prioritized? Is there a clear sense of the AI impact opportunities across mission areas to frame investment decisions? In those cases where AI is part of a larger system, what amount of effort on AI development versus the effort on other elements of the solution? As we discussed in the Chapter 2 project types, these performance questions are not straightforward; they deserve more analytical rigor than simply gut-level investment decisions.

3. Are those AI resources paying off? Is the before and after impact of AI investments captured? A number of confounding factors can make it difficult to create a clear picture of current performance, but this requires attention to both advocating for needs and demonstrating payoff. AI will not necessarily improve performance; the payoff is a function of the type of deployment, as discussed in Chapter 2. Additionally, a lack of clear baseline performance is a consistent point of critique from the Government Accountability Office regarding DoD business transformation efforts.

4. How are programs adapting in organization or capability? AI solution development spans a wide range of activities from policies, to prototyping, production, operations, and maintenance. How do you decide what AI work can be centralized and what can be executed in a decentralized structure? When AI models are a component of a larger solution—the normative case—how do you work the technical, organizational, and interpersonal challenges created by having to integrate across multiple seams?

Effective leadership at the program level is essential to the United States winning the AI competition for national security. In this chapter, we help program leaders succeed by equipping them with enduring truths for program-level leadership, experience from case studies, and a set of best practices for leading AI at the program level.

Program Axioms
Axioms for Leading AI Programs

In addressing the challenge of widespread AI implementation in major programs, we believe four axioms are true regarding AI and advanced analytics solutions. These axioms shape how we can successfully expand the use of AI across the national security sector. These axioms are interrelated and intended to shape how we communicate, fund, co-fund, integrate, and engage diverse programs across organizations. The axioms represent enduring truths and shape the character of the AI challenge for program leaders at all levels. AI is each of the following:

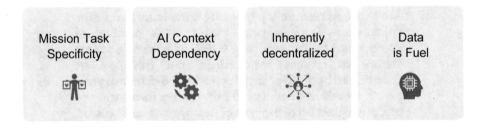

| Mission Task Specificity | AI Context Dependency | Inherently decentralized | Data is Fuel |

Mission Task Specific. All AI implementations are "mission task specific." AI introduces the capability to navigate tasks customarily or historically addressed by a human. In a workflow, we might think of AI at various decision points, ranking, scoring, matching, and approving, and so on; the AI is explicitly focused on a mission-task. In the logistics arena, this might recommend shipping parts to a location. In the maintenance area, this might mean recommending a preventative maintenance inspection on a piece of gear. In personal communications, the task could be using face identification models to verify you are the authorized user of your phone. AI is connected to a specific mission task. As noted in Chapter 2, the efforts toward general AI will continue evolving over many years, likely decades. However, over the foreseeable future we are best advised to think of AI as tightly connected to a mission task. As Andrew Ng points out regarding manufacturing, the problems are distinct and required tailored AI solutions. This will be the dominant reality.

Context Dependent. Once we identify a specific mission task, we immediately grapple with the context to bound potentially successful approaches for AI solution development or advanced analytics. Face identification algorithms designed to work on your iPhone with a single sensor input and fairly controlled parameters are quite different than facial identification running in an enterprise with multiple sensor-type inputs and highly varied data capture parameters (i.e., distance, angles). Running an AI model on your phone only for your face is an entirely different context from a solution running real-time against diverse inputs to identify particular people of interest. Some models must run in real-time and on edge devices. Other AI models can run offline and provide periodic outputs into workflows. The context fundamentally shapes the work of a solutions team and their integration with broader development teams.

Inherently Decentralized. AI is not represented in one program or even a handful, but rather a diverse range of decentralized decision points and functions across thousands of IT programs and other systems. In this context, tens of thousands workflow decision points or discrete capabilities that might benefit from AI solutions represent potential insertion points for AI. In structuring larger efforts to drive the broad adoption of AI, we must recognize the systems and problems we want to impact are independent and decentralized. Importantly, as this pertains to programs of record and various systems, each of these efforts has requirements, current funding limits, and current challenges related to expected performance, schedule, and cost. This reality presents specific leadership challenges if we are to rally these diverse efforts effectively to improve performance.

Fueled by Data. If no data, then no AI model and, thus, no performance improvement. The easiest way for an organization to choke off progress in this area is bureaucratically restricting access to data. AI solutions or the exploratory analytics that precede solutioning require access to data—typically not from a single system or database. The fact that the environment is inherently decentralized and requires access to multiple systems creates many opportunities to slow the pace of work or stop it altogether. The fix here is not technology alone—in fact, viewing it that way can be unhelpful. Whatever the purview of the program, leaders must act to ensure data is made accessible so associated exploration and model development can happen briskly. The workload for systems administrators, competition between contractors, control concerns between organizations, security concerns—all these and other factors contribute to slow-rolling data access, which stalls the work of teams.

Illustration of AI Program Contexts

Case studies can help leaders think in practical terms about the opportunities and challenges presented to AI at the program level. In this section, we first consider a set of DoD programs at multiple levels to share insights from experience, interviews, and research on important leadership issues; these issues are important to consider when establishing a new program or improving existing efforts. We start with a major program of record, the Navy's Aegis Weapon System, then move up the organizational chain to the Department of the Navy and the DoD overall.

As we move up the chain from major system programs to departmental AI efforts, the questions regarding prioritization of AI investments naturally become more complex. For example, how do the Chief of Naval Operations or Chief of Staff of the Army structure activities to ensure maximum progress on AI across the service consistent with naming the area a top priority? How does the Office of the Director of National Intelligence (ODNI) foster progress across the diverse agencies in the Intelligence Community? Leaders will better appreciate the magnitude of the department-wide challenge as we consider the tremendous degree of complexity in just the Navy Aegis program itself.

We also examine three cases with large scope and relevance. First, the DoD's implementation of Lean Six Sigma across the department. Second, the Department-wide Counter-IED initiative during the wars in Afghanistan and Iraq. Last, the commercial smartphone vendors' use of facial recognition. Note, while neither LSS nor the Counter-IED efforts were centered on AI, the implementations provide insight on opportunities and concerns regarding centralized approaches. The facial recognition case puts the program axioms into a practical context.

The Aegis Weapon System (AWS)—The Operational and Functional Environment for a Major Program. With almost four decades of service history, this weapons system is central to the U.S. Navy's afloat air and ballistic missile defense capability and a major part of our global maritime combat force. The AWS is deployed aboard both Arleigh Burke class destroyers as well as Ticonderoga class cruisers—a total number of about 80 vessels in the Navy's fleet of some 300-odd ships and submarines (Figure 3-1).

Figure 3-1. Arleigh Burke class destroyer

Even to a relatively untrained eye, the destroyer bristles with a variety of features (weapon systems, helicopter landing pad, and environmental covers for various radars or communications antennae). These destroyers and cruisers are comprised of many important programs spanning propulsion, energy, command and control, weapons, logistics, and more. They are built to serve 30-plus years with the expectation of various modernizations over time as technologies change. The Aegis Weapon System is central in processing inputs from high-performance SPY radar and other on-board sensors as well as sensor and platform data from other navy and joint systems. Aegis also orchestrates a range of weapons on the vessel. In sum, Aegis is central to the primary missions of these vessels: air and ballistic missile defense.

Figure 3-2. Combat information center—Arleigh Burke class destroyer

The photograph in Figure 3-2 shows the Combat Information Center (CIC) on an Arleigh Burke destroyer. The name is meaningful, this center deals with combat and tactical information—a good example of the sense-making and decision-making activities outlined in Chapter 2. The decisions made by sailors standing watch in the nerve center for the ship can be enormously consequential. They process data from various sensors and on-board systems to constantly assess the environment, identify potential or actual threats, and direct appropriate responses. As you study the scene, note the tight quarters and wide variety of systems and displays. AWS is a central facet of this environment, but the CIC is illustrative of "context" for any potential AI-centered activities. Adjacent systems of record, whether sensors, software applications, or the hardware and network environment, define the context for solution development. While new elements might be introduced, that is not a casual activity—this ship has limited opportunities available to modernize with new equipment. It all must be integrated seamlessly with the current combat information systems, then be readily maintainable during extended underway periods.

The CIC picture provides some visual sense for the AWS environment while the architecture graphic (Figure 3-3) gives insight into the range of systems of record and capabilities that comprise the Aegis, provide crucial inputs, or receive outputs. Capabilities reflected in red are weapon systems. Those reflected in blue are various sensors. The green elements focus on command

and control functions as well as associated communications. The Aegis weapon system is in the center of the graphic. It includes several major elements: the AEGIS Display System, Command & Decision (C&D), and Weapons Control System (WCS). Note the SPY radar is central in this capability—it has been since its inception. Notably, C&D integrates inputs from many sensors or data sources. This suggests it might be fruitful ground for AI, but the larger point is this is an ecosystem of many systems of record and capability. Each of these has 1) requirements and performance expectations, 2) funding constraints, 3) current deficiencies in schedule, time, or cost, 4) technical limitations, and 5) potential constraints associated with industry contracts.

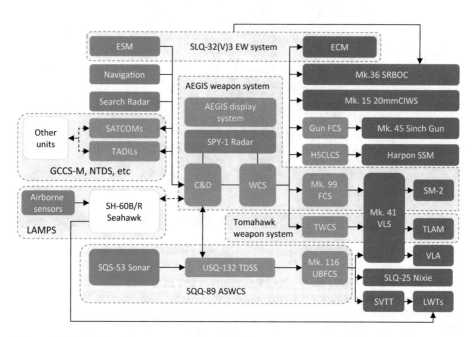

Figure 3-3. High-level component view of Aegis weapon system and related systems

Program Executive Offices. AEGIS in its programmatic context. Individual systems of record or programs do not exist in a vacuum, as illustrated in Figure 3-3. The pictures and functional architecture illustrate the operational environment and the range of adjacent capabilities that may be implicated in any individual effort to introduce AI or conduct advanced analytics around performance. Across the military services, almost 40 Program Executive Offices provide crucial acquisition coordination in addition to ensuring adequate operations and maintenance support. This is another level of leadership and oversight that may accelerate the insertion or adoption of AI. However, PEO has many challenges that are broad and an environment that requires as much persuasion as direction. The illustration shown in

Figure 3-4 is of the Navy Program Executive Office for Integrated Warfare Systems (IWS)—an expansive and critically important effort to the service. Note in the bottom left that the PEO spans 124 programs/ projects. High priority missions are reflected in the "Acquisition Category" or ACAT level.

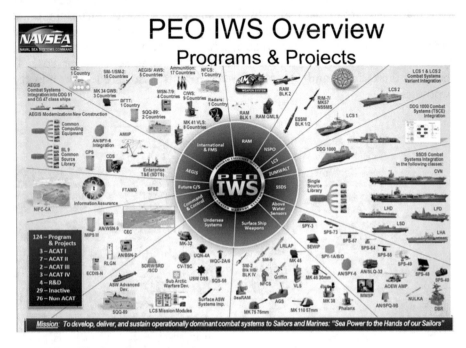

Figure 3-4. Navy PEO for integrated weapon systems—including Aegis weapon system

The PEO director and staff play important roles in coordinating, integrating, prioritizing, and producing Congressional Budget Justification Book inputs, but they cannot shift money across these programs unfettered. Effectively, the PEOs may need to foster integration and coordination without being allotted additional funds by Congress explicitly for this purpose.

■ **Gray Zone AI Solutions** Not all AI solutions begin as systems of record or as part of a major technology program. For operational capabilities, the major technology programs and systems of record are dominant, but far from the only path.

The government runs a number of non-technology programs often focused on analytics and AI-related work. Many of these are supported by industry on multi-year contracts.

Teams working in these environments can create AI solutions or conduct experiments that progress to smaller-scale capabilities (prototypes, proofs of concept) not yet formalized as systems of record. A common form would be a dashboard that may apply advanced techniques to process and transform data then served to decision-makers via a dashboard.

We hold a simple view based on numerous experiences with different agencies and departments through the years: 1) AI projects in these environments are very important, 2) organizations must take care that any work crafted to be enduring is actually supportable long-term. PEOs and system programs are very focused on sustainment. In contrast, the service-type programs are often more focused on operations support, performance assessments, and experiments over creating and sustaining capabilities. Consider a simple example.

In a DoD staff environment, an organization wanted more discrete and detailed tracking of select activities. A creative military member and data scientist accessed some data sources (via advanced programming interfaces) and fashioned a pipeline that included various computations and transformations to feed a dashboard. All this was in a particular programming language. The military member rotated out and the replacement lacked the skill and knowledge to operate and adapt the capability. The organization was left to consider migrating the capability to another group for sustainment/support, adding contractor support, rebuilding in an easier to support construct (problematic), or shutting the capability down. In our experience, this is a classic dilemma in the non-systems program environments.

In the absence of transition, these organizations become mired in sustainment activities or struggle to maintain performance and meet other requirements. Service program leaders should pay careful attention to transition planning to migrate capabilities or make necessary plans to adequately support prototypical solutions for periods longer than expected.

Envision the challenge for the Director of PEO IWS: drive deeper integration of AI into Navy systems. This leader is persuading, coordinating, motivating, and advocating, but is limited in his or her ability to shift substantial resources by the inherent constraints around all the "subordinate" programs/projects. As stated previously, each of those has 1) requirements and performance expectations, 2) funding constraints, 3) current deficiencies in schedule, time, or cost, 4) technical limitations, and 5) potential constraints associated with industry contracts. They have independent leaders working with their own set of industry partners to create and sustain capabilities. A variety of reasons cause competing dynamics and forced choices. The PEO clearly spans a set of related warfare systems—capabilities in which data sharing and optimization across related functions holds great promise. But introducing AI-centered solutions across this portfolio poses a complex, multi-faceted challenge. When we think about moving AI forward from a programmatic perspective, we paint on this complicated canvas.

Service/Departmental-level Program Leadership. Imagine being the senior uniformed or civilian leader of a military service. How do you drive AI and advanced analytics adoption? For example, following the model with the AEGIS Weapon System and PEO IWS, the Army has multiple PEOs and over 1,500 systems of record, each of which is a potentially fruitful deployment environment for AI. This is the reality for all the services, agencies, and departments in the national security community. The deployment environment for AI is highly decentralized—thousands of independent, but linked, systems of record and programs.

Two techniques to foster AI integration are important: large experimentation and exercise efforts or establishing large, new projects. The military services implemented a variety of approaches over the last several years to push toward organizational change. For example, the Navy formed task forces around warfare domains (e.g., aviation, surface) to identify beneficial areas for experimentation and improve coordination and crosstalk. These task forces provide input to PEOs and programs along with context on which the Office of Naval Research focused R&D. In parallel, the Chief of Naval Operations initiated Project Overmatch, one of the top priority Navy efforts intended to improve the network, hardware, and software factory environment for command and control. For its part, the Army created a new Army Futures Command in Austin, Texas, which is charged with rapid experimentation and prototyping regarding autonomous systems and AI. Additionally, the Army-wide Project Convergence provides a venue to focus and showcase related advancements.

Arguably, one of the most important things the senior leader can do is to track progress across the organization against clearly set expectations about AI adoption. Given that AI is task-specific, context-dependent, and decentralized across many programs, one might expect a large number of AI-centered projects. Creating a clear framework is crucial to capturing the impact of these initiatives. This is a new area rather than a classic business intelligence reporting problem—the data on how AI improves baseline performance goes largely uncaptured. Consequently, not unlike many areas in government operations, a clear expectation must be set around the data to be captured and how it is to be reported. For the military part of the national security community, unit readiness is reported monthly against a structured framework. This regularized reporting then becomes fuel for executive leadership discussions on progress against strategy. Do we have enough projects? Are we making sufficient progress? Are we applying sufficient resources? AI leaders should aim to make these conversations less conceptual, more data-rich, and more practical.

Joint AI Center (JAIC). The Office of the Secretary of Defense is working to accelerate AI adoption. An illustration of this comes in the formation of the Join AI Center (JAIC) in 2018 "to seize upon the transformative potential of Artificial Intelligence technology for the benefit of America's national security." The explicit intent was to make the JAIC the focal point for AI in the DoD—a substantial charter, given the highly decentralized challenge. Mission initiatives are a major element in the JAIC effort, focusing on major functional areas that are present in multiple military services. For example, JAIC's "warfighting" function includes command and control, joint fires, and other activities. The JAIC further invested in the creation of a Joint Common Foundation to bring data together in support of exploration and model development.

Notably, a DoD-wide charter for AI acceleration presents many challenges. One of the senior leaders in JAIC remarked in late-2020, "I think the challenge right now is access. We're trying to find out where all the data is and where all the previous work has been done," he explained, "So part of our job is to also encourage developers to bring their projects into the Joint Common Foundation (JCF) so that we can build a DoD repository." Now we only need to reflect back to the discussion of numerous programs like the AEGIS Weapon System to grasp the nature of this challenge; each of these programs has a unique data environment and constraints as well as contract constraints, equities, or other limitations. It is no small effort to bring all the AI projects to one central development environment.

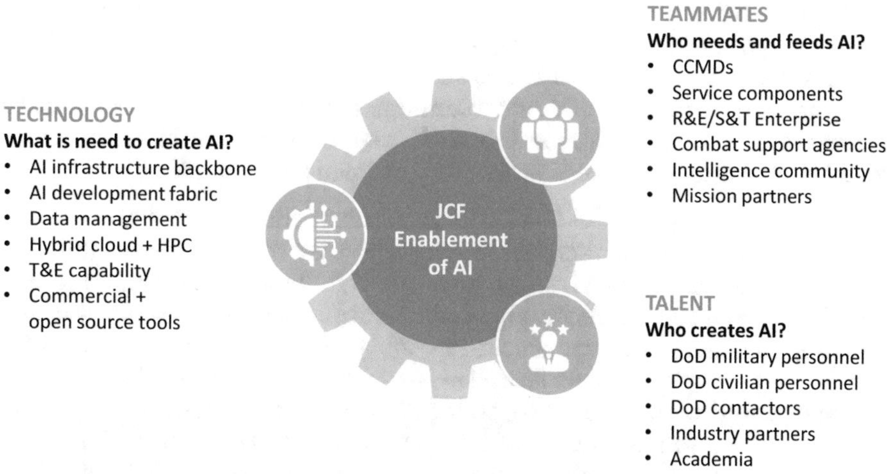

TECHNOLOGY
What is need to create AI?
- AI infrastructure backbone
- AI development fabric
- Data management
- Hybrid cloud + HPC
- T&E capability
- Commercial +
  open source tools

JCF
Enablement
of AI

TEAMMATES
Who needs and feeds AI?
- CCMDs
- Service components
- R&E/S&T Enterprise
- Combat support agencies
- Intelligence community
- Mission partners

TALENT
Who creates AI?
- DoD military personnel
- DoD civilian personnel
- DoD contactors
- Industry partners
- Academia

Figure 3-5. JAIC joint common foundation role in AI enablement

The JAIC executes its charter through a range of activities, some of which are quite complex. The Joint Common Foundation is an important initiative, creating a computing environment that allows a range of users to perform AI-related development. The JCF approach is illustrated in Figure 3-5. In parallel to JCF, the JAIC has teams working to address challenges in the warfighting, intelligence, cyber, and other military missions. These teams work to understand requirements, rally stakeholders, and develop or co-develop AI solutions. As leaders craft and adapt AI programs, it is necessary to recognize that AI activities span a range of complexity, and all are not equally suited to perform from a centralized posture. AI is still so relatively new in terms of broad adoption and widespread deployment of solutions at enterprise scale. Leaders need to advocate for and adjust programs as drivers of effectiveness and inhibitors are clarified through AI assessments, experimentation, and operational development.

Case Example: Centralized DoD Program to Counter IED Threat

In 2003 insurgents and other hostile combatants in Iraq began to use improvised explosive devices (IEDs) to attack and kill U.S. and coalition soldiers. The IED threat presented an end-to-end problem. Bomb makers assembled IEDs using a number of widely available commercial parts, such as the transmitter and receiver used by a garage door opener. Instructions for making IEDs were widely available, and manufacturing could occur almost anywhere; capital expenditures to get started were minimal but financiers were an active component. Attackers could emplace and detonate IEDs at times and places of their choosing. Once emplaced, an IED was very difficult to detect without substantial effort, such as a U.S. or coalition patrol slowing its pace to sweep the road and roadsides for IEDs. IED attacks steadily increased over time. Each month of 2005 saw an average of 35 U.S. soldiers killed by IED attacks. Dozens more were maimed and wounded.

DoD created the Joint IED Defeat Organization (JIEDDO) in 2006 to organize and execute department-wide efforts against the IED threat. JIEDDO had a very focused target: i.e., the network of IED manufacturers, attackers, and devices in a specific geographic and operational context, initially Iraq and then Afghanistan. For select acquisition efforts, JIEDDO was responsible for the full system development lifecycle – from research and initial acquisition. Without entering the debate regarding JIEDDO effectiveness, it is plain the organization served as a central (joint) effort to rapidly screen technologies or solutions and move select ones into acquisition. For example, JIEDDO drove early screening and acquisition of the Mine-Resistant Ambush-Protected (MRAP) vehicles. As this program ramped up, acquisition oversight transferred to the MRAP Task Force, with the vehicles being used by multiple military services and Special Operations Command. JEIDDO also played a central key role in pushing a family of electronic warfare jammers developed on a wide range of vehicle platforms. At some point with all these efforts, however, military service programs took over the efforts and pushed the equipment into operations. In this context, JIEDDO is a useful reference in considering what to centralize and what to leave to diverse services or programs to action.

With respect to AI, what is the best role for a centralized multi-departmental program? The defense-wide implementation of Lean Six Sigma (LSS) is presented as a case study, not to prescribe a solution, but rather to provoke thought. As you read this case, ask yourself: Is the nature of implementing AI across DoD and/or the national security enterprise more like the counter IED effort or more like the nature of DoD's efforts to implement LSS across the department?

Case Example: Lean Six Sigma: Centralized and Decentralized Program Elements

Case Context. This case uses the DoD implementation of Lean Six Sigma to explore useful boundaries on what can be centralized at higher organizational levels and what might best remain decentralized. In 2007, the Deputy Secretary of Defense, Gordon England, directed that Lean Six Sigma (LSS) become the department-wide continuous process improvement technique—all organizations were to use this to drive improvement. Not unlike aspects of AI, the goal was to improve Department-wide performance using LSS. DepSecDef England further directed the Deputy Undersecretary for Business Transformation to establish a Program Office to drive the adoption and use of LSS across the department. LSS focuses on speed and quality outputs in process performance. Processes for inventory management having little in common with processes for acquisition or security clearance approvals make this another inherently decentralized challenge.

History of LSS. When Deputy Secretary of Defense, Gordon England, directed the wide-spread use of LSS, the technique was well-established and successful in the DoD. It had a suite of tools that could be applied to any process, irrespective of its domain. LSS is a merger of Lean, which is integral in the Toyota Production System and Six Sigma which both originated in the 1980s. Lean is focused on increasing process speed effectively. Six Sigma focuses on error reduction. Fundamentally, LSS aspired to deliver cost savings. The LSS method targets eight types of process waste; teams pick from the toolkit to assess a given process and implement improvements. LSS is not a software development process, nor does it focus on organizational redesign or process redesign. By 2007, LSS was in wide use with associated training programs for staff members using a belt system. The most basic training (yellow belt) provided essentials. Staff could progress through green belt, black belt, and master black belt levels of training credentials.

DoD LSS Implementation. Recognizing successes scattered across the Department, the Deputy Secretary of Defense declared LSS a major initiative with the creation of a program office in the Office of the Secretary of Defense (OSD). Then, this resulted in a series of cascading activities. A DoD instruction was issued in July 2009, making it clear that LSS would implicate the entirety of the department including combatant commands, the individual military departments (e.g., Department of the Army), the Joint Staff, defense agencies, DoD field activities, and "other DoD components."

The DoD instruction specified four elements for all DoD components:

1. LSS would be an "essential tool" across the full range of DoD activities

2. LSS would focus on cost management and process performance

3. "Demonstrated performance improvements and results achieved as an outcome of CPI/LSS projects shall be documented and maintained in an automated, transparent fashion for purposes of management review, assessment, research, knowledge sharing, and historical reference"

4. Components could retain the savings due to LSS projects

The new Chief Management Officer established a program office for LSS consistent with earlier guidance. The essence of the program office's task was to ensure standardization of implementation with a clear set of training and implication expectations. Additionally, they would ensure activities and results were posted to a central database. Further, the program office would conduct periodic reviews on effectiveness and annual symposia to promote the method.

Individual components, in turn, initiated or enhanced activities to comply with this guidance and support the department-wide effort. For example, the Army assigned this effort under the Office for Business Transformation to integrate it with other change activities. Training was organized for both service members and civilians. Additionally, the office created reporting guidelines and mechanisms. By 2011, the Army trained over 5,700 green belts, 2,400 black belts, and 175 master black belts across the service.

Project execution was highly decentralized for the vast majority of the effort; in 2011, the Army counted over 2,100 projects underway with an estimated savings of over $3.5 Billion. These projects spanned the service with significant activities in materials and health. A prominent success was the Army's effort to speed the refurbishment of damaged HUMVEEs, slicing days off the total cycle time and substantially increasing the monthly throughput.

Observations on the LSS Work. As we search for guideposts around structuring AI-related programs, three aspects of the LSS effort stand out. First, the nature of LSS is quite different from that of AI in that the latter is founded in software and system development. LSS projects by contrast can be relatively quick. But they share some common challenges in execution. Second, the DoD placed a centralized effort on training and standards but expected decentralized execution. Lastly, the entire program placed customary LSS emphasis on capturing and documenting both potential and actual savings. As AI leaders, we should consider these when establishing or improving AI-related programs.

Unlike AI, LSS was not a major software initiative but both efforts need realism in setting expectations and framing projects. LSS is chiefly focused on improving existing process performance and eliminating waste or error. While some small software tools may be a facet of a particular solution, LSS is not a software-centered activity. LSS might look at issues like when to reorder components, when to forward work to a next step, how to synchronize work between activities, or how to organize small teams. Using the Army as an example, LSS is distinguished from larger-scale "business process redesign." During the LSS journey, some teams identified quite large targets such as improving the security clearance process. Some of these large efforts underperformed substantially; even 10-12 years later, groups are still trying to tackle these security clearances and it is vexing as is crosses multiple organization boundaries, implicates personnel guidelines, requires significant software change, as well as representing significant cultural change. Realism is framing larger efforts is a lesson we might take away from LSS.

LSS featured common training and certification. As the DoD pushed this initiative, there was a well-established body of training materials and knowledge to draw on, creating the basis for a standard approach. Thousands of DoD members, both military and civilian, were trained to varying levels and worked full- or part-time on LSS projects. The project frameworks of "Plan-Do-Check-Act" or "Define-Measure-Analyze-Improve-Control" bounded a standardized approach to a variety of challenges. Leaders had confidence that the work was being approached in a way that reflected best practice because of the natural stages integrated into a project progression. In the AI arena, there is no similar widely-used standard on training or progressive certification. We are not entirely bereft of materials on which to draw. However, we have highly variable materials without the standardized training standards of the LSS context. This is not necessarily a deficiency—some critiqued the LSS focus on training over outcomes. Nevertheless, keep in mind that there is no industry standard approach to AI solution development.

Capturing Cost Savings/Budget Impact. As explained, the entire department policy incentivized improvement by allowing the components to retain the savings from their LSS projects. The department also emphasized the estimated and actual cost savings for projects. This effort demonstrates to the legislature the commitment to improving efficiency and effectiveness across the operation. However, our discussions with participants suggest driving this from the enterprise level brings some challenges with it. The essence of the executive choice may be beyond driving the requirement for reporting, but in the nuance of the reporting standards. The key performance indicators (KPIs) in one part of the enterprise may make no sense in another portion. Consequently, the LSS roll-out emphasized scoping potential savings and capturing reportable items while leaving latitude to subordinate elements to tailor the measures.

Summary and Implication. The DoD LSS program effectively integrated centralized and decentralized elements appropriate to the mission challenge. Policy, training, and results tracking were centralized while execution was decentralized to the military services and subordinate elements. Decentralized execution in the DoD context and more broadly across the LSS community is necessary because solutions require expert insight to numerous processes and workflows. LSS is performed best close to the workflow by experts in the work but trained in the technique.

Case Example: Smartphone Face ID and Implications to Program Design

Government teams often learn from commercial practices and mimic them in Federal development efforts. While wise in some instances, the mimicry may be based on myths or misimpressions. We believe in commercial best practice and believe that the government should draft on commercial technology development wherever appropriate. We also believe government leaders should recognize the limitations of transferring commercial capabilities to Federal service. Leaders should spend time understanding the implied and explicit limitations of pursuing these solutions and whether the mission tasks and contexts allow for successful adoption whether for individual programs or cross-department common solutions.

In the AI arena, some commercial activities provide fantastic references for the art of the possible and the tradespace in approaching development. We share this case of smartphone face identification as it illustrates three of the axioms in practice—mission task specificity, context dependency, and inherent decentralization.

Case Context. This short case explores some of the boundaries to creating cross-program or cross-platform solutions with an AI-specific commercial example that will be familiar in function to almost all readers. This case builds on the LSS case to fuel further thinking on where to draw the centralized versus fully decentralized boundary in any domain.

Smartphones are a great case study to understand applied AI as well as some of the challenges that rise in attempts to create common solutions across multiple programs. Apple, Samsung, Motorola, LG, and Nokia are major non-

Chinese smartphone manufacturers. Over the past decade, companies moved to bring face identification to these devices as a fast method to authenticate users by applying AI. In this market, no dominant software emerged to address this mission task.

Relevant Issue for Government Executives. At a fundamental level, all these smartphone devices perform a similar family of tasks. User identification and authentication is a common mission task—face identification is its AI-enabled approach. The mission task is to use the camera or sensors on the device along with AI to authenticate the user. If this is a common mission task, we might ask why no common method and software provider has emerged? To answer this question, we look at two of the other AI program axioms: context dependency and inherent decentralization.

Context Dependency. Smartphone development environments are not abstract or conceptual; they are practical and bounded by specific constraints. These include hardware, software, device, and network constraints. These constraints differ between manufacturers, from sensors to processing capabilities. While the manufacturers share a common task, they must perform it in different contexts. We share a more detailed insight from Apple's Vision product to illustrate larger system integration and performance issues impact AI approaches. The following paragraphs that describe the issues Apple had to address in making Face ID viable on their iPhones:

> *"Optimizing   [Face   Identification]   for   On-Device Performance*
>
> *The joy of ease-of-use would quickly dissipate if our face detection API were not able to be used both in real time apps and in background system processes [emphasis added]. Users want face detection to run smoothly when processing their photo libraries for face recognition, or analyzing a picture immediately after a shot. **They don't want the battery to drain or the performance of the system to slow to a crawl** [emphasis added]. Apple's mobile devices are multitasking devices. Background computer vision processing therefore **shouldn't significantly impact the rest of the system's features** [emphasis added].*
>
> We implement several strategies to minimize memory footprint and GPU usage. To reduce memory footprint, we allocate the intermediate layers of our neural networks by analyzing the compute graph. This allows us to alias multiple layers to the same buffer. While being fully deterministic, this technique reduces memory footprint without impacting the performance

or allocations fragmentation, and can be used on either the CPU or GPU.

For Vision, the detector runs five networks (one for each image pyramid scale). These five networks share the same weights and parameters, but have different shapes for their input, output, and intermediate layers. To reduce footprint even further, we run the liveness-based memory optimization algorithm on the joint graph composed by those five networks, significantly reducing the footprint. Also, the multiple networks reuse the same weight and parameter buffers, thus reducing memory needs.

To achieve better performance, we exploit the fully convolutional nature of the network: All the scales are dynamically resized to match the resolution of the input image. Compared to fitting the image in square network retinas (padded by void bands), fitting the network to the size of the image allows us to reduce drastically the number of total operations. Because the topology of the operation is not changed by the reshape and the high performance of the rest of the allocator, dynamic reshaping does not introduce performance overhead related to allocation.

To ensure UI responsiveness and fluidity while deep neural networks run in background, we split GPU work items for each layer of the network until each individual time is less than a millisecond. This allows the driver to switch contexts to higher priority tasks in a timely manner, such as UI animations, thus reducing and sometimes eliminating frame drop.

Combined, all these strategies ensure that our users can enjoy local, low-latency, private deep learning inference without being aware that their phone is running neural networks at several hundreds of gigaflops per second."

Those paragraphs capture the context dependency of this Apple engineering team. They are mindful of hardware specifics; power usage and loads demanded by other applications concurrently on this edge device. They are working specific processing techniques on the processing unit to meet service level requirements (e.g., processing in milliseconds for specific tasks). They also leverage specific functions on the phone—including shared ones in their ecosystem—to optimize performance.

Importantly, other brands and engineering teams in this industry may choose different approaches. Some vendors provide cross-platform solutions with some adoption. As an example, a company named Sensory offers its TrulySecure solution—adopted by at least two of the smaller smartphone market share companies, Nokia and LG. But all these options come with trade-offs in cost and performance.

Inherent Decentralization. The smartphone industry includes more than 15 brands; Apple and Samsung represent the two largest market shares. Each of these companies has separate investors and shareholders. The smartphone is hardware with specific operating systems and application environments that are developed and upgraded over time; different portions of the devices are on different development timelines. Each manufacturer writes its own software or outsources it, codes its architectures internally or contracts it out, and makes many other decisions unique to their brand. The nuance of each brand differentiates it from its competitors.

In this diverse market, some common standards and cross-cutting organizations provide guidelines and promote sharing. For example, the European Telecommunications Standards Institute (The Standards People) publishes important content for the industry. In 2021, ETSI released a Consumer Mobile Device Protection Profile to define security and assurance requirements for smartphones and tablets. However, standards like these still allow a wide latitude for companies to create performance- or price-differentiated products.

The operating system level represents the greatest area of common software use. Google writes the Android operating system that powers the majority of smartphones. Additionally, Apple devices use the iOS operating system. Some smaller entrants remain in the operating system space, but effectively these two operating systems predominate. Essentially, the Android operating system is so popular because it is open-source and works across a diverse range of devices.

Summary and Implications. Leaders structuring programs must think carefully about attempts to build common AI-services, like face identification in this smartphone case, that bridge many programs of record. In the smartphone market, some vendors do opt to leverage shared capabilities (software as service) where the cost and performance trade-offs make sense. In others, smartphone vendors are building their own tightly integrated AI-solutions with a keen eye on managing hardware burdens, power management, and the ability to leverage other shared software on the phone. In DoD program of record environments, especially for tactical systems on the edge, this can present substantial challenges if the goal is centralized development of shared solutions. It is not impossible, but leaders should approach with eyes wide open and a recognition that integration into individual programs of record may be very difficult.

Key Leadership Issues and Best Practice for Program Design, Operation, Adaptation

Program-level Activities. When we consider these various levels from the discrete system of record (program) through PEOs and senior leader initiatives, a variety of functional activities are required, but not all are equally valuable at each level. Table 3-1 defines the functional activities required by a major program.

Table 3-1. Potential Major Activities for Any Program

Potential Program Activities	Description
Solution Development	Applying appropriated funding to create a capability (some combination of software, hardware, networks) to meet a national security requirement
Research & Prototyping	Exploring potential advantages in new hardware, software, and techniques that can impact existing programs or support entirely new efforts against requirements
Monitoring & Reporting	Regularized reporting of performance and critical activities
Coordination & Integration	Sharing information and resolving issues around shared capabilities or solutions
Funding/ Co-Funding	Applying funds to focus effort against organizational goals and encouraging systems of record to adapt
Training & Education	Any new fielded capability will require training, either in the schoolhouse or in operational units; education on capabilities and limits is also key for leaders
Staffing Support	Assigning staff from a work center to support distributed programs or activities with skilled personnel
Advocacy	Explaining capabilities and accomplishments in a compelling way not only to support Congressional decisions but for others in service to grasp contributions
Policy Development	Promulgating standards and approaches across multiple programs

Six Best Practices for Leading AI at the Program Level. Given the work activities that must be conducted by a major program, we suggest there are seven best practices for leading the execution of these activities:

1. **Be particular about what to centralize and what is left in individual programs.** The chart in Table 3-2 illustrates several types of programs discussed earlier in the chapter as well as the range of their potential activities. Not all activities are equally effective at all levels of potential AI program implementation. The following paragraphs highlight considerations in centralized efforts in an arena which is inherently decentralized. Solution development may be the most crucial area of decisions around establishing various centers or enhancing performance. AI can impact thousands of systems of record and be integral in a number of new, evolving systems. However, the individual programs are the driving force in building these. Particularly as it pertains to non-enterprise business systems, each program office will have an overall architecture, hardware approaches, software approaches, requirements, schedule constraints, and funding limitations. Trying to develop capability that can be readily leveraged by multiple programs in the AI arena is not impossible but will not be the primary means to introduce AI capability. In our view, the decision to charter new centralized development aspiring to influence multiple programs/projects should be scrutinized carefully. In addition, stakeholder programs should be aligned in advance of activity. For existing centralized efforts, closely monitor the degree of integration with decentralized programs and the degree to which capabilities are meaningfully used.

Table 3-2. Potential Program Activity by Program Type

Potential Program Activities	System of Record— Foundational Layer	Program Executive Office	Agency/Service-specific AI Center	Cross Agency/ Service AI Center
Solution Development				
Training & Education				
Staffing Support				
Funding/ Co-Funding				
Policy Development				
Research & Prototyping				
Monitoring & Reporting				
Program Advocacy				
Coordination & Integration				

■ Expected function   ▨ Approach with care

2. Several other activity areas are worth close consideration for establishing new or enhancing existing centravlized AI-activities; these are shaded yellow in Table 3-2. Training around AI solution operation and maintenance is something we might expect to come chiefly from the programs building solutions. Those teams know their solutions expertly and gain valuable insight through training interactions with the user community. Programs can effectively run train-the-trainer efforts with formal schoolhouses while staying linked to receive feedback. But, it is beneficial to keep training close to the program with these emerging solutions. On the other hand, general education on data science, AI, and related programming is something that lends itself nicely to centralized approaches spanning multiple programs and even entire agencies or departments, not unlike the LSS example. Creating a central group of experts who can be deployed to support various programs or operations is another organizational strategy. In this model, the center handles hiring, training, and managing deployment of staff. These staff are locally responsive to the supported element where they are assigned. This method may be especially helpful in early phases of accelerating awareness of data science and AI capabilities. However, unlike training and education a centralized office may have little influence over how assigned staff are actually used. This approach may be less valuable over time than having decentralized hiring and workforce management of data science and AI practitioners.

3. **Create a framework to measure progress and performance impact across projects.** Every government organization needs a framework to judge whether sufficient resources are applied and expected performance gains are emerging. Government leaders at multiple levels can prioritize and can (to varying levels) allocate proportional resources to drive progress. Information on progress across projects is critical to navigating these decisions.

   The trap many organizations fall into is producing anecdotal "success stories." One military service vice chief commented that "seeing all these small stories is not helpful. What are we actually doing?" To measure progress, leaders must ensure a framework is in place for standardized reporting. For example, in the DoD, this is accomplished for readiness with the Defense Readiness Reporting System (DRRS). This highlights that the department created a structured means to gather data at a regular time interval on the status of forces. Thousands of units report monthly in this system. Similarly, AI leaders can specify a framework for reporting the presence of projects, proportional resourcing, key performance indicators (KPIs), and progress. Each military service maintains an established task list; the crucial tasks the service must be capable of conducting for operational success. These task lists are one way to approach enterprise-wide monitoring of the AI implementation progress. These frameworks address fundamental areas such as maneuver, application of fires, intelligence, command and control, and so on. These are the exact areas in which AI must create advantages; the tiered composition of the task lists provides a potential ready-made framework to capture AI progress.

4. **Identify the high potential pay-off areas and resource them.** Across the national security enterprise, organizations are emphasizing AI. For some, it is formalized priority for the organization both internally and publicly. Returning to the Navy as an example, hypersonic weapons, autonomous systems, and AI are priorities for the service. Prioritization of organization goals is both necessary and helpful. However, AI should be prioritized because of its wide-spread potential application and the range of methods that can be used to progress it. Unlike the Lean Six Sigma challenge, which centers on process and focuses on fast-paced progress, AI solutions bring significant technological change. Leaders at multiple levels can create the greatest impact by ensuring priority problems are receiving coordinated treatment. This challenge will manifest at all levels, but the greatest needs for attention are within Program Executive Offices and at the military service/department level. Command and control receive tremendous attention across the Department of Defense—it also intersects with the intelligence activities in national security. It is particularly important to prioritize chained effects because battle management aspires to gain near-machine speeds in critical functions. Leaders can focus attention on end-to-end activities with a mission focus to

ensure crucial elements are not left unattended or held at lower priority because of competing demands. Returning to the Aegis Weapon System example from earlier in this chapter, multiple systems must interact quickly to engage successfully into the future—sensors, command and decision, and fire support. Leaders must analyze interconnected chains such as this to craft a comprehensive approach.

5. **Take action to make data available and accessible.** Data is the fuel for training and deploying AI-enabled solutions—it must be rendered accessible. Physical limitations may limit or prohibit local data capture and storage without technological change. This being said, it is important to ensure that, within programs and PEOs data can readily be captured and shared to support development of an AI solution. Collectively, leaders should not assume data is being captured in sufficient volumes or for sufficient time periods. To illustrate, consider sensors like a closed-circuit TV (CCTV) used for security applications. Many CCTVs in the private sector overwrite their storage every day or so. In a number of tactically focused systems, insufficient communication connectivity may prohibit sending data back continuously for storage. Additionally, physical limitations may prohibit local storage without technological change. To return to the Aegis Weapon System example again, the multitude of sensors onboard each ship creates a substantial volume of data each day. Are each of those ships rigged to store that data? Are the Navy networks rigged to support moving the data to centralized storage environments? These are questions that the AI leader needs to address to accelerate the development and deployment of AI solutions. Chapter 8 discusses this in further detail, but it is important for senior leaders to not only set expectations about data sharing but also to link evaluations in this area to prioritization decisions regarding new capabilities. A variety of options are viable, each with its pros and cons which must be matched to mission needs and budget realities.

6. **Work the seams between programs of record and innovation groups.** Multiple studies show that only a fraction of AI-related work in the commercial sector is deployed into operations. There are natural obstacles, including and especially the gap between innovation groups and production programs. The National Security Commission on AI laid out an ambitious goal to make the DoD AI-ready by 2025—a major emphasis on speed given the sweep of the problem. A host of practical, every-day dynamics can slow the pace of implementation to a crawl without adequate leader engagement. In this context, one focus for leaders can be ensuring emerging capabilities nurtured in R&D or central innovation activities migrate into programs of record. A range of legitimate issues can slow the conversion of R&D into operational capability. Program managers are constantly balancing competing issues with limited funds; integrating new capability presents cost and schedule impact. Programs of record typically have architects and system engineers in addition to development teams. These leaders set frameworks to guide extended development efforts over the course of years. Some innovation presents challenging choices about how to integrate particular AI-centered functionality—typically with impacts to cost and schedule. For example, an innovation-oriented group might argue "we have created a model for text processing and it is only 100 lines of Python code." The group responsible for production software might see the potential for additional work including major changes to other components in order to deploy the model into operations. Leaders must support acceleration of capabilities by engaging on both sides of the problem— innovation and production. For example, leaders might direct innovation groups by asking them about how they can apply promising work to a program of record. When the implementation is unclear, the team must 1) identify candidate programs to integrate the capability, 2) engage programs to screen emerging capabilities and plan integration, and 3) support integration and capability transition. For priority capabilities to transition, innovation leaders should consider regularized interaction with the receiving programs of record in the planning phase as well as in the integration and transition phases.

7. **Be proactive with contracts and intellectual property.** As with any major capability change area, AI progress leans heavily on industry expertise and technologies; the government will acquire these via contracts. Particularly for leaders coming from operational roles into dedicated programs or larger centralized programs, it is essential to think through the contractual posture of the program. We are capitalists and believe in competition. However, choose carefully where you focus the industry competition. The macro-objective is to rapidly introduce AI-enabled capabilities across the national security enterprise. The government recognizes that important facets of this change will come from non-traditional vendors and from small businesses. In parallel, this is a significant integration exercise at the individual program level and certainly where any centralized programs work to impact multiple individual programs. When procuring AI-related services, government buyers have two high-level options. The first is single award contracts with the expectation the prime contractor will nimbly add players to meet the needs. The second option is multi-award contracts where then competition continues with each task issued. Procurement officials are often biased toward multi-award contracts, which can be helpful at times. But government leaders must not be blind to the problems these can create with regard to collaboration and working integration. When the competition is constant, companies will necessarily be concerned with protecting themselves—notions of "check the company badge at the door" are sincerely naïve. Furthermore, leaders ought to structure tasks end-to-end. This approach is consistent with agile development; it charges a project team to grapple with requirements, a development and testing approach that flows through to deployment. The alternative, contractually, is to carve these functions up across companies. In many situations, this can create conflict that impedes organizational progress. No perfect solution exists, but our experience indicates that project-focused teams that are responsible for a product from end to end produce the best results.

Government Programming and Budgeting for AI Leaders

"If you look at it by any metric, we have a lot of money, and I think what we are trying to do is go after this with more of an abundance mindset, not a 'gosh I wish I had this much more.' What that leads to is we are starting with what we have, starting with the people that we have, with the funding that we have, with the technical expertise that we have, which is eye-watering."

—Rear Admiral Douglas Small
Commander, Naval Information Warfare Systems Command

© Chris Whitlock, Frank Strickland 2023
C. Whitlock and F. Strickland, *Winning the National Security AI Competition*,
https://doi.org/10.1007/978-1-4842-8814-6_4

"This is not a time for incremental toggles to federal research budgets or adding a few new positions in the Pentagon for Silicon Valley technologists. This will be expensive and require a significant change in mindset. America needs White House leadership, Cabinet-member action, and bipartisan Congressional support to win the AI era."

—National Security Commission on AI Final Report

Summary

Program authorities and funding already exist for creating some impact on national security through AI. The President's priorities and Congressional actions stemming from the NSCAI create opportunities for additional AI programs and funding. AI leaders must collaborate with their department's financial and congressional affairs staff to drive budgets in three contexts: the current Fiscal Year (FY); the next FY; and the FYs that come after the next. The process is not key; the program content is key and AI leaders own that content. This chapter demystifies the programming and budgeting process, equipping leaders with sufficient understanding to secure the funding required for global scale AI impact at a brisk pace.

This chapter begins with five axioms that provide AI leaders with strategic perspectives on engaging the federal programming and budgeting process. We then provide best practices for leading AI programming and budgeting in four areas:

- Demystifying the budget process so that leaders understand the essential elements.

- Leading execution of the current Fiscal Year (FY) budget, and why this is foremost.

- Leading formulation of future FY budgets, and how this prepares you to defend your program to Congress.

- Leading the defense of your next FY budget request to Congress.

The Challenge. We defined the four types of projects in an AI portfolio: performance assessments, experiments, dashboards, and deployed models (Figure 4-1). We defined and illustrated with case examples the importance of studies to shaping a portfolio. However, if national security leaders are going to create mission advantages over adversaries at global scale using AI, then leaders must drive beyond just studies to develop and deliver the many operational capabilities required to offset competitors' advantages. Given the global threats, chaos, and uncertainty of this century, leaders must get to widespread operational deployment at scale at a brisk pace.[1]

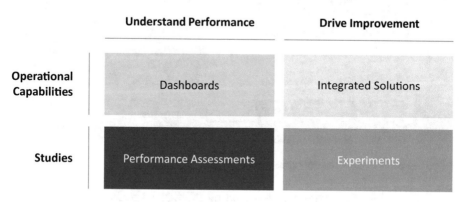

Figure 4-1. Four AI project types

This requires leaders to do what leaders are uniquely charged to do—deliver on the present with approved programs and funding while preparing for the future with proposed programs and funding. As summarized in Chapter 3, the funding for major system solutions comes to national security departments and agencies through formal *programs* that are authorized and appropriated by Congress. AI program leaders and their supporting project leaders request and receive the necessary funding through the four paths outlined in Figure 4-2.

As depicted in green, the funding immediately within a program manager's control is the funding authorized and appropriated by Congress for an existing program of record within the current government Fiscal Year (FY). The other three paths—depicted in gray—have yet to pass through the budget processes in the executive and legislative branches of government.

---

[1] The NSCAI called for DoD to be "AI ready" by 2025, fewer than five years after the commission published its report.

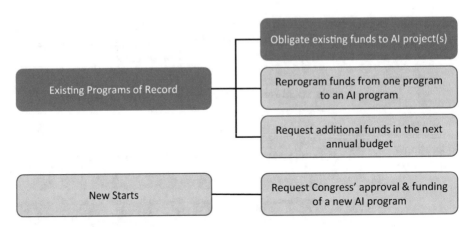

Figure 4-2. Program manager funding environment

In 2021, the Government Accounting Office (GAO)—a government consultancy that supports Congress—profiled current AI-related projects in DoD (Table 4-1). GAO found 602 AI projects funded through research and development (R&D) funding and 82 AI projects funded through procurement funding. R&D and procurement in this context refer to different types of Congressional Appropriations. (We define these and discuss salient implications for AI later.) These 685 projects also represent the green path in Figure 4-2—the point being that Congress has already authorized and appropriated funding for some initial AI work across much of DoD.

Table 4-1. Artificial Intelligence (AI) Projects by Identified DOD Components, as of April 2021

DOD component	Number of AI projects funded through research and development	Number of AI projects funded through procurement	Total number of AI projects[c]
Air Force (including space force)[a]	74	6	80
Army	209	23	232
Marine Corps	26	7	33
Navy	176	39	215
Other DOD entities[b]	117	8	125

Source: GAO analysis of department of Defense (DOD) information. I GAO-22-104765

a. DOD's methodology combined AI projects from the Air Force and Space Force.

b. Other DOD entities include combatant commands and other unspecified DOD components included in the Joint AI Center's methodology.

c. DOD's initial inventory does not include classified AI projects or those funded through operations and maintenance.

GAO's survey does not capture all the projects within DoD, much less the entire national security enterprise, wherein thousands of program managers have the latitude within existing programs and budgets to begin clarifying the value of AI to their missions using assessments and experiments. Consider all the intelligence, C2, weapons, business systems, and other existing programs of record that have approved funding for gathering, storing, and processing data. Those programs are opportunities for the departments and agencies to at least experiment with AI using their existing authorities and funding.

Deployed models will take substantial effort not only in model development and maintenance, but importantly in the integration of models into operational systems. Full autonomy will normally require the development of entirely new systems. These requirements will demand sufficient funding.

The national security enterprise's understanding of where and how AI will drive mission results is still at a relatively low level. As more assessments and experiments clarify specifics on the use of AI for a given mission and system, program managers will need to engage the budget process to sustain or increase the funding level for the existing programs of record and request funding for new programs—the gray boxes in Figure 4-2.

Whatever your personal views on government spending and debt may be, government must make choices about AI funding priorities as the federal budget is not infinitely elastic. Given the clear linkage between the budget process and AI programs, leaders cannot afford to be either antagonistic or apathetic about the budget process. If you must, think of this process the way you think about an adversary. You don't have to admire an adversary, but you must respect and understand them in order to win.

This chapter gives you the knowledge and the key skills to effectively engage in the budget process, explaining the process with an emphasis on national security programs. We examine the formulation of programs in the President's Budget (PB)—a process that best case takes months and not infrequently takes years. We explain what happens to the PB in Congress, giving you an understanding of the old maxim "the President proposes, but the Congress disposes." We dig beneath the process to surface some of the contextual factors that shape the ongoing dialogue between the executive and legislative branches regarding programs and the budget. These principles and best practices are derived not only from our experience, but also those of several friends who have served in key programming and budgeting roles in the Congress, Office of Management and Budget, Office of the Secretary of Defense, Office of the Director of National Intelligence, and other key Executive Branch agencies.

The best AI leaders will apply these axioms to drive the budget process:

| Three Budgets Not One | An Ongoing Dialogue | Substance Drives Process | Performance Underpins Budget | Dispassionate Defense |

Programming and Budgeting Demystified

It isn't important for AI leaders to understand all of the byzantine machinations of this process—your department has budget and congressional affairs/legislative staff for this purpose—but it is essential that you understand and apply some key best practices to ensure your AI program is properly funded. Your department's staff know the process; you must bring the substance. A sufficient understanding of the process will enable AI leaders to effectively work with their budget and legislative staff.

Figure 4-3 summarizes the actions of the Executive Branch and the Congress to appropriate funds and authorize AI programs and projects in law. Appropriations law is grounded in the U.S. Constitution, Article I, Section 9: "No Money shall be drawn from the Treasury, but in Consequence of Appropriations made by Law...". The federal government's fiscal year (FY) nominally begins on 1 October, assuming that Congress passes and the President signs an Appropriations Act prior to 1 October. This normal Appropriations cycle has only happened four times since FY 2010; the other nine FYs have required a Continuing Resolution (CR).

A CR is a stopgap Appropriations Act that keeps the government funded and running in the absence of a new FY Appropriations Act. For the vast majority of programs, a CR funds only those programs from the previous FY and at the same funding levels as the previous FY. By preventing the start of new programs in the PB and constraining existing programs to the previous FY's funding levels, a CR can inhibit the scale and pace of AI deployment. Given the past 13 Appropriations cycles and the current state of U.S. politics, program managers should assume a high probability of a CR for some portion of every FY. Consequently, AI leaders must do what they can in program planning to prepare for operating under a CR.

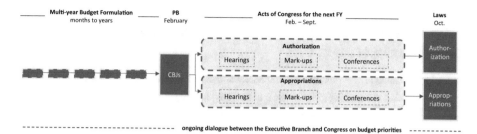

Figure 4-3. Authorization and Appropriations cycles

As seen in Figure 4-3, some national security departments receive an Authorization Act, which provides policy and other Congressional direction for government programs. Congress' use of Authorization Acts varies across the national security enterprise—DoD almost always receives a National Defense Authorization Act; the IC normally receives an Authorization Act; DHS rarely receives an Authorization Act; and the Department of State never receives an Authorization Act. When departments and agencies do not receive a separate Authorization Act, their programs receive legal authorization language through the Appropriations Act. For DoD and the IC, Authorization language is important to AI programs, as it will often convey Congress' official view—and sometimes direction—on program priorities and other operational details. Thus, DoD and the IC must work effectively with their authorization committees.

There is a natural tension between Congress and the Executive Branch in terms of how much policy and program direction Congress may give before it encroaches on the President's authorities. The most successful AI program managers will work with their budget and legislative staffs in the ongoing dialogue with Congress, striving to elicit the funding and authorization language from Congress that your programs need.

In 1999 then Major Mike Folsom stood at the whiteboard and began to explain the budget process to me (Frank). Most of my career to that point had been in the development and support of analytics capabilities to apply satellite reconnaissance and other intelligence data to military operations and national intelligence. Despite the honor of becoming the National Reconnaissance Office's Director of Legislative Liaison, I confess to feeling at that moment some contempt for the budget bureaucracy—what Keith Hall, the NRO Director, sometimes referred to as "the perversity of the budget process."

The process and its many detailed activities and tasks would soon become very familiar as I worked through three congressional budget cycles. What remains fresh in my thinking, however, is the wise counsel Mike concluded with that day. When he finished his explanation, he put the marker down and said:

"Now, this looks like a nice neat linear process with clearly defined milestones leading to an end point. However, the budget process is more than this. It is an ongoing dialogue between the Executive Branch and Congress."

"An ongoing dialogue…"—his point immediately struck me as strategically important to forming effective working relationships on the Hill and securing funding for major programs.

Harvard professor Joel Barker has said that the leader's job is "to secure the future." AI leaders are focused on current execution while also thinking ahead. You naturally think ahead about the cost, schedule, and performance factors of your program or project. You must also think ahead in terms of the funding your program or project will need in coming fiscal years. In doing so, AI leaders must be engaged in three budgets, not one, at any point in time. Those three are:

- Executing: This is the budget enacted by Congress and signed into law by the President, which you are currently spending to create AI capabilities.

- Defending: This is the budget request for which you are engaging with Congress as your department's oversight committees make their "marks" on the PB.

- Formulating: This is the future budget your department is developing within the Executive Branch for the President's approval and submission to Congress.

Figure 4-4 highlights the three budgets as they occur in the overall budget process. In terms of fiscal years, you are *executing the current FY budget; defending the next FY budget* request to Congress; and *formulating the budget* that will go to the President and Congress *after the next FY*. Just as you think about and plan for the technical and operational coherence of your program, you must also think about the financial coherence of your program or your program's impact may be stunted by lack of funding.

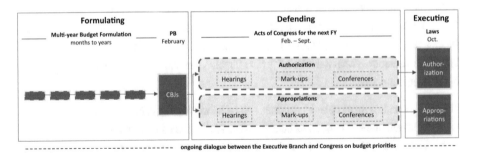

Figure 4-4. Three budgets in the total budget process

The Congressional Budget Justification (CBJ) or Congressional Budget Justification Book (CBJB) is that portion of the PB for your department or agency. It is naïve to think that the oversight committees for your department or agency will constrain their attention to just the CBJ you have submitted for the next FY. Depending on your program's size and a committee's priorities, the committees will also look closely at your execution in the current FY as well as the funding plan your department is formulating for future years beyond the next FY.

Indeed, the failure to obligate and expend current FY funds at rates set by your department can lead to your department and/or Congress taking money out of your program. Obligation generally refers to an act that an authorized government official takes that legally binds the government to incur expenditures, such as obligating funds to a contract. Expenditure generally refers to payments the government makes. Your budget/financial staff will understand these targets in detail. However, they do not start the actions to meet the targets; program managers do.

If you don't pay attention to the financial coherence of your program over multiple years, Congress will do it for you. When you are engaging with your department's financial staff and the Congressional Committee Staff, trying to box them out of your planning for future FYs does not help the defense of your budget proposal for the next FY. You don't have to express every thought you have about the future but, when necessary, demonstrate that your analysis and planning appropriately address requirements and budgets in the out years.

Executing: The Underleveraged Starting Point for Programming and Budgeting

Time is the most precious commodity of any senior leader. Government AI leaders can find their time dominated by future matters—defending the next FY budget request and formulating the FYs that come after the next FY. At the senior staff level, it is tempting for government leaders to focus most of their attention on future concepts. We believe the strongest position from which you can think about and plan for future funding of your AI program is being firmly grounded in the present performance of your program's impact on mission. A focus on current FY execution has several benefits to AI strategy and execution: 1) begin delivering mission impact with what you have; 2) clarify needs with hard data; 3) reprogram funds as required; and 4) perhaps the most underleveraged tool in your arsenal, informed acquisition planning.

Begin Delivering Impact: Because AI is a means of creating insights from data, it is likely that your department's existing IT, analytics, intelligence, C2, or other programs have the latitude to conduct some amount of AI work without further authorization. The military's Joint All-Domain Command and Control

(JADC2) concept, along with the myriad of C2 and weapons systems programs across DoD, all have some form of data processing authorized and funded within the existing programs. The IC, DHS, the Departments of State and Justice will have similar programs.

As one example, RADM Douglas Small is the executive agent for the U.S. Navy's Project Overmatch—a capability concept for accelerating the speed of the operational cycle used in Chapter 2, that is, sense-making, decision-making, and action-taking, across the vast scope of a command and control (C2) network that includes all domains: air, surface, sub-surface, land, and cyber. His charge is to modernize the underlying and critical infrastructure— hardware, networks, and software factories—so that others can develop and deploy AI solutions.

In cases like Project Overmatch, AI can be a means of executing existing responsibilities. From a programming and budgeting perspective, no additional authorization from Congress is required. AI is the "how to" not the "what" in these cases.

Clarifying Needs: The strongest budget requests you can form are those based in practical terms, clearly defining the mission impact you will achieve and how you will leverage AI to achieve that impact. Given that government is just on the cusp of widespread application of AI—and potential applications of AI to national security missions are voluminous—you need to ground your funding requests not simply in your vision for the future, but also in your grasp of the present. We therefore urge leaders to have a robust set of data-driven assessments and experiments as part of their AI portfolio and budget formulation. The relatively low cost of these projects is such that much can be accomplished within a program's or department's existing resources.

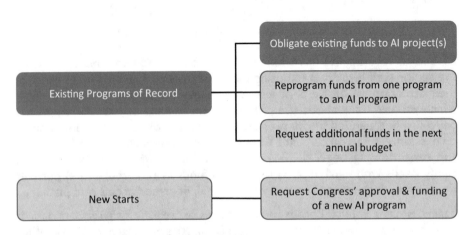

Figure 4-5. Program manager funding environment

Reprogramming Funds: The three budgets in Figure 4-4 imply that the program you are executing in the current FY was formulated a year or more ago. Consequently, the objectives and potential for AI development in your program may have changed. If an existing program lacks sufficient funding for objectives that have emerged, leaders may need to wrestle within their departments to reprogram the necessary funding for AI development in the current FY—one of the paths available to increase funding on an existing program shown in Figure 4-5.

Reprogramming is essentially taking funds from the purpose for which Congress appropriated the funds and applying the funds to a different purpose. The Appropriations committees understandably set controls on reprogramming. In some cases, your department can reprogram funds within an appropriated account up to a ceiling set by Congress with only a notification to Congress. Reprogramming within an appropriated account for an amount above the ceiling set by Congress requires prior approval from all of your oversight committees. Reprogramming any amount of funding whatsoever from one appropriated account to a different account requires prior approval from Congress.

Most of the reprogramming controls are on small amounts relative to major development programs. For example, here is a $2.5M reprogramming request by the Air Force in FY 2021:

> Funds are required to develop a cloud-based software suite to automate and synchronize the Air Force Air Reserve Component (ARC) utilization process to rapidly generate ARC capability, increase lethality, facilitate the timely issuance of orders, and enable predictive analytics and data-driven decision making. This is a new start.

Your budget and legislative staffs are intimately familiar with the reprogramming controls set by Congress Thinking ahead, AI leaders should work with these staff to organize AI portfolios such that you have maximum flexibility to move funds without crossing a reprogramming control line set by Congress, thus reprogramming becomes less necessary. When congressional approval is required for a reprogramming action, a department must receive approval from all of its oversight committees—one committee can veto the process.

Congressional committees recognize reprogramming as a fact of life given the long timeline of the budget process. Thus, your department's staff and you can successfully get approval for reprogramming with sufficient time and good staff work. This is yet another reason for senior AI leaders to have strong working relationships with their department's budget and legislative staffs. We empathize with AI leaders' passion for mission impact and technology.

At senior leader levels, however, you recognize that these results require funding and funding requires good staff work in the budget process.

As seen in the Air Force example, it is even possible to get approval for a new start program through a reprogramming action. However, the Appropriations Committees cordially loathe approving new start programs outside the normal Appropriations process. You may be able to get a few small new starts approved through reprogramming actions, but do not plan on getting approval for a major new start through a reprogramming request.

Acquisition Planning: Beyond existing programs of various types where some AI work can occur, the NSCAI report recommended that additional funding and new programs are required if the United States is to create and maintain an edge in national security using AI. This leads to what may be the most important and least appreciated element of your department's AI effort—an acquisition strategy.

There are a number of AI experts in the government and, in select cases, government officers and staff will develop and deliver AI capabilities. However, the government will acquire, not develop, most AI capabilities. While a few government AI experts might chafe at this notion, we suspect that most government AI leaders will recognize it as a logical deduction—the overwhelming leadership in AI is in commercial industry not the government. As discussed in Chapter 7, we also hope government leaders will embrace this reality, as government-industry partnerships are essential to America winning the AI competition.

It is typical for major program planning to start with the programming and budgeting process and only then create an acquisition strategy, if at all. Therefore, the implied logic goes like this—get the money and then figure out in detail how you will spend it. This is one of the major causes in departments having difficulty with the obligation and expenditure targets mentioned previously.

There is always a strong lament about the state of government acquisition. Much gnashing of teeth occurs over the time it takes to acquire a major system, as one of many examples. Dropping below major system acquisitions, even the simplest contract actions can take many months, sometimes years. More than one senior official has left the government of late citing their concerns with the acquisition process.

Congress has taken one bold action that can improve AI acquisition in the 2016 NDAA. The long-standing procurement legislation governing Other Transaction Authority (OTA) was modified such that some departments can move from a successful OTA prototype contract to a full production contract without further competition. AI leaders should have a detailed understanding of how they can leverage OTAs for their programs. While more action in legislation and government policy is required to streamline acquisition of AI capabilities, we encourage leaders to focus on a major lever that they control—acquisition planning.

The failure to properly plan for procurements in a realistic acquisition strategy is one of the root causes of the problems in government contracting. It is not the only cause, but it is a major cause and one that AI program managers can control. As you gain clarity on AI mission and funding requirements, it is essential that you not only drive the formulation of programs and budgets, but you must also drive an implementing acquisition strategy. By "gain clarity," we mean that your acquisition strategy is based in realism, for example, you are using tech that is proven for a given problem or you have baked in alternative paths for higher risk tech. The objective here is not an artifact that checks a box, but rather an acquisition strategy rooted in facts about performance, cost, and schedule expectations. A solid acquisition strategy is the key bridge between your grasp of reality in the current FY and your aspiration for future FYs.

The National Reconnaissance Office (NRO) is one of the largest contracting agencies in the national security enterprise, executing 90+ percent of its multi-billion dollar budget in contracts with industry. The NRO's roots go back to the 1960s, when it was essentially three covert organizations hidden within the Air Force, CIA, and Navy, known as Programs A, B, and C, respectively. Our analytics journey began in Program C, then housed at the Naval Research Laboratory.

We and others would argue that the core competency of the NRO's government workforce was not in any form of engineering—although there were and are amazingly talented engineers in the NRO—but rather in acquisition. NRO program managers were expert in creating acquisition strategies and managing the contracts required for executing those strategies. AI leaders seeking to learn more about acquisition strategy may benefit from NRO lessons learned and best practices in acquisition strategy.

Formulating: Defending Starts in the Executive Branch Not in Congress

Justification for AI programs begins in the Executive Branch, starting with the budget formulation process in your department or agency. Every national security department and the IC has a budget office, under a chief financial officer (by whatever title), and a staff devoted to engaging Congress in the budget process (commonly referred to as "legislative liaison" or "congressional affairs" staff). Major national security organizations also have staffs dedicated to analyzing the requirements and priorities for all programs in a department or agency—the SecDef's Cost Assessment and Program Evaluation (CAPE) staff being one of the best known examples. Your department's senior leadership, supported by these staff elements, has a process for evaluating and prioritizing what does and does not make it into a CBJ.

Beyond your department, the budget request and justification must pass muster with the President's budget staff in the Office of Management and Budget (OMB). OMB examiners, including those focused on national security, ensure that all CBJs align with the President's priorities and guidance, both in terms of the funding amounts and the associated programs' contents. OMB staff and program analysis staff, such as OSD CAPE, think like Appropriations Committee staff—meaning they are expert in examining your program with a critical eye. AI leaders—especially leaders of major programs—should form close working relationships with these budget and legislative staff to communicate the strongest justification of AI programs and projects to Congress.

Taking the Air Force as an example, an AI program manager in, say, Air Combat Command must get their request for AI funding through a review within ACC. Then, multiple elements of the Air Force Secretariat and Air Staff—Air Force Headquarters' civilian and military staffs respectively—will review the budget request on behalf of the Secretary of the Air Force and Chief of Staff of the Air Force. If approved inside the Air Force, the Secretary of Defense's civilian staff—the Office of the Secretary of Defense (OSD)—will also review the request as part of formulating the combined DoD budget request. The OSD CAPE staff consists of program and financial analysts who thoroughly analyze select programs and portfolio areas, such as AI, advising the Deputy Secretary and Secretary of Defense on what does and does not make it into the final budget submission. The Joint Staff—a military staff under the President's senior military advisor, the Chairman of the Joint Chiefs of Staff (CJCS)—also participates in these reviews.

AI leaders should neither be surprised nor offended when Executive Branch and Congressional staff ask questions that imply skepticism about their program or requested funding. The process is designed to critically examine the need for a program and the funding requested. Yes, the process is messy and inefficient. Push past this; anticipate skeptical questions beforehand and form dispassionate fact-based answers. Doing so will help the AI leader form a stronger program and budget request.

While earlier we encouraged AI leaders to begin implementing AI with current programs and funding, the potential of AI models deployed to a vast number of mission and business systems is such that additional funding to some existing programs and the creation of new programs will be required. There are capabilities that have AI as the primary reason for the system, for example, developing large data engineering and data management capabilities; developing, deploying, and maintaining large numbers of models within software applications at enterprise-scale; and of course development of autonomous solutions. The creation and operation of major AI centers of excellence within your department or agency would also fall into this major program category. This requires AI leaders to formulate a strong request for additional funding and/or a new start program inside the Executive Branch. Table 4-2 provides AI leaders with the five criteria for formulating a strong budget request.

Table 4-2. Criteria for Budget Formulation Submissions

Criteria	Defined
Compelling	• Why is the program or project necessary?
	• As a natural part of any AI project, you define anticipated mission impact. Use that understanding to explain the resource request in terms of mission value. This may seem straightforward in the abstract. In practice, budget justifications are too often weak on specific mission impacts.
Concrete	• What data do you have to substantiate your request?
	• Data-driven arguments come naturally to AI practitioners. Use data from assessments, experiments, and other sources to make a fact-based argument for resources. Here also, many budget requests are sparse on hard data/facts.
	• Being a political organization, Congress is accustomed to spin. Be dispassionate in your justification; hyperbole will hurt your argument.
Coherent	• Can the reader or listener easily follow your story?
	• Your budget justification is a story. Good storytelling will enhance good content. Bad storytelling will diminish good content.
Clear	• How well does your story communicate to a non-AI expert?
	• Avoid jargon; use plain, accessible terms as much as possible.
	• Apply the fundamentals of good writing that you learned in English 111—topical paragraphs; subject-verb-object sentences; 90+% active voice; among other good writing techniques.
Concise	• Have you scrutinized every sentence and paragraph so only that which is necessary remains?
	• Long form content isn't nearly as long as it once was. Economize your words.

Additional funding for AI programs and projects is not simply a matter of increases to the top line of your department's budget. The formulation process within the Executive Branch also includes trade-offs between programs—more of program "x" and less of program "y" in effect. This is especially relevant to AI, as operational AI models will often be deployed in a mission or business system, such as a C2 system or an enterprise financial system. AI is a component—a key component—but not the system itself. AI program managers' ability to demonstrate and communicate mission value will also help advocate for AI in these trade-offs within the Executive Branch.

Defending: Authorization, Appropriations, and Congressional Oversight

The third context for considering AI programming and budgeting is defending your portion of the current PB to Congress. Some would start the discussion of the budget process here. We believe that leaders' attention to the best practices in the executing and formulating phases will best prepare them to defend the next FY request "on the Hill." Execution provides the hard data and substantive details for strong formulation.

Applying the best practices in formulation best positions you to defend your program's budget request. There are orders of magnitude more financial oversight in the Executive Branch than Congress can execute with its relatively small committee staffs. If an AI leader completes the PB formulation with a strong budget justification, then they are well prepared to defend that request to Congress—through the written justification and, as required, briefings and meetings with committee staff and members. Therefore, the best practices we commended to AI leaders in Table 4-2 are also the best practices for defending your budget request to Congress.

For the majority of AI programs and projects, your budget justification will only be in the written CBJ with the potential for questions posed by committee staff to your department's legislative and budget staff. As you rise in the leader ranks and manage larger programs, however, you will at some point find yourself communicating your request to committee staff or perhaps even committee members through briefings and demonstrations. Your legislative staff will prepare and support you if this need arises. This section will give you a solid grasp of the fundamentals, which in turn equips you to effectively work with the legislative and budget staff in your department or agency.

Congress allocates its focus through the committee structure with 25 committees in the House and 20 Senate committees plus four joint House-Senate committees. Most committees are mirrored between the House and Senate, such as the House and Senate Committees on Appropriations. A committee will further divide its work into sub-committees. With omnibus

Appropriations of $1.5 trillion dollars in FY 2022, you can see the need for the Appropriations committees to divide oversight of the federal budget into 12 sub-committees. Your budget request will follow parallel paths in each chamber, House and Senate. Figure 4-6 reflects the path for Appropriations.

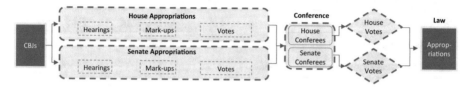

Figure 4-6. Congressional appropriations cycle

The House and Senate Appropriations sub-committees with jurisdiction over your department's or agency's budget will hold a hearing or hearings to review the budget. The Senate's Appropriations sub-committee on defense, for example, will invite the SecDef, CJCS, and other key DoD leaders—as the committee chooses—to present the budget in a formal hearing. Given the classified and sensitive nature of national security topics, many of these hearings are closed to the public. Based on these hearings and the ongoing dialogue between your department and Congress, the sub-committee will "mark-up"—or make their changes—to the proposed budget.

National security departments and agencies will have different Appropriations sub-committees and Authorization committees. Your congressional affairs staff will help you understand the committees with jurisdiction over your budget.

The President doesn't sign a House bill and a Senate bill; he or she signs a single bill representing the Congress as a whole. In order to resolve differences in how they have marked the proposed budget, House and Senate committees will each send representatives to a "conference" whereby the two chambers will agree on the same budget numbers and language.

Table 4-3 is an illustration of this process at work in the FY 2005 DoD budget. The House Appropriations and Senate Appropriations Committees sub-committees on defense (HAC-D and SAC-D, respectively) have made different marks on two of the President's proposed programs. You can see that the severity of the marks are somewhat inversely proportional between the two chambers. This reflects the House and Senate sub-committees' substantive judgments on the two programs. It is also plausible that an element of these marks is one or both of the committees positioning for conference. For example, the Senate sub-committee observes that the House would reduce the Space Based Radar program request by over 80 percent, therefore the

Senate reduces the Transformational Communications Satellite program—likely a program the House supports—by over 50 percent. This creates room for negotiation in conference.

Table 4-3. Illustration of Senate-House Dynamics in Budget Review

Program	PB	HAC Mark	SAC Mark
Space Based Radar	$327	($275)	($100)
Transformational Communications Satellite	$775	($100)	($400)

A senior official in the IC once presented the committees' differing marks to an audience of program managers, decrying how "incoherent" Congress is. This is a good example of cynicism regarding Congress that, while well-earned in other areas, is misapplied in this case. Program managers should be thankful when the committees are incoherent. The lack of coherence across committees provides a vulnerability the Executive Branch can and does exploit. When the committees cohere—that is, when they make pretty much the same mark—then there is no negotiation; the committees' marks drive the budget.

Suppressing cynicism about Congress best equips you to defend your budget request. If you must think of Congress as an opponent in the process, then engage with the strength that dispassionate determination gives you when meeting any opponent. Occasionally, some congressional committee staff can say or do something that tempts you to a passionate reaction. Keep the reins tight on yourself and focus your energy on achieving the objective, which is making the best possible defense of your budget request versus winning an argument with some staffer on what too often is a peripheral point to your objective.

When each committee publishes its marks to the PB, Executive Branch staff will prepare formal written appeals for their principal leaders and engage in informal appeals through meetings with committee staff. In practical terms, your department will seek to optimize the overall outcome for its mission in negotiating marks with Congress. This may mean that a mark to your program is essentially left without strong Executive Branch appeal as your department chooses to prioritize other appeals. Once again, AI program managers' relationships with their budget and congressional affairs staff are key to effective appeals. For those leading the largest AI programs, you should build these relationships at multiple levels in the Executive Branch including and especially the OMB.

As seen in Figure 4-6, there are multiple votes that must take place throughout this process. Congressional hearings, debate, and voting take time; this inefficient process truly earns the metaphor "sausage making." As Churchill said, "No one pretends that democracy is perfect or all-wise. Indeed, it has been said that democracy is the worst form of Government except for all those other forms that have been tried from time to time...". Guarding yourself from cynicism about the process is one of the most straightforward yet difficult best practices an AI leader can pursue. The world's authoritarian regimes are generally much more efficient, but you may wish to consider whether tyranny over liberty makes greater efficiency a good trade-off.

Perhaps the worst impact of the congressional budget process is the high probability of a CR to begin each FY and the fact that CRs prevent new start programs. This is especially annoying when you have successfully sold the new start program through the Executive Branch process as well as Congress' review, but the Appropriations committees do not deliver a bill to the President by 30 September. You can try to do as much within your existing programs as legally authorized in this circumstance, but you won't have the required funding or the latitude to launch a new program as you normally would.

There isn't a good solution to this problem. As previously discussed, you can request a reprogramming through Congress along with approval of a new start. That may work in select cases, especially for relatively small amounts, with good staff work in coordinating with and across the committees. Worst case, you can push your development schedule to the right until Congress completes and the President signs a new Appropriations Act funding and authorizing your new start. A 2018 initiative sponsored by the Chief of Staff of the Army, the Army Leader Dashboard (ALD), had to do just that. There is no amount of seniority in the Executive Branch that can push past the Appropriations Committees' tight control over new starts. Expect the effects of a CR in your formulation and structure as much flexibility as possible in your programs.

Data Science for AI Leaders

"A data scientist is someone who can obtain, scrub, explore, model, and interpret data, blending hacking, statistics, and machine learning"

—Hillary Mason
Founder, Fast Forward Labs

Summary

Data scientists are problem solvers who use programming languages, technology, and a range of statistical and math approaches to create solutions that deliver insights from data. Leaders can engage these teams and individuals successfully by raising their own professional knowledge over time. While some data science leaders will rise from the front-line work, others in leader roles may not have that exposure. Building awareness around five or six significant realities can raise leader effectiveness. While much of this work may be smaller scale problem solving, enormous modeling efforts around imaging and text data in particular are yielding breakthrough capabilities that can benefit many. Natural language processing illustrates this progress. As DoD learned in the software boom of the early 2000s, leaders with just

© Chris Whitlock, Frank Strickland 2023
C. Whitlock and F. Strickland, *Winning the National Security AI Competition*,
https://doi.org/10.1007/978-1-4842-8814-6_5

technology backgrounds are unlikely to make good AI leaders. You must gain sufficient understanding of data science.

The chapter is laid out around six axioms of data science and associated work, culminating by exploring one of the major advanced modeling areas—natural language processing:

- Programming skill required
- Statistical understanding required
- Labeled Data is One Path
- Foundation Methods Are Key
- Advanced approaches can Generate Lift
- Text Is An Asset

The goal for the remainder of this book is to teach the dynamics of leading large-scale change enabled by AI rather than to teach the technical details of AI and data science. This includes increasing your ability to navigate the people and technological issues associated with this domain. In this portion of the book, we provide further insight into technical aspects of data science work and AI model types to arm leaders with richer context for conversing constructively with their teams. In this regard, the content is a complement to the project chapter as well as the chapter defining AI projects.

Data scientists and AI experts will find the material in this chapter familiar. These readers may find value in the level of technical detail being conveyed to non-data scientists. Data scientists, we encourage you to engage leaders in your work in a way that does not drag them inordinately into deep details.

Non-data scientist leaders should finish reading this with a clearer sense of relevant language, increased knowledge of modeling, and a grasp of data types that will help them engage with teams. Detailed AI knowledge is neither assumed nor necessary. Leaders involved in these projects will discover handholds to engage with their team in the project section, but that is a process view. In contrast, this chapter provides some handholds that pertain to matching general model types to mission problems as well as areas to probe with teams early in the process.

We love data scientists and their work. We have led all four types of AI-related projects. We started an analytics company committed to the notion that decision-makers should have access to insights beyond subject matter expert panels; we believed they should be informed by detailed analytical results. To plumb native data sources and derive insights, we needed teams with multi-disciplinary backgrounds and expertise in a range of software tools. Performance assessments and experiments demand an exploratory, expeditionary posture to find relevant data, understand it, and probe technical angles to derive insight. Consequently, We have led teams building AI-enabled dashboards as well as AI models in larger systems of record. Our work focused on advanced analytics for many years. Over the past 20 years, we have focused on cultivating and deploying data scientists. Their work is fascinating; even average data scientists are quite capable.

We want to provide insight on what data scientists do as well as some of the prominent techniques they employ, which will be relevant across a range of AI projects.

Programming Skill Required

Over the past 15 years, "data science" has become trendy. A number of notable studies and articles speak to the importance of the function. Yet, if you gather a number of non-data scientists to talk about the field, they may founder when asked to define a data scientist.

We have hired many people into analytics roles. Therefore, we have a clear criterium for a data scientist: data scientists can write software code. Big analysis software companies are focused on creating graphical user interfaces (GUIs) in which you can drag and drop items on a canvas to create analytical solutions. This functionality is important, but these companies also always provide the ability to write code in some set of languages so practitioners can directly prepare data or implement software functions. An analyst working only in the drag-and-drop environment can contribute; there is a place for them. However, data scientists are the data MacGyvers; their capabilities center on competence with programming languages.

Capable data scientists can write code in some combination of programming languages and are typically quick to pick up new functionality. In a database context, they will all feel comfortable working in SQL databases and writing queries in the appropriate language. These are foundational capabilities. Many will also be quite competent in navigating NoSQL and graph databases with the relevant query languages. Moving beyond the databases, data scientist can write code in some combination of R, Python, SAS, Scala, and other languages. These programming languages require specific syntax and include libraries of pre-built functions that a competent programmer can call to accelerate their work. The window in Figure 5-1 is a snapshot of R Studio, the programming and work environment data scientists most commonly use. In this way, they can organize dataframes, write discrete processing steps, call functions, and visualize outputs. This is no drag-and-drop environment for a general analyst who lacks programming competence. College courses commonly teach R today. Additionally, job postings frequently request that applicants be proficient in R.

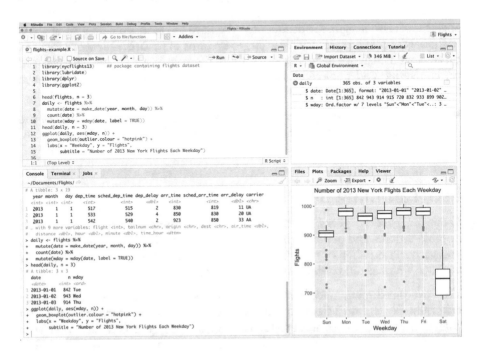

Figure 5-1. Example R console

*"A data scientist is someone who can **obtain, scrub, explore,** model, and interpret data, blending hacking, statistics, and machine learning." (emphasis added).*

Data scientists access data in a variety of ways. But once it is in hand, the data scientist must be able to explore and manipulate the data by writing code. We illustrate this with a package in R called "Dplyr"—a common work environment to explore and manipulate data as preparation for subsequent analytic or modeling steps. Working in the R Studio environment shown in Figure 5-1, data scientists often use Dplyr to create a dataframe (a set of data they will work with for exploration, advanced analytics, or AI modeling). Once in the frame, the data scientist can properly format the data. For example, they can transform rows and columns, rename columns, "mutate" the data, or add new columns, filter the data, sort the data, and more. Some of the functions that are used in Excel can also be performed in R. The data science programming environments widens the range of functions and the volume of data with which a team can work.

Thinking About Common Software

The capability differences in data manipulation and the range of options are radically different between data science packages and Excel. As a leader, it is important to probe teams on the tools planned for different types of work. A couple of common questions we have heard over the years are: 1) why not just use Microsoft Excel and 2) what is the difference between R and Python?

Excel is a fantastic desktop tool that gets wide usage. Much of this is to organize and track information. In one large company, staff were asked to characterize ability on a five-point scale. Many scored themselves very high on the use of Excel. This same population, however, on average scored themselves modestly regarding analytics. This illustrates a common boundary with Excel. Many users leverage this for tracking, sorting, organizing, rather than complex work. Excel does include the ability to program (write macros) and offers about 80 ready-to-use math formulas (e.g., "SUM" to total data in a column).

Data science work revolves first around "data." Often for teams this is quite voluminous. At the first level, this is where Excel is separated from software like R and Python. As one simple example, Excel can accommodate roughly one million rows of data. R by contrast can accommodate 2^31 rows, or roughly two billion rows in a dataframe.

The science element is both practice and methods (accessed via functions or libraries in the open-source packages of R or Python). While Excel has 80 ready-to-use math formulas, in R there are literally thousands of functions with new content being added regularly. These are searchable and represent capabilities these data MacGuyvers can readily employ as they explore data or craft solutions.

Data scientists often affinitize to either R or Python as their preferred environment. Both are very capable open-source software environments for data science and leaders can run into sometimes fun debates between the "tribes" as it regards this software. For leaders, does it matter which type a team is using? We believe it does and have a general point of view that informs our approach to these decisions.

When thinking of the project types, we are inclined to emphasize Python for the top row focused on enduring solutions. R can certainly be used here for dashboards and AI-centered solutions, but the range of tooling available in Python and performance for enterprise applications inclines us to that when working initiatives on the top row of the Project types two by two. R is very effective as pertains to data exploration and performance assessments. The functions available also are robust to perform experiments and test concepts.

> "A data scientist is someone who can obtain, scrub, explore, model, and interpret data, blending **hacking**, statistics, and machine learning."

Hillary Mason's definition is useful in highlighting "hacking" as an element of a data scientist's work. While "hacking" might have a negative connotation for some, the word conveys the MacGyver mentality; the data scientist must have this attitude because of the sheer number of problem-solving tools available. We mentioned Dplyr, but many packages and functions are available to aid a data scientist in data cleaning and manipulation. The data scientist must artfully identify the best tool for the job (Table 5-1).

Table 5-1. Select Packages in R for Data Cleaning and Wrangling

Package	Functionality	Description
purr	Data wrangling	Applies a function to items in a list and returns desired format
tidyxl	Data wrangling	Deals with complex Excel files including merged cells, and so on
jsonlite	Data wrangling	Parses JSON files within R or pushes an R dataframe to JSON
XML	Data wrangling	Handles a variety of tasks for HTML, XML files
rvest	Data import	Supports web scraping to pull data from HTML pages
data.table	Data wrangling	Supports a variety of manipulation in exceptionally large datasets

Statistical Understanding Required

*"A data scientist is someone who can obtain, scrub, explore, model, and interpret data, blending hacking, **statistics**, and machine learning."*

Data scientists must be able to derive insight from and make sense of complex, large datasets using common software packages. We continue to illustrate basic tasks using R Studio and R. Visual exploration of datasets is an important early step for most teams, especially with structured data, which we explain further later in this chapter. Immediately below is a foundational output available in R known as "plot." In Figure 5-2, the plot illustrates potential relationships between data in five columns in a well-known training dataset, "Iris." The columns are Sepal Length, Sepal Width, Petal Length, Petal Width, and Species. Plot creates a visual comparison of the variables. In this instance, two of the variables (Petal Length and Width, annotated in red) are positively related as indicated by the upward-trending array of data points in the two graphs beside both Petal Length and Petal Width. As one increased the other increases and vice versa. It is apparent looking at the graph even for a layperson, not all the variable pairs inter-relate in that way. This is a simple and common form of data exploration readily performed in R.

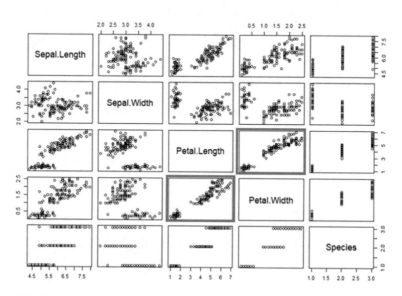

Figure 5-2. Exploratory data view in R

Data science work leans heavily on statistics for tasks from describing complex datasets to interpreting sophisticated model performance. One aspect of this work is choosing appropriate visualizations for various datasets. The software environments (i.e., R or Python) provide a robust set of tools to accelerate data exploration as well as sharing outputs with stakeholders and users. In R, several commonly used packages include ggplot, plotly, and lattice. Once a data scientist has data properly prepared in a frame, packages like these enable visualization. Numerous visualization options are readily available. The following figures illustrate the packages, plotly (Figure 5-3), ggplot (Figure 5-4), and lattice (Figure 5-5).

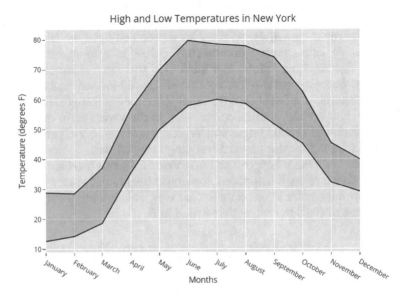

Figure 5-3. Example of R plotly output

Source: https://plotly.com/r/filled-area-plots/

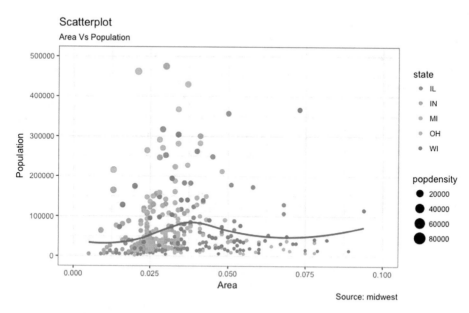

Figure 5-4. Example of R ggplot output

Source: http://r-statistics.co/Top50-Ggplot2-Visualizations-
MasterList-R-Code.html

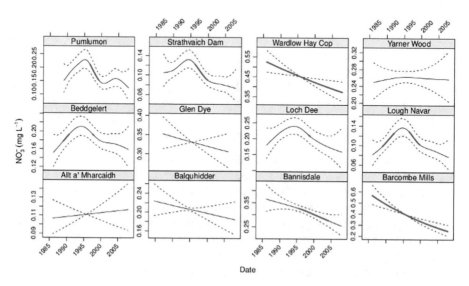

Figure 5-5. Nitrate concentrations in rainfall at UK deposition monitoring sites showing estimated trend and point wise 95 percent confidence interval. Periods of significant increase (blue) or decrease (red) are indicated by the coloured sections of the trend

Source: https://fromthebottomoftheheap.net/2013/10/23/time-series-
plots-with-lattice-and-ggplot/

Plotting data and creating stories with it requires solid knowledge of elementary statistics—chiefly emphasizing descriptive statistics. In many instances, teams can work with a population of data to understand relationships, ranges, and basic distributions. Where possible and advisable, teams should work with population data (tank gunnery qualification data across the Army for a year or more) as opposed to sample data (tank gunnery qualification data for a few randomly selected units in randomly selected windows). The available software packages will support large-volume data processing, but other constraints may limit these approaches; such constraints include data availability or limitations of the computational environment.

In classic social science research and other common applications, data collection may be limited, so teams work with sample sets of information. As a practical and highly visible example in the national security space, the Army worked diligently to develop a new fitness test; the Army Combat Fitness Test (ACFT). This effort included identifying the elements of the ACFT and developing an appropriate scoring system. In development, not all soldiers were tested (as an example, as of August 2021 prior to the roll-out, 49 percent of active duty enlisted women and 71 percent of enlisted men had been tested at least once). While these are large percentages, the gaps create potential uncertainties. Further, in initial development of scoring the Army worked toward a gender- and age-agnostic approach, but significant questions of potential bias emerged.

In instance like this when working with samples or portions of the overall potential data, the team must have strong statistical knowledge. R, Python, SAS, and other software have an array of packages or libraries to tackle these problems. In these situations, the team makes inferences from observations on a sample or multiple samples regarding the likely situation at the population level. In R, the DataFlair package supports hypothesis testing. The package supports t-testing, correlation, and analysis of covariance (ANCOVA)—techniques important to the team's approach to sample data.

Figure 5-6 shows the output of a two-sample t-test, a particular form of hypothesis testing. While leaders need not understand every aspect of the analysis, they should appreciate that teams must deal with technical statistical measures for data processing. The red box in Figure 5-6 annotates these. Software packages easily generate these results, representing a risk for teams if members do not have adequate experience understanding and interpreting these auto-generated results. Do not take this understanding for granted, as teams process data to produce complex technical outputs.

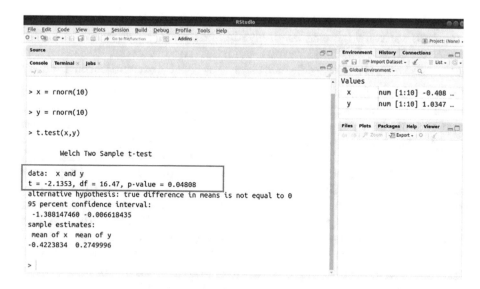

Figure 5-6. Example of statistical test measures in R console

Source: https://data-flair.training/blogs/hypothesis-testing-in-r/

Labeled Data is One Path

*"A data scientist is someone who can obtain, scrub, explore, model, and interpret data, blending hacking, statistics, and **machine learning**."*

In machine learning efforts, data scientists apply a particular type of algorithm to data to enable various types of predictions. One form of model is "supervised" and leans heavily on structured data and "labeled data." The other major form of machine learning model is "unsupervised" which can be used with structured or unstructured data sets. The following sections discuss aspects of different models, but an appropriate starting point is in defining basic data terms: structured and unstructured.

Structured Data. This is common in machine learning efforts. It is generally defined as well-organized data captured in columns and rows. Generally, it is the type of data teams would historically analyze of manipulate using Structured Query Language (SQL). The rows represent individual entries (e.g., a parts order for an aircraft), while the columns represent attributes of the data (e.g., part number, part name, price, or availability). We expect structured data to have stable fields or columns and a data dictionary. When these are not present, the data should be stable and readily understood by experts who use it regularly. A leader can know the data is structured if any of the following common software is being used: MySQL, PostgreSQL, Microsoft SQL, IBM DB2, or Oracle RDBMS. Various estimates suggest about 20 percent of enterprise data is structured, yet it plays a key role in machine learning activity.

Unstructured Data. This has become increasingly prominent over the past 20-25 years along with the rise of the Internet and public-facing software applications. In a general sense, unstructured data encompasses text and image data. In an enterprise, emails represent a large body of unstructured data. Microsoft Word documents, PowerPoints, PDFs, and pictures are all unstructured. Streaming video inputs, video repositories, or images are unstructured; this is true whether the images are x-rays, weather satellite photos, or ground photographs taken by a Defense Attaché. Data on web pages, in SMS messages, and comments on social media sites are also unstructured data. There is an enormous amount of potentially valuable unstructured data available. Many machine learning practitioners focus on deriving insights from this data. Significant breakthroughs have occurred in this work during the past 15 years. Be aware that a whole family of database software enable storage and manipulation of this type of data, including Apache Cassandra, Apache HBase, Apache CouchDB, MongoDB, DataStax (a graph database), and Neo4j (a graph database).

Labeled Data. In the context of work processes, labels are applied to a range of data regarding cases, targets, documents, applications, and so on. To use a familiar example, consider images with names for people in the scene or labels on types of equipment. Document tags specifying topics are quite common. In the medical field, diagnostic codes are assigned to various procedures and patient visits. Such labels give machine learning algorithms the answer key. Consider soldiers seeking selection for Army Special Forces. Some number pass through Special Forces Assessment and Selection (SFAS) over a three-week period each year. A fraction of those aspiring to attend the Special Forces Qualification Course are selected to be in SFAS. The outcome of SFAS for each soldier constitutes a label—selected, voluntary withdrawal, and so on. These labels allow data science teams to explore machine learning models that compare data on soldiers who attended SFAS with their outcome, deriving insights about the profiles of successful soldiers. This allows the Army to classify SFAS applicants on their likelihood of successful completion.

Labels are available in a variety of environments, but one of the largest of these which virtually everyone can relate to is in social media. Figure 5-7 shows the fuel for social media advertising and content management: the response labels for content shown in a Facebook timeline. Knowing what users like or love, makes them laugh, makes them sad, or makes them angry is based on labels applied to largely unstructured data. Data science teams use the labeled data generated by social media platforms to train and test machine learning models that direct content and ads to a particular user timeline.

TASKANDPURPOSE.COM

This Army 'Best Ranger' competitor showed soldier ingenuity that had instructors face-palming

4 Comments

Figure 5-7. Example of social media labels users apply to content

Source: Facebook, 2022. Standard labels to respond to posted content.

Labeled data can be very important for machine learning and this is true with regard to the DoD Project Maven in a similar way to Tesla autonomous driving system. With unstructured data, organizations will sometimes employ staff to perform data labeling. For Project Maven this entailed junior military staff and others looking at image data and apply labels so the dataset could (e.g. "F-22," "aircraft," "tank") then be used to train supervised machine learning models. Meaning, the machine now has the answer key in the form of labels and can learn from the underlying data how to accurately label future data.

Unlabeled data lacks the answer key but can still be used in machine learning. For text data, as an example, unlabeled data would indicate there are no topical content tags that can be used to train a machine learning model to accurately identify certain types of information or to apply tags automatically to new text documents. With labeled data, as an example, machine learning might use content tags on maintenance-related information to identify all the reporting that deals with helicopter rotary blade failure or deterioration and then train a model to apply appropriate tags to future reporting. With unlabeled data, different techniques can be employed and two primary ways to leverage unlabeled data are with clustering models or in what we described earlier as "dimension reduction." Suffice to say that with clustering models, as an example, the machine looks for similarities in the unlabeled data to create groups of like data, files, cases, reports that lack labels. Data scientists and domain experts can then evaluate the groups to see if useful categories emerge forming the basis for segmentation, topical tags, classifications, or labels of different types useful to operational users.

Foundation Methods Are Key

A great debate can erupt among passionate practitioners on what models/ approaches are included in machine learning. We believe foundational techniques have a prominent place in most tasks, if for no other reason than to establish baseline targets. While this is not relevant for all problems, leaders should encourage the use of techniques like linear regression, logistic regression, and decision trees. These are foundational techniques that, in some instances, provide the bones of more complex approaches. For example, logistic regression is a machine learning workhorse that can generate strong predictive performance. But these also provide the bones of much more complex neural net implementations. A single decision tree usefully classifies cases, applicants (as with SFAS), or events. Multiple decision trees comprise the more sophisticated, capable "random forest" machine learning models. Linear regressions establish relationships between variables (e.g., height and shoe size) that can data scientists use to predict volumes, prices, and inventories. Additionally, advanced techniques to attack sparse matrix data arrays effectively apply multiple linear regressions.

In grasping these foundational models, leaders gain insight into more sophisticated efforts. For teams, these approaches serve as a baseline performance to try to beat with more sophisticated machine learning approaches. Advanced machine learning methods can be more computationally intensive and harder to explain to users. Therefore, data scientists should explore foundational approaches first, including logistic regression, linear regression, and decision trees.

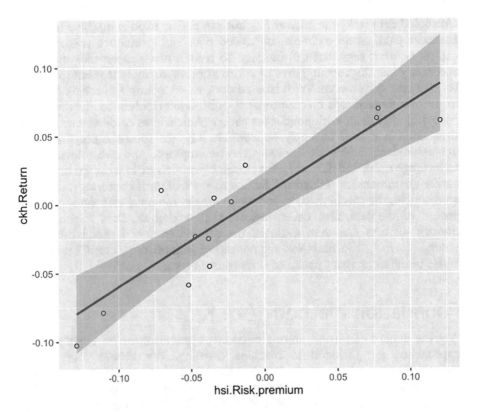

Figure 5-8. Example of linear regression output using R ggplot

Figure 5-8 was created in R using the ggplot package to show results of a linear regression. This graph plots the relationship between investment risk (horizontal axis) and return on investment (vertical axis). A similar plot could include variables such as age of a part or time since last engine maintenance in the horizontal axis and time to expected parts failure on the vertical axis. This is a linear regression, in which teams use one or more variables to predict the likelihood of another.

Source: `https://t-redactyl.io/blog/2016/05/creating-plots-in-r-using-ggplot2-part-11-linear-regression-plots.html`

Potential Leader Questions

As leaders interact with teams, questions like these can open up constructive dialogue:

- Why is a linear regression appropriate here?

- What data underpins the work (structured or unstructured data)?

- What labels in the data might be important?

- How confident is the team based on the amount of data used to train?

- How is that confidence level articulated?

Linear regressions answer questions like how many or how much, comparing one or more variables against a target output. In the notion example, age of a part or time since last maintenance might help predict time to parts failure.

Logistic regressions are related to linear regressions, but focus on categorical outcomes—admission, failure, injury, completion, and so on. Developing a logistic regression requires labeled data on the target outcome or the dependent variable. The predictors are any number of potentially related variables pulled from structured data to determine the probability of the occurrence of the target outcome. The SFAS example—Special Forces candidate selection—is a good prospective application for a logistic regression. Labeled outcome data is available for all soldiers who participate in SFAS. A variety of common variables are available to build the model (e.g., if the soldier is Ranger-qualified, the soldier's physical training scores, the soldier's years of service, the soldier's rank, etc.). Some of these factors may be important to predicting outcomes, while others may be of little value for outcome prediction. Logistic regression will attach value to the different variables during model training and form an equation that predicts the prospects for any given candidate in the future.

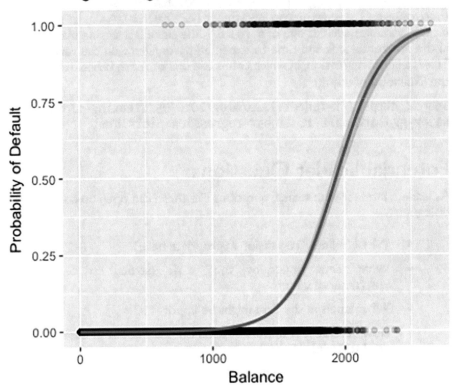

Figure 5-9. Example of logistic regression output in R

Figure 5-9 shows the output of a logistic regression run in R. The dependent variable in this plot is the probability a loan holder will default. The predictive variable (a single one in this instance) is loan balance. Note that the loan balance is a continuous variable, not unlike linear regression problems. However, the regression predicts whether the loan will default: a categorical outcome. The vertical axis (y-axis) shows the probability of default). Now, imagine logistic regression for the Army SFAS example. The predictive variable might be the overall physical fitness test score, which can range from 180 to 300 points. The target outcome is the probability that the candidate completes SFAS and is selected for special forces. That is a simple application of logistic regression.

Source: https://uc-r.github.io/logistic_regression

One of the concerns with any model is overfitting—training a model to great precision with training data but making it vulnerable to low performance in operation. One aspect that can drive overfitting is the number of predictive (or independent) variables, such as the Army Physical Fitness test score. Some data science practitioners have rules of thumb for the maximum number of variables.

We simply encourage two things for leaders: 1) strive toward the smallest number of variables and simplest models with adequate predictive power and 2) engage the team regarding their thought process in evaluating model performance. This is an area where foundational statistical knowledge and experience is valuable. If performance looks overly strong, discuss this with the team and the potential causes of very strong performance bearing in mind that an overfitted model put into operation on new data will not perform well.

Decision Trees. Decision trees are another important foundation method. Data scientists conceptualized this technique almost 50 years ago and still use it frequently. As mentioned earlier, random forests models combine many separate decision trees to create a more sophisticated model. However, there are advantages to using a single decision tree over a decision tree forest. Multiple decision tree forest options are available to teams including adaboost, xgboost, and random forest (which we mention further later in this chapter). Parsimony, or simplicity, is crucial in data science practice. As mentioned, the simplest technique that provides adequate precision, recall, or accuracy is the best model for the situation. Decision trees are a simple technique that can be readily implemented in R, Python, and other software. One valuable aspect of decision trees is how they reveal the most powerful features in reaching an answer. This is referred to as "feature importance" and different methods center on this in evaluating more complex decision tree forests.

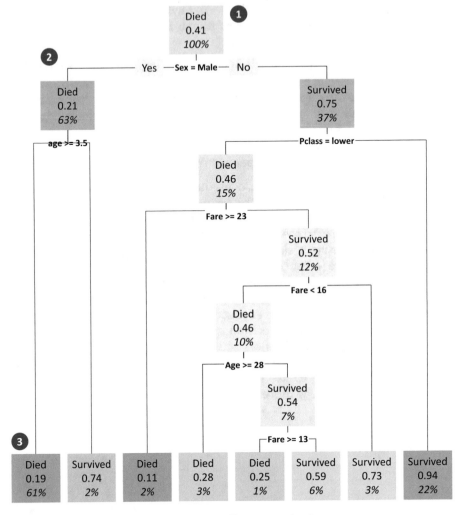

Figure 5-10. Example of decision tree using Titanic casualty data

Source: https://www.guru99.com/r-decision-trees.html

A data scientist created the chart in Figure 5-10 to illustrate the use of a decision tree in R, applying the model to data on survivors of the *Titanic* tragedy. First, the top of the tree represents that 41 percent of the passengers and crew survived and that 100 percent of the observations are filtered through the tree. The decision at the top of the tree is gender; is the person a male? If yes, break to the left side of the tree and the second red annotation. This node includes 63 percent and 21 percent. This indicates that 63 percent of the passengers were male, 21 percent of whom died. The question at this node focuses on passenger age; the model identifies which questions to ask as it trains itself using the training data. Based on gender and age, the reader flows to the bottom classification of results. On the left, 61 percent of passengers were males older than 3.5; 19 percent of these individuals died. In contrast, the next class to the right, males younger than or equal to 3.5, represented 2 percent of passengers, 74 percent of whom survived. The analysis of the classes carries on to the right.

The decision tree function analyzes the training data for useful breakpoints in the data. These form the basis for the classification. In R, data scientists can bound the complexity of the trees (i.e., tree depth, pruning criteria and other factors shown in R or Python). Then, data scientists evaluate the performance of the tree based on common model metrics.

Advanced Approaches Can Generate Lift

If the three foundation model types were sufficient for all mission tasks, we would not have seen the evolution of other approaches over the past 20 years. Contemporary computing environments and advances in software performance have opened paths to substantial gains in machine learning and AI performance. These sections provide a high-level view of some of these dynamics as well as the concept of "lift." Then the content will shift to an exploration of text and natural language processing work, fields in which practitioners have made substantial progress in the past 15 years.

Before plowing into a couple of the model types, leaders should be mindful of two different approaches to machine learning—supervised methods and unsupervised methods. Many of us have seen movies about or heard stories of jail breaks—prisoners who escape and are tracked. Conjure up the image of the tracking bloodhound presented with a piece of clothing with the prisoner's scent, then the dog running off on the prisoner's trail. Dogs are trained for a range of missions such as narcotics or explosives detection. In some raw form, this is an example of supervised learning. The handler gives the dog a specific pattern in the context of scent and they seek that scent. Similarly, with supervised machine learning, data scientists train the model with labeled data that includes the desired pattern and events or observations that do not fit that pattern. The model learns to detect the pattern over and over. Then, the model scores the probability that a particular observation fits the pattern. Unsupervised machine learning approaches seek to make sense of data, forming clusters of similar observations or identifying potential patterns in the data.

It is particularly useful in adversarial settings to run *ensemble model approaches* (multiple models in parallel), which have supervised and unsupervised models running in parallel. The supervised models look for the known or historical target pattern (the "scent," if you will). Meanwhile, the unsupervised models are testing for new patterns, new behaviors. In an adversarial environment, the bad guys change behavior. If an organization's detection posture is limited only to known patterns, then there is a risk they will be surprised, failing to detect changes in behavior that are material. Separately, certain types of data and mission task combinations require unsupervised methods to achieve high performance.

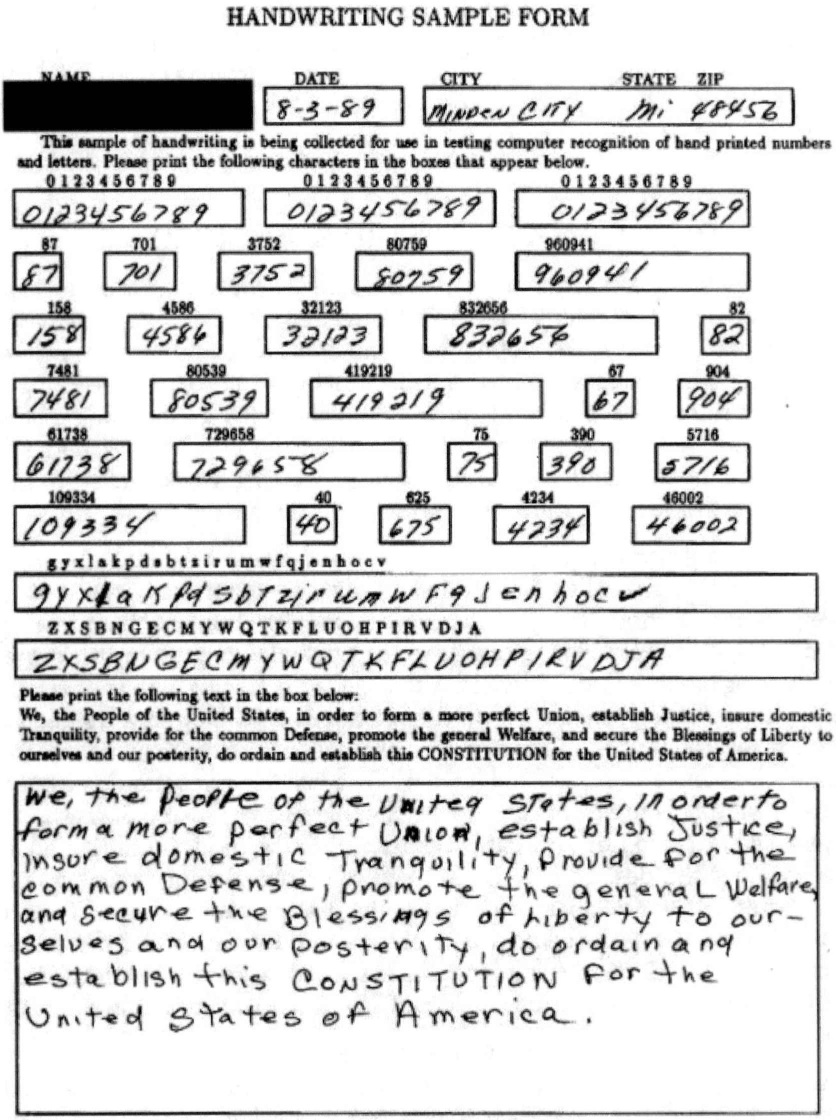

Figure 5-11. Example of NIST handwriting data often used for NLP testing

Source: https://www.nist.gov/srd/nist-special-database-19

The National Institute of Standards and Technology provides important datasets that support machine learning research and model development. One of these is a handwriting dataset. Figure 5-11 is an artifact from this dataset. This form contains both structured and unstructured data. Converting handwriting to text is a challenging task for machine learning models.

Not all models perform equally well in this task of conversion. As a leader, it is important to ask your team about the relative performance of their models. The team should establish baseline machine learning performance with a foundation model. These foundational models include linear regression, logistic regression, and decision trees. Models like these or status quo processing can form the baseline performance in a mission process.

As teams explore different model performance, they are looking for "lift" (or improvements over baseline performance) in key metrics such as accuracy. An apples-to-apples comparison of models on the same training data allows the team to understand which approach will perform best. Furthermore, having several options arms the team to interact with the larger software development organization in large systems contexts. Some of the higher-end models have more demanding computational requirements. As mentioned earlier, these requirements can raise interpretation and trust questions with operational users. Consequently, exploring multiple models is helpful. A long-term colleague of ours, Michael Greene, is a fantastic data science leader. He performed research and experiments to understand variations in model performance for converting handwriting in the NIST dataset to text. This work is not only interesting for exploring performance differences between models, but also represents an example of best practices for teams. In the NIST array of handwritten numbers, there are ten options for accurate conversion for any given number. For reference, a human randomly guessing would have a ten percent expected accuracy. In the table, the baseline model is essentially logistic regression; it has an accuracy of 75 percent. Then, "lift" is measured by comparing the performance of this model with that of other model types. The point is not to explain each of these models in the test, but rather to highlight that performance will vary. Further, the gaps in performance will not always be this consequential. Across the range of mission tasks, foundational approaches may perform quite well and result in a lower computational burden. In others, the foundational model may be far outpaced by more advanced or ensemble techniques. See Table 5-2.

Table 5-2. Model Results for Different Approaches on Handwriting Conversion

Technique	Accuracy
Random Guess	10%
Logistic Regression	75.3%
LASSO Regression	85.3%
Neural Network (One Hidden Layer)	91.3%
Convolutional Neural Net *	97-98%*
K-Means**	73.6%
Random Forest	95.1%

Source: Independent research, Michael Greene, Deloitte Consulting

* - CNN results reported by Nielsen (reference below)

** - K-Means results based on using an unsupervised technique rather than a supervised technique

References: Michael A. Nielsen, "Neural Networks and Deep Learning," Determination Press 2015 LeCun, Yann and Cortes, Corinna. "MNIST handwritten digit database." (2010) - source of the MNIST dataset of handwritten digits.

Source: https://www.nist.gov/srd/nist-special-database-19

For example, consider the random forest as an advanced technique. In the example of handwriting conversion, the random forest far outperformed the logistic regression model. Similarly, a team might expect a random forest to outperform a single decision tree. When training a decision tree, the model identifies important issues (e.g., in the *Titanic* example gender and age were highly predictive of survival outcome using the tree). In many operational and enterprise processes, variables are present to inform the creation of a decision tree. Creating a single decision tree leaves a number of potential tree variations out of the picture. A random forest is a collection (or ensemble) of varied decision trees. As the model processes a new observation for prediction, each of the varied decision trees in the forest processes the data and arrives at an independent prediction.

The choice the random forest recommends is the majority prediction of the output of each of the trees, as shown in Figure 5-12. For example, if a random forest is comprised of 50 trees to deal with accepting a candidate for a training program and 40 trees result in "accept" predictions and 10 result in "deny," then the random forest would recommend "accept." Source:https://towardsdatascience.com/understanding-random-forest-58381e0602d2

Practitioners can apply random forests to classification or regression problems. For example, in the context of a predictive maintenance system for aircraft parts, a model like this might predict the probability of a part needing replacement. This first aspect is classification, not unlike logistic regression. The probability of part failure might be the target outcome of the prediction. Data scientists typically use a random forest regression to predict a value (price, time until an event, etc.). For leaders, it is a more complex task to train a random forest compared to a decision tree; it is valuable to recognize that there are different types. Further, if the team has not previously worked with random forests, be sure explore what is driving predictions. Ask the team about the importance of different variables. The answers should align with your operational or business intuition.

Neural nets are another advanced model type leaders should understand at the basic level. Fundamentally, neural nets mimic the function of the brain and nervous system. A neuron in the human body receives signals from the body's sensory system, processes those signals, and transmits its own signals. When we wince, pull our hand back from a hot surface, or reach to cover our ears in presence of a loud noise, neurons and the nervous system are at work. In an autonomous driving vehicle, neural nets process various sensor inputs and output signals to other neural networks that process this situational data and issue commands (e.g., accelerate, brake, signal, steer). In essence, these neural nets seek to mimic the actions of neurons and nerve cells in our bodies by receiving a set of inputs, processing them, and issuing outputs.

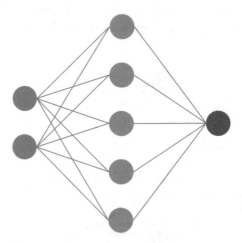

Figure 5-12. Shallow, one layer neural net

Figure 5-12 depicts a simple neural network with the three constituent layers: input, hidden layer for processing, and output. The output is not unlike a logistic regression in that it represents a probabilistic classification. The far left nodes represent the input layer. In this context, the input layer is a data format that the neural net is prepared to receive and process (e.g., images). The lighter-blue nodes in the center represent a processing or perceiving layer. Data scientist will often refer to this as a "perceptron layer." Finally, the output layer is annotated in darker blue on the right. Neural nets can be as simple as this conceptual representation, or they can be "deep" with multiple hidden layers. Each node in the hidden layer processes data and issues a signal to the output layer. Then, the output layer applies weights and biases to produce a prediction. In software like R or Python, the data scientist sets the number of nodes in a simple network. Additionally, in more complex networks, both the number of hidden layers (blue) and the maximum number of nodes are specified. Some data scientists remark that a single hidden layer network like the one pictured is similar to a logistic regression. For simple problems, a leader may ask about their team's point of view on the relative value or risk of using a simple neural network over a logistic regression. At some level, overfitting is more likely with a simple neural network unless the team is careful. The output is against a range of specified values (e.g., "Accept," "Deny," "Defer," or outcomes categories relevant to the mission problem). In simple terms, imagine a model trained to differentiate trucks, cars, and main battle tanks in overhead image data. This is a classification, and the output layer represents the model's prediction (e.g., truck).

Neural nets can have significant depth in terms of the number of hidden layers as well as the number of nodes per layer. "Deep learning" models are neural networks with many hidden layers that are often focused on unstructured data processing. Neural network packages or libraries can be called in R and Python that represent advanced capability to accelerate work.

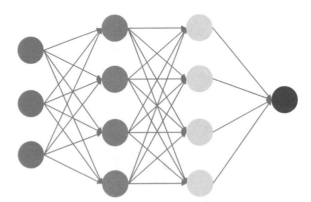

Figure 5-13. Multiple hidden layers in neural net

For example, in R, the neural net packages readily available to teams include TensorFlow, Keras, nnet, and neuralnet. A data science team will know or be able to learn these packages. Take TensorFlow and Keras as examples. Google created TensorFlow as an open-source capability for machine learning, including neural nets. Keras is a high-end deep learning package running in concert with TensorFlow, allowing the team to experiment with and train deep neural nets. Returning to the MacGyver analogy, part of the team's job is selecting packages appropriate to the mission task, then experimenting with the parameters around input, hidden layers, and output layers. The team may be able to train a neural network on a simple task with a fast feedback loop within days, while a complex network against a challenging mission task could take months. Running these experiments is something any good data science team can do. However, be sure to ask the team about their experience working with these models. Ensure that they have a thoughtful approach to the training and interpretation of results. To return to the handwriting analysis experiment shared earlier, neural networks can do everything a logistic regression can do, potentially with substantial gains in accuracy. More importantly, neural networks can be built to address tasks well beyond the capability of logistic regression.

Text Is An Asset

Text is messy and filled with potentially valuable information; natural language processing (NLP) methods allow data science teams to tackle this and create insight. A tremendous amount of the global data is unstructured. Much of this consists of text such as emails, data on web pages, comments in social media, text on collaboration sites, and an array of common documents in operational environments. NLP methods convert text to insight, convert it to a more useable and searchable form, and increasingly position automated capabilities to generate text with surprising realism. Some of the more common techniques in operation include:

- Stopping (removal of articles and unnecessary words like "the"
- Stemming or lemmatization (techniques of varying sophistication to isolate the root of words)
- Tokenization (grouping connected words or elements)
- Topic identification
- Text classification
- Parts of speech identification
- Named entity recognition (people, places, etc.)
- Sentiment analysis
- Translation
- Text summation
- Text generation (Natural Language generation, a subset of the NLP field)

NLP is relevant in each of the four AI project types. For performance assessments, NLP packages can discover insights. For experiments, NLP may be an adjunct to other primary exploration, providing collateral information or context. Alternatively, NLP may be the focus. For example, a data science team was tasked to explore whether changes in foreign leader thinking and sentiment over multiple years could be derived from speeches and commentary. A body of NLP techniques were applied to ten years of content to identify topics over time, and assess sentiment as well as associate particular people, policies, and issues with changes.

With respect to dashboards, NLP can be applied in data pipelines to enrich information. Imagine a system like the Defense Readiness Reporting System, which includes highly structured inputs as well as unstructured, free text entry in select fields. NLP could potentially be applied to the free text entries to identify specific entities, applying tags that could further enrich dashboard views. Lastly, NLP is the cornerstone to major AI-enabled solutions that provide user support via chat and email response. In addition, it enhances search, summarizes reports, and more. Each type of AI project can benefit from NLP.

NLP packages can be used across a variety of computing environments, but some leading applications are computationally intensive. Leaders know that open-source software environments provide a robust range of packages and libraries. For example, the capabilities of Python can substantially accelerate a team's work. Useful packages and libraries abound. PolyGlot is not the most used library, but it has the built-in capability to tokenize (breaking text into logical chunks) in over 165 languages, detect almost 200 languages, perform named entity recognition in 40 languages, and more. Additionally, SpaCy is one of the most prolifically used libraries with a fantastic range of capabilities including text classification, text tagging, part-of-speech tagging, sentence segmentation, and named entity recognition. GenSim is another package worth mentioning because it supports capabilities like chat bots and text generation. Every team has options applicable to their work. However, while some packages run efficiently, others require sophisticated computational infrastructure to support training new models. These can exceed the computational resources available to a team, even in a cloud environment; leaders must be attuned to these challenges. The following paragraphs provide more insight on these issues as well as three capabilities, BERT, ERNIE, and GPT.

BERT. Bi-directional Encoder Representations from Transformers (BERT) is an NLP innovation created by Google to enhance search and related text activities. It represents a fascinating NLP breakthrough. Additionally, its open-source capability is available in Python, working with a variety of libraries like TensorFlow and Keras. This capability is remarkable in that the language model was trained using unsupervised techniques across English Wikipedia and the Brown Corpus (another large body of text). As a capability, BERT is pre-trained language models that comes in various sizes (e.g., BERT-Large). A significant body of material is written on BERT, but it essentially processes text in such a way that deals with the common ambiguity associated with words. It also has an ability to predict what word or sentence should come next. Google developed the capability to enhance search, but it applies to various text challenges such as question answering, text summarization, conversational response generation, and sentence prediction. Think of BERT as a neural net with a deep set of processing layers and an extremely large set of parameters that can capture base language learning. BERT-large has about 340 million parameters and 24 transformer layers. So, while BERT is available to teams, they need to exercise the MacGyver problem-solving skills to judge the appropriateness of BERT given the computational environment. As a general rule, if a team is going to use BERT and fine-tune it to a particular problem (e.g., question answering), this will require a GPU. GPUs are not a given in a computational environment; depending on the training task, the team might need numerous GPUs for a period of time. The BERT community is increasing its computational efficiency, but leaders should be conscious that its high-end capabilities come with extensive requirements. The data science team will typically need to work with larger development, engineering, or cloud support teams to judge its viability.

ERNIE. Enhanced Language Representation with Informative Entities (ERNIE) was created by the Chinese firm, Baidu, as an open-source NLP capability. With a number of similarities to BERT, ERNIE performs NLP functions centering on text classification with a word-aware capability that can predict capitalization and sentence ordering, and can learn semantic relationships. Similar to BERT, a team can run ERNIE on a CPU or CPU-virtual machine, but the processing is intensive; it will perform best on GPUs, especially for fine-tuning large models. ERNIE was trained on 64 NVIDIA cards—a major computational commitment. But the pay-off can be high for large-scale operational systems that need to accurately interpret and respond to text in real time. Like BERT, ERNIE is largely based in the Python programming language.

GPT. Generative Pre-Trained Transformer (GPT) is an OpenAI initiative most remarkable in its advanced NLP capabilities. This deep learning capability is in its third version (GPT 3.0). It generates text with a quality eerily similar to normal human interaction. Trained on over 175 billion parameters drawn from a variety of text sources, it represents the leading-edge NLP capability. Microsoft invested $1 billion in OpenAI. Additionally, Microsoft is integrating GPT 3.0 into its product suite; the capability will be a component of the Azure Cloud environment via an API. As with BERT and ERNIE, there are a variety of implementation issues to work through, but the nature of this capability is different in being able to render text from relatively scant prompts.

Rather than describing this fascinating development, we provide an example of text generated (the following two pages of text) by GPT 2.0 with some basic topical prompts:

"GPT-2 Generated "Global Warming" Article 79

Global Warming/By GPT2 Text Generation

Input: What needs to be done to stop Global Warming?

Generated Text:

Global warming occurs when carbon dioxide and other greenhouse gases are added to the atmosphere. Greenhouse gases trap heat inside the Earth's atmosphere, which causes air to get colder. That causes things on the Earth's surface to get colder, and so on. The Earth's surface and the items on it that are closest to the surface become colder. The objects that are farthest away from the surface and the most rapidly getting cooler are the objects that are getting warmest.

Warmer temperatures are correlated with illnesses and problems for many normal individuals. For example, in areas where the average summer temperature has increased about 1◆C (1.8◆F), all ages in 2017 had a greater chance of being hospitalized with an illness related to temperature, compared with those in areas with cooler temperatures.

The data is from the U.S. Census Bureau's 2017 American Community Survey, summarized by the U.S. Department of Health and Human Services. It shows U.S. health impacts from climate change for the years 2010-2016.

An upcoming story in *Science Magazine* tells the story of a student from South Central Los Angeles named Chris Mosier, who is using math to mitigate the effects of global warming. Here's a bit more about his project:

His quest: Find a mathematical formula to translate from the real world—one where streets are getting swelterier and more dangerous—into a form his classroom will understand. He and his class are part of a pioneering effort to apply rigorous scientific tools to a vexing public-health issue. "If you think about it, climate change is kind of a perfect storm of a lot of different issues," says Mosier, a sophomore at Cal State Northridge. "One of them is the weather, one of them is the economic impact, one of them is the environment. It really goes to show you how interconnected everything is." Mosier began exploring the subject after learning many working-class kids his age were skipping lunch to save money to buy groceries. After seeing the impact of air pollution, he wondered if air quality—and the cost of living driven up by it— were mirrored by climate change. His research took him around the world, from Shanghai to El Paso, visiting some of the world's leading climatologists to get their perspective on the subject. He has also joined a small but growing band of high school students around the country embarking on such journeys.

You can read the rest of this story at *Science* magazine: "Climate Change, Public Health and the Undergraduate." It talks, as well, about the future public health implications of a changing planet.

The effects of climate change on human health have been the subject of numerous scientific studies, reviews, and public statements, including the Fourth Assessment Report of the Intergovernmental Panel on Climate Change, which was released in 2013. The full text of the AR4 report can be found at http://www.nap.edu/catalog.php?record_id=12897.

There is a growing body of scientific evidence that climate change alters the global environment, directly affecting climate, precipitation, temperature, the hydrological cycle, ocean ecosystems, and the radiation budget of the climate. Many of these changes take place quickly, causing the climate to change more rapidly. Others may take many years to emerge, and may cause changes to the climate that are less obvious, but still important. Changes in the global environment are expected to cause wide-ranging changes to the health of human populations. These changes include, for example, changes in access to food and water, increased frequency of violent storms and tropical storms, changes in the distribution of agricultural products around the planet, changes in the timing of trade visits, and changes in travel patterns.

The Intergovernmental Panel on Climate Change (IPCC) assessment of the scientific evidence indicates a significant human influence on Earth's climate. This influence, which is evident in observed hotter days, darker cool evenings, and heavier downpours, is attributed to a warming Earth increase in the growth of atmospheric CO2 and other greenhouse gases, and to absorption of solar radiation by the Earth's energy barrier. This warming is a consequence of these influences and not a cause.

Increased confidence in recent warming because of more precise observing systems and improved model forecasts. Less consensus on attribution of recent warming to natural drivers of climate change, for example, changes in land and ocean surfaces or in aerosols; and doubts regarding the safety of greenhouse gases blamed for recent warming, especially CFCs and sulfates. Ever-increasing emissions of greenhouse gases are changing the climate, an act of creation the atmosphere contains gases which are said to have caused the warming. The atmosphere contains more evidence for creation the second Law of Thermodynamics (changes in the ratio of gases would take up less space so the atmosphere had to be created more quickly).

Human activities have contributed to a warming of the climate in the past, but now there is scientific evidence that natural causes also contribute (SWITCH project).

Generated Using: GPT-2 1558M (1.5Billion) parameters base model fine-tuned further on our custom dataset for Global Warming specific text."

Source: https://blog.machinewrites.com/gpt-2-generated-global-warming-article-79/

Incorporating these advanced text processing capabilities is not trivial and this challenge is illustrated in a relatively simple research experiment by a data scientist and former colleague, Andrew Marvin. Curious about the ability to adapt neural networks to generate text similar to the GPT example, he performed some initial training of a neural net-based model in about one hour using historical military strategy texts (e.g., Corbin, Jomini, Clauzwitz). He then seeded the text-generation request with a simple word string, not unlike the GPT example. The point for leaders is conceptually many things are possible, but it is easy to underestimate the work required to create a reliable, high-performing solution. The following outputs illustrate the challenge when we compare a small, untuned model to a large-scale work like GPT and the training done around specific problems. The simple experiment rendered these results:

Prompt: "The offense is"

Partial Results:

"the offense is the pursuit_than on some single sciences of defences

Against what shakens only in the operations of an army, disturbed or

sufficiently, then lust this path of eccentric lines are not generally regarded enough to be saved by, to make use of all history, for it stands themselves by separate combats.

Prompt: "convoy operations are"

Partial Results:

"Convoy operations are not quite a difficult undertaking. The direct essence of the

moment when it behind him with a system which can only be occasions before the defender's start spon by believes, best Holland throughout better decisions

which happens his retreat"

Source: Andrew Marvin, independent research, May 2022.

The types of high-end text processing capabilities illustrated in BERT, ERNIE, and GPT have pertinence to a range of tasks in the national security arena, if they can be successfully adapted. The opportunity space is potentially quite large. As one example, it is common to create daily summary reporting of information flowing into various commands. This is an area for potential duplication of effort across different commands and components. Creating text summarization capabilities by adapting technologies like this can free front-line staff from the routinized activities so they can focus on more in-depth work to understand context, background, and changes. But we rely on human intuition today and human effort to select which items to include in summaries and to write them. In this respect, potential application also illustrates the common AI-related challenge in needing to think about the work process and the right fit for these solutions. As the experiment with military history illustrates, however, the training and adaptation of models is not trivial and certainly not the integration of the large-scale solutions like GPT.

Summary Regarding Data Science

Data science is fundamentally a problem-solving discipline that applies technology to create solutions and other outputs. As Hillary Mason put it so well, "A data scientist is someone who can obtain, scrub, explore, model, and interpret data, blending hacking, statistics, and machine learning." Having read this chapter, we trust you have a clearer view of some of the fundamental aspects of this work, the reason programming languages are important, and a clearer sense of the techniques and models available. This work requires talented people—as outlined in Chapter 7—who work in a structured way with quality oversight—as outlined in Chapter 6. Options are heavily shaped by the technological choices outlined in Chapter 8. Taken together, leaders should have a clearer view of where and how to engage to accelerate the deployment of compelling AI solutions.

Leading the Project

"Smart people often fail to recognise when they need help, and when they do recognise it, they tend to believe that no one else is capable of providing it."

—Travis Bradberry, President, TalentSmart, 2015

Summary

AI projects create solutions that deliver insights from data on their own or as a component of a larger system. Advanced techniques are pertinent to each of the four project types—performance assessments, experiments, dashboards, and operational AI capabilities. Projects can fail to deliver an inspiring, accurate, and timely result. Success is not a given and some AI concepts will simply not pan out. The leader must ensure failures are not a function of execution issues by the team. This work is technical in nature and requires a rigorous team approach to maximize impact. Leaders can engage and apply quality checks in five discrete phases around any given project to create effective team engagement and minimize the risk of a project failing to deliver the desired mission impact.

© Chris Whitlock, Frank Strickland 2023
C. Whitlock and F. Strickland, *Winning the National Security AI Competition*,
https://doi.org/10.1007/978-1-4842-8814-6_6

This chapter reviews the four AI project types outlined in Chapter 2, then explains five project-level axioms. What follows are six major project activities and a leader emphasis and engagement guide:

- Selling the project
- Project initiation
- Data acquisition/exploration
- Model development/advanced analytics
- Solution deployment/conveying results
- Monitoring/adapting AI model performance
- Leader emphasis and engagement issues quick reference

Individual projects answer advanced analytics questions and build the AI models required to improve operational performance; projects convert ideas and aspirations into results. We can structure the right programs and build portfolios of projects, but if we perform poorly in project-level execution, little will be gained. Over the course of our work, three project-level failure modes are always possible: creating uninspiring results, getting incorrect answers, and taking too much time. Effective project leadership is crucial to ensure the resources applied to AI create the desired payoff as well as to ensure teams avoid these failure modes.

Revisiting AI Project Types

In Chapter 2, we introduced a simple framework to cover four types of projects. We laid out our rationale for referring to all of these under the simpler umbrella of AI. Machine learning and various forms of AI can be present in all four of these types, while those with the purest focus on developing AI models are in the right column of Figure 6-1. However, we have performed a number of studies that leveraged AI tools to perform studies, such as assisting in one-time natural language processing. Dashboards pull tables from specified locations and display them for monitoring and decision-making. AI models can create critical values by using models in the data pipeline to feed the dashboard.

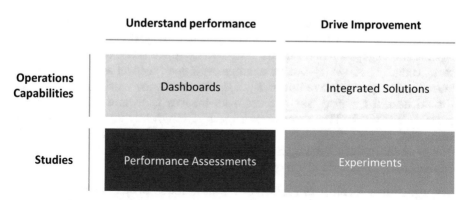

	Understand performance	Drive Improvement
Operations Capabilities	Dashboards	Integrated Solutions
Studies	Performance Assessments	Experiments

Figure 6-1. Four AI project types

This chapter focuses on successfully executing these project types. Many resources on enterprise dashboards are available; consequently, we give dashboards less attention in this chapter, though the project approach is still relevant to them.

Project Axioms

Looking back over our history working on or leading hundreds of projects, several core truths span them all. These six project level axioms are as follows:

Engaged Leadership is Required

Data Science is a Capability

Quality Approach Essential

Data Access A Leader Challenge

AI development Speed Not Uniform

Seams Require Management

In this chapter, we address several major aspects of project-level leadership. First, we elaborate on these axioms, explaining why every leader must be vigilant and engaged around them. Then, we illustrate some of this with select case studies. Last, we lay out an example of a project-level approach; this we intend not as prescriptive but as a guide. Any company working in the space should have a method, seek to train its leaders in it, and use it to guide project-level work. The absence of a method inherently increases risk. That being said, there are different ways to approach method creation; we would not presume to offer a single best solution, but rather desire to illustrate components to include in a method.

Engaged Leadership Is Required. Data science projects can go awry in several major ways and must overcome some common hurdles especially around data access and connected to end users or decision-makers. Leaders in this area must engage from beginning to end to ensure success. Over-delegation or failure to check on teamwork creates significant risk for the project. Leaders should aspire to drive not ride. Focus on active engagement; meeting with end users and decision-makers, performing checks with the team, and engaging in discussions on methods and options. In this chapter, we lay out specific areas to probe with the team and principles to apply to the work.

Leaders need not be expert in all the details but must strive for excellent process understanding and comfort around critical factors in projects. This is technical work, described in more detail in the chapter on data science. As a consequence, leaders will always have team members with deeper technical insight, knowledge, and skill. This does not eliminate the need for engagement in the least. Rather, it brings some not insignificant expectation for leaders to develop knowledge especially and to guide the team around the organizational and domain dynamics.

Data Science Is a Capability. To deliver on AI projects, leaders need a data science team with an appropriate environment, including hardware and software. Teams work with data. For this, they need either access to on-premises or cloud-based servers to store data and to run various processing. Leaders must ensure access to these hardware and software assets. We discuss these issues more in the technology chapter, but there are a range of software options, from commercial off-the-shelf to open-source.

With respect to the team as part of the capability, we might rephrase our chief concern as "beware solo data scientists." Those who have worked with us know this refrain well. As software has changed, cloud computing has increased the availability of resources, and more people have become trained, it is important to view the data science work necessary to create AI as a capability. "Give me a data scientist." These five words should immediately raise caution flags unless the data scientist will be joining a team with others. This work is highly technical, requiring advanced knowledge and skill in multiple areas. It is unwise to load all this risk on one "smart person." Multiple negative potential outcomes come with this approach. Over the years, we have run into a variety of reasons project-level leaders discount this issue and want just a single "smart person" or solo data scientist: cost, underestimating the challenge/risk, and marketing around technologies. We can all immediately resonate with the cost component. However, the hidden costs of having a solo data scientist are unclear until you run into major problems, and we discuss this further in this chapter. The second issue revolves around the leader's understanding of the mission task and environment, which should lead to a clear expression of the data science need, which in our experience is typically a team with a mix of complementary skills. Especially when there is cost pressure, we crave to simplify and minimize costs, but this can lead to other consequential problems. Rather than starting with a "give me a data scientist" view, we recommend considering, "What should a data science capability look like on this project team?" Lastly, we benefit from advancing technologies in data science—we should capitalize on all of them appropriately. But we must maintain a sense of realism while doing this. "Democratizing data science," "AutoML (automated machine learning)," and other buzz phrases capture realities of some emerging technologies, but these have hard limits. A savvy leader must develop discernment regarding the boundary between hype and reality as it pertains to structuring effective projects. Thinking holistically about the data science capability will minimize risks.

To drive home the risk of solo data scientists/modelers working without competent checks, consider this excerpt of an article about a commercial example; the much-discussed London Whale Trade which resulted in a $6B loss for JP Morgan:

> "You blink a few times at the screen and realize what you're seeing is not a typo. $6.2B has left your bank due to some rogue trader making untimely bets on the market. That's B as in billion. You call up the modeler who was supposed to make sure this never happens to your bank. The modeler takes a closer look at his model and realizes that he made a fundamental error in how he calculates one value that caused the dominoes to fall. This is the story of the "London Whale" at JPMorgan Chase in 2012 who cost the bank $6.2B and a breakdown of the Excel error that may have caused the whole thing."

A Quality Approach Is Essential. To complement treating data science as a capability, leaders must ensure there is a structured quality approach with periodic reviews throughout the project across multiple dimensions of the work. Quality is not something added at the end of a project, it is a stem to stern activity throughout the project that requires leader engagement. The following sections provide specific pointers to issues for leaders to probe and explore with teams. We outline a process later in the chapter as an illustration, but our intent is not to prescribe. Rather, we want to inform leaders who can then explicitly test for the presence of a quality approach, engage at specified points, and monitor some set of leader indicators regularly to help ensure success.

The opposite of this is a passive approach, which assumes teams are smart and will logically navigate a process. In this posture, the leader is a rider, not a driver. In the absence of a structured approach that directs engagement at pre-agreed points and offers a list of regular issues to monitor, the leader quickly ends up in a reactive posture. Negative dynamics can unfold: the project progresses too slowly because the team is mired in data access issues. Seeing interim results, the leader may be left surprisingly unimpressed, or worse—mistakes become apparent to the project leader when incorrect outputs or problems are highlighted by users or decision-makers. As with the London Whale Trade, these risks are real; no company or organization is inoculated against them, especially in the absence of structured thoughtful reviews.

As an example of attributes to check in a quality approach, DoD has promulgated a policy pertaining to ethical AI. Five tenets are specified in the policy, which a project leader can tacitly review and test in a regularized review. Importantly, these checks cannot be performed only at the end of the project without substantial risk of costly rework. According to the policy, AI solutions must be the following:

- Responsible
- Equitable
- Traceable
- Reliable
- Governable[1]

Data Access Requires Leader Engagement. Gaining access to necessary data can be one of the most frustrating aspects of AI projects. It is unwise to overly delegate around this critical activity—no data, no AI. To create outputs or solutions, teams must access data, explore it thoroughly, train models, and test models. None of this is possible without data access.

Data is typically managed by particular programs (whether prototypes or programs of record), which have legitimate reasons to restrict or be concerned about access. The two most common obstacles are concerns about security and concerns about data interpretation. Security issues are relatively straightforward in one sense: the data's level of classification. The more

---

[1] "A Closer Look: The Department of Defense AI Ethical Principles," *The Joint Artificial Intelligence Center*, 24 February 2020, https://www.ai.mil/blog_02_24_20-dod-ai_principles.html

common discussion topic is need to know. Why do you need access to this data? This can lead to legitimate questions from as about a project teams' ability to properly interpret the data in an AI context. Datasets in complex organizations may not have well-defined data dictionaries, can include embedded domain-specific codes, and usually include characteristics that inherently reflect the operational process. In our experience, project teams should consider these concerns to be legitimate—they must address both explicit and implied objections.

AI Development Times Are Not Uniform. We all want results quickly, but it is important for leaders to recognize that the pace of AI training, testing, and deployment is tightly linked to the cycle time of the operational process being supported. To illustrate, consider something away from national security but which we can all relate to in some way: paying taxes and tax administration. Each year, the Internal Revenue Service (IRS) selects some small percentage of tax returns for examination. Sophisticated models are used to select these returns based on the likelihood an examination will result in a "change" to the return by the taxpayer. The taxpayer may have made a mistake or attempted tax fraud. New model innovations are tested periodically. The time required to know whether these innovations work is the cycle time of the examination process (2-3 years). For a range of maintenance or supply issues or other problems in national security, the feedback loop will not be immediate. Leaders must plan realistically and shape stakeholder expectations around the cycle time for AI projects.

Seams Around the AI Team Require Management. AI teams produce outputs, either in the form of models to be employed in some operational setting or insights in the form of a report. Leaders must focus on the seam that can develop between AI teams and larger development teams in programs of record. Development teams, whether operating in an agile or waterfall development environment, have preferences, architectural constraints, cost constraints, and schedule constraints. Development teams are responsible for creating deployable, functioning systems. To orchestrate the work of many developers, these teams will have preferences on code type, comments on code, and methods of interacting to achieve deployed code status. AI teams, which may operate with some autonomy in exploring potential approaches and models, can stumble when approaching development teams to integrate their capabilities as part of the broader solution. Leaders must recognize up front that these AI solutions are typically part of something larger. This is not to say they cannot stand alone as tools, but leaders need to pay attention to the target implementation environment. If the implementation environment is in an existing development program, then they must expect that the seam between the AI and development teams will require attention. Development teams must operate in an architecture context, which implies the interaction of hardware and software, service-level agreement approaches on functions, and so on. Importantly, these development teams have cost and schedule constraints. AI teams must integrate into these environments constructively.

Two other facets of this require leader attention and should not be taken for granted. High-performing development teams tend to have an engineering bent—they value discipline in creating solutions with all the associated componentry. System architects, software architects, software engineers, and developers are common job titles. Overall, many in the AI field are much more exploratory in nature and oriented toward analysis rather than engineering. This is not to say there is no overlap. But a cultural differences exists between development and AI teams that can become a challenge to actively manage.

We have also observed management challenges in multi-company environments. The simple message is this requires leadership and management from government and industry leaders. We live in a capitalist system—competition is a core aspect of what happens in the market. Government leaders should be tuned to protecting intellectual property where appropriate and ensuring obstacles to progress are not actually competitive dynamics cloaked in "technical issues." Exhorting industry partners to operate in a "badge-less environment" and act as if their companies do not exist can only carry projects and programs so far. The major challenges hinge on access to data, information sharing, collaboratively problem-solving, and collaboratively prioritizing work. These factors can be actively managed by strong leaders.

Six Major Project Activities

Government and companies in industry will have project-level approaches; there are some in industry to draw on such as the Cross Industry Standard for Data Mining (CRISP-DM). Our intent is not to prescribe or recommend any particular existing method; we believe various approaches can work. This high-level, six-part framework equips leaders to evaluate proposed approaches or to structure reviews of existing projects no matter the particular process in use.

These project activities are not strictly serial. As an example, the solution deployment may require some early work in coordinating with development teams, setting boundaries on technical options, and so on. Waiting until much of the work is done to perform these tasks is a fast path to rework. Generally, solution deployment is an activity that culminates after substantial work has been done. See Table 6-1.

Table 6-1. Six Major Project Activities

Major Project Activities	Key Tasks
Selling the Project	Whether government or industry leaders, new projects must be "sold" to garner the resources and support required to see the effort through
Project Initiation	Problem framing, project planning, data scoping, assessing technology environment, finalizing team composition
Data Acquisition/ Exploration	Engage data owners, agree to terms on data use, arrange batch or API access, explore data parameters and labels, build data dictionaries where absent, perform some common feature engineering
Model Development, Advanced Analytics	Finalize model types for evaluation, perform feature engineering, perform training and test, evaluate results; for performance assessments, structure and test operational hypotheses and seek new results/insights daily
Solution Deployment, Conveying Results	Solution deployment: finalize integration approach, work schedule with development team, evaluate/monitor early operational deployment
	Conveying results: on analytics studies, create decks that speak to findings, interactive visualizations or dashboards to make findings more accessible
Monitor, Adjust AI Model Performance	For deployed models, leaders must ensure models are monitoring and re-trained as required to meet performance expectations

Activity #1: Selling the Project

Whether you are a government or industry leader, selling the project is crucial to establishing a successful project. Projects require organizational support: contractor resources, government resources, potentially hardware/software resources, access to data held by other organizations, and so on. Consequently, any given organization can only undertake a finite number of projects at any given time. To get a new project approved, you must sell it.

Case Example: Setting Realistic Expectations

Modernizing existing systems and building new ones requires advocacy for funding. It also may require new acquisition initiatives. These must be sold to stakeholders and decision-makers.

The Defense Readiness Reporting System (DRRS) is a well-established monthly mechanism to capture the status of units across DoD against a structured framework as well as capture each commander's assessment of mission-essential capabilities.

Some desire advanced modeling capabilities in DRRS as it modernizes. Concepts have included building a "what if" capability to answer investment questions for various programs. For example, could an AI solution readily address, "What is the readiness impact if we invest $5B in this program?"

This is an easy-to-conceptualize capability, but it is enormously prone to over-selling and quite challenging to implement. It is easy to think this might be "one button" or one capability when in fact the differences between programs require a tremendous amount of task-specific, context-dependent work. Would we believe a model that works for a main battle tank series like the M1 Abrams will also work for aircraft like the Apache? Consider the range of aircraft type series in DoD. Would each type series require system dynamics models to underpin such a capability? Could a model that renders a reasonable answer for the C-130 family also output an accurate and relevant answer for the F-22 fighter? Would every major equipment program require specific modeling solutions?

We believe the answer is clear—this is the type of concept very prone to overselling. Leaders can avoid overselling projects like this through benchmark research and detailed assessment.

- **Initial problem framing: connecting mission value to cost.** After experiencing many different organizations over time, we found varying approaches to AI-related project prioritization. The forcing function is limited resources. So, most of the organizations we have supported require periodic evaluations of new potential project ideas, often along with regular reviews of progress around existing projects. In these environments, a new potential project needs an advocate. Enough spadework must be done to outline the potential cost-benefit ratio and feasibility of the project. A project proposal may be as simple as a single page to explain the proposed task, current situation, benefits, resources required, and timeline. In other environments, a multi-page proposal is required. Some of this is linked to the size or importance of the potential task. Whatever the format, the process centers on a mission problem, then links the cost-benefit ratio and feasibility to the proposed effort.

- **Be thoughtful in setting expectations.** The cost-benefit ratio and feasibility representations of the project in this selling phase can implicitly and explicitly set expectations for the project outcome. Therefore, leaders remain thoughtful. We outlined earlier three project failure modes: uninspiring results, incorrect outputs, and projects running too slowly. The seed of these failure modes can be planted in the selling phase through overly aggressive representations of potential results or small requests for resources. In software sales, there is well-established tension between marketing or sales staff and the engineers who actually have to implement the software in the client environment. This well-known industry tension illustrates the core risk here: over-selling projects up front leads to lofty expectations that can be dashed by the realities of the environment. Uninspiring results in a project can trace back to unrealistic expectations set in the selling phase, particularly as it pertains to operationalizing models or conducting AI experiments. For example, overselling a text processing concept on the frontend can easily leave stakeholders cold when seeing the actual results. Similarly, under-resourcing a project, down-playing data access, or underestimating computational challenges can directly lead to slower-than-expected progress.

- **Anchor anticipated value to benchmark examples.** Realistically linking the benefits to current baseline performance while estimating required resources based on similar efforts inoculates against over-selling. The challenge for some organizations is that AI projects, especially experimental ones, may be very new to them. In our experience, when your organization lacks a deep background in the area, you must refer to external examples. However, this opens you to the vulnerability of underestimating context-dependent factors in the benchmarks cited. This overselling risk compels leaders to lift the hood and understand assumptions behind external benchmark claims. How similar was the mission task? What was the extent of model training? How is the data different? Are the hardware and software situations similar enough? Questions like these can create a more realistic vision of a project's potential benefits. Commercial examples can be helpful, but they need to be relevant. Google supports over five billion queries per day;

Facebook over 250 million new posts daily and reportedly a repository of over 500 billion images; Instagram over 500 million posts daily. Most leaders use these applications but can readily underestimate the gap between the environment in these companies and that in national security as regards training and deploying AI models. As Andrew Ng, a leading AI innovator and chief scientist behind the high-performance Baidu text-processing capability says, few AI solutions will outside the consumer space look like these large text and image processing capabilities. For the most part, there will be a lot of tailoring and smaller-scale modeling and it is important for leaders to understand the relevance of the benchmarks in setting expectations.

- **Plan to use existing software and computational infrastructure wherever possible.** For AI experiments or performance assessments, we recommend using existing software and hardware (or cloud environments), if possible. The realities associated with introducing new hardware and software for these projects can immediately create extended timelines, resource hurdles, and implementation difficulties. New software and hardware invoke procurement processes, security reviews, technical support requirements for implementation, potential financial hurdles, and even privacy concerns in some situations. These are all potentially necessary for implementing new operational capabilities, whether in the form of dashboards or AI models. However, they are not necessary for most performance assessments or AI modeling experiments. How should a leader judge exceptions to this rule? Consider a practical and functional example. Graph processing is a particular method to not only store data about network relationships on a complex topic but also implement a variety of AI models to highlight activities or changing relationships in the graph. To perform an experiment on the potential value of graph processing with an organization's problems/data, some graph software must be available on the network. This will often be the case if the organization has deployed open-source data science software such as Python or R. If these tools are unavailable, then the project advocate must think through how graph software will be added during the "selling" phase. A realistic view of implementation challenges will help avoid the slow project failure mode.

- **Engage stakeholders to build support.** In the selling phase, it is also important to engage various stakeholders in at least a preliminary way. These groups include supported operational commands or programs of record, procurement, and relevant IT components. The purpose here is not detailed plan review but ensuring the concept in consideration is viewed as feasible. Additionally, it ensures that the necessary organizations are ready to support.

Activity #2: Initiating the Project

This phase sets the foundation for high performance in the project, shifting from the conceptual assessment of the opportunity and "selling it" to forming a team and performing detailed assessment. In our experience, involving a multi-function team early on adds value to the project. Several other activities are critically important in this early activity phase, including establishing baseline performance, scoping the data, assessing the technical environment, finalizing team composition, and finalizing planning. Leaders need to direct and check a series of important actions:

- **Finalize problem framing.** In selling a potential project, both government and industry leaders must make some assumptions about the operational problem being addressed and the potential methods, but as the project actually initiates this must be finalized. While we never formally collected data on this aspect of projects as the root of failure, our intuition and experience strongly orient to this task as crucial in setting up success or project failure. The team must formalize the focus on target operational tasks and measures for the AI-related work and structure thinking on the broad approach. This document serves as a touchstone for the team and is used to engage end users and set expectations.

- **Engaging end users.** Nothing is more frustrating to a team than creating a solution only to find that the target audiences will not use it or do not find it as helpful as anticipated. For a wide range of AI projects, early user engagement is important to bound the acceptable space for a solution. This is true for dashboards, performance assessments, experiments, and operational models, but especially dashboards and operational models. With AI-related projects, users must trust the results. A core activity for the team is ensuring sufficient visibility into how the outputs are developed and what assumptions were made.

Accuracy and confidence become especially important. Irrespective of the AI project type, discovering that an output is incorrect corrodes trust that can be difficult to rebuild. Therefore, teams must communicate the expectations of solution performance with users. Using two of the common model performance measures, recall and precision, we can illustrate some common trade-offs. In some operational applications, it is important not to miss potential problems. For an AI experiment or operational model, this measure is referred to as model "recall." What percentage of the legitimate cases or instances of a potential issue does the model flag? If users are concerned with achieving high recall (not missing a potential problem), then this can drive performance on "precision" in the wrong direction. Precision is a common measure of model performance around the correctness of the output: "I said the animal was a dog, was it in fact a dog?" It is crucial to engage users early to understand what they value.

- **Establishing baseline performance.** Project benefits will be assessed relative to the current state. For example, implementing an AI model should improve performance— an obvious expectation. But what improvement do we expect against what baseline performance? For example, the target is to decrease manual processing time for certain supply chain functions (inventory management, parts approval, etc.). As another example, Aegis Weapon System leaders may be concerned about the number or percentage of ambiguous air contacts or time to resolve them. To capture the AI pay-off, the project team needs to understand baseline performance; this should not be taken as a given. In some instances, there is a clear, readily available metric. But, in others, this is not the case. Often, operational leaders observe challenges like big manual labor traps, but they do not necessarily know the performance level. Capturing baseline performance typically involves working with the stakeholder organization to access data, understanding metrics they may be evaluating currently, or even performing direct observation of the work environment. Whatever the combination of methods, it is important to establish the baseline and contextualize targeted performance improvement.

Some common baseline approaches include fully manual processing with written guidelines, rules engines, custom algorithms, and regression models. Manual processing remains common in a variety of national security functions. Notionally, consider a task like visa approval for a foreign national. A State Department officer might conduct a search on several different systems for the applicant's name and background information. According to a specified standard, they directly adjudicate the request or review it with a manager. In contrast, rules engines are status quo in some environments for scoring or ranking options. Each rule (e.g., flag if the supply order volume is greater than 10,000) is developed and refined through some periodic analysis. Rules tend to be inherently static; AI models offer the prospect of a much more dynamic posture. Custom algorithms and regression models also represent common baseline implementations. Where present, they should produce structured outputs to serve as baseline performance. For example, each pass around the earth for an imaging spacecraft presents numerous potential imaging targets. Some optimization model likely determines which ones will be imaged on a given pass. This would represent the baseline for any notional AI-driven upgrade.

- **Finalizing team composition.** Depending on the phase, team composition might vary. However, certain competencies must be covered throughout the process. All the work is rooted in mission tasks, which requires domain knowledge of organizations, processes, guidelines/laws, data sources, and data field interpretation. Often, the team will need to lean on subject matter experts from a stakeholder organization, but the core team needs sufficient domain knowledge to avoid problems and wasted time. Leaders must be conscious that data sources are often not well-documented in the form of data dictionaries, but yet teams must understand and properly interpret fields. This can potentially be achieved through document reviews, but the best path is access to subject matter experts. Statistical, mathematical, and programming expertise is important in these AI-related tasks. Programming expertise in open-source environments like Python and R are a strong indicator; leaders should press to understand the relative proficiency of team members. On the quantitative front, much of this work is rooted in advanced statistics—expertise here should not be taken for granted. Many of these data science functions—even basic ones like regressions—output technical metrics that team members may not fully understand. It is fine to have varying levels of expertise but beware teams lacking strong statistical understanding. Three other areas can be important to teams throughout a project lifecycle depending on the focus: user experience, applications development, and data management.

- **Scoping the data.** In this step, the team should evaluate data access, storage options, and potential bias issues in the data.

  Early on, the team should meet with data owners to ensure necessary access. In some instances, this will include using established application programming interfaces (APIs) to access data according to standards specified by the API owner. In other situations, the team must arrange batch downloads to support the project. Well-established environments may have data lakes or central repositories with some or all of the required data. In these situations, the team must scope the data to determine where any special processing will be required. For example, it may be necessary to anonymize data or standardize certain data fields. The focus in project initiation is not to do this work, but to refine the understanding of the work to be done and to request and review data dictionaries and schemas.

  Planning for data storage and management should also occur in this step. Whether for performance assessment or AI model experiments, the team will need to store data and manage modifications—this is a facet of feature engineering. The team may have a dedicated on-premises environment that will accommodate this or may require cloud resources. Either way, it is important to evaluate this and ensure resources are available. Work can begin with a team working across desktop machines in some instances, but a shared server environment is ideal.

  In this early data scoping, the team should also identify potential for systemic bias in data sources. Bias is typically rooted in the data sources and can take a variety of forms. Teams can test for geographical bias, sensor or input types, temporal or seasonal bias, gender bias, and so on. The potential biases depend on the mission task and the data domain. The team should take some explicit steps to identify potential issues in the data; these can be more fully explored in the next step. In some situations, the root causes of early biases could prompt a different approach or a need to engage stakeholders on additional data sources. In this phase, leaders should probe what explicit steps the team performed to avoid the effects of bias. In subsequent phases of work, probing for bias and testing results rises in important and is discussed in more detail later in this chapter.

- **Assessing the technical environment.** The team will need technical resources to perform projects. This initial phase should assess those needs and take any necessary up-front administrative tasks such as securing logins. Depending on the project, the team will need to move data, store data, process data iteratively, and manage models and data. AI tasks vary in computational intensity or demands; the team should test their proposed approach relative to the available infrastructure. Any individual project may require access to some specialized functions. Additionally, the team may need to manage workload so as not to disrupt other teams working in parallel. This assessment should output some specific requests linked to milestones in the project plan.

- **Finalizing the plan.** The project plan can vary in format, especially based on project type, but its purpose is to set expectations for activities over time. Leaders should look for these plans to reflect important engagement with outside groups, key work steps, and progress reviews. For different types of tasks, especially as they implicate larger development teams, the format and approach can vary. For example, agile development teams for larger solutions will have specified formats and reviews the team can leverage. For stand-alone AI efforts, the team will develop their own. But the content should serve to set expectations between team members, between the team and government project leaders, between the team and supporting elements (like IT), and between supported groups (operational commands, systems of record, etc.).

The plan should capture critical assumptions in the approach, including those around data access and the technical environment.

Activity #3: Data Acquisition and Exploration

For any AI-related project, this activity can be a major focus with respect to time required. Missteps in this activity can directly lead to project failure modes of "getting it wrong" and "being too slow." From a leader perspective, pay close attention to five facets of this work: gaining data access, exploring data, making initial data modifications, managing datasets, and checking for data bias.

- **Gaining data access.** For this data acquisition and exploration activity, there are effectively two types of projects. The first is wonderful: all the data the team needs is readily available in a data warehouse or data lake where they have full permissions and access to data. In these situations, the team can move directly to exploring the tables and datasets related to the task. The second type of task is likely to be the norm in national security, meaning the team will need to seek access to various datasets held by a range of owners. This effort can take several forms. Gaining access to existing data lakes or warehouses is one type of task. Leveraging an application programming interface (API) to regularly access data on an existing program is another. Alternatively, arranging batch, bulk data transfers when necessary is another option. The last is the most difficult—it requires gathering data from organizational nodes where storage is local. This is common in many tactical environments. This is also especially relevant in performance assessment efforts. For this last manifestation of the data acquisition challenge, simply recognize that the network capacity does not exist to readily move data from tactical nodes into a more centralized storage environment. Very tactically focused systems present challenges and the Aegis Weapon System example illustrates this case— terabytes of local data production per day but both limited local storage and limited network capacity to move the data.

Leaders must monitor data access issues closely and engage to facilitate progress. Over-delegation or an expectation that these issues will resolve quickly at the working level can lead to delays that compromise the project schedule, leading to "this is too slow" failure mode outcomes. Data access delays trace to three fundamental sources: technical challenges, security processes, and organizational concerns. In our experience, organizational concerns chiefly revolve around concerns about interpretation and use of the data by teams outside a program or organization. These concerns are legitimate, but may become political. Security processes are necessary and expected, but can also become back-logged. Technical challenges occur most commonly on large, bulk transfers or while solving data collection for distributed local repositories. Whatever the case, leaders should take a proactive approach to data acquisition to limit delays. Engage data owners and, as necessary, leverage mission owners to advocate on behalf of the team for access.

- **Exploring and modifying data.** For any particular AI project, leaders should expect data to not be ready for the project team to use. At the conceptual level, it may seem very simple to expect all data to be well-organized, free of jargon or codes, aligned on the use of labels, time standards, locations, and so on. However, this is typically not true, especially when combining multiple data sources. A data dictionary for any given dataset describes the fields. Most commonly, it is in the form of columns and rows in a tabular type array. As a project leader, expect non-uniform quality on data dictionaries. even where they are solid, the team must interpret this data appropriately. This exploration of the data is where domain knowledge meets the data science skill. A major project vulnerability centers on misinterpreting particular columns or fields in the data.

Case Example: Misinterpreting Data—A $10B Error

A common AI modeling problem is scoring or prioritizing work in environments that are resource-constrained in labor hours, inventories, physical space (e.g., hangar capacity), and so on.

In transitioning to a new project, we took on an AI experiment designed to save money. Prioritization based on risk and financial commitment was central to this project. The team previously working this year-long experiment implemented two "random forest" models, a family of more sophisticated machine learning or AI models.

In the status quo prioritization approach, the organization saved approximately $1.5 B annually. The experimental models looked to increase that to almost $12 B annually!

However, as our teams inspected the models during transition, we found several issues. One of the most fundamental was that a crucial field in the model was inappropriately signed—what should have been negative was positive. This was a domain knowledge problem. The fix reduced the potential gain by $10 B/year.

The leader's challenge is to ensure a balanced team effort with checks on the interpretation of the data fields and checks on the results.

In the early phase of data exploration, the team should look for areas important to the project results that require some degree of standardization across datasets. As a simple example, most data will have some form of time-tagging. This may be simple a calendar date, time of day, and so on. Across datasets, time may not be uniformly rendered. If this is important to the modeling, then the team should not only identify issues but take early steps to standardize the data.

- **Managing data.** The moment the team begins to change the native data (they *will* need to do this), the project takes on a data management challenge. Leaders probe the team on how they are maintaining native data and modified datasets to ensure traceability of changes. Any effort to change data introduces an opportunity both to improve the usefulness of the dataset and to introduce errors. Traceability to the native dataset is especially important in this regard. In these activities, leaders may hear the term "feature engineering." This is common in data science. It refers to the process of creating new elements from the data that will be helpful to further analysis or modeling. To stay with the example of time, imagine that the native dataset includes the calendar date and time of day. However, the team has a hypothesis working with domain experts that the "day of week" is important in the output. Effectively, the team will create a new column in the data and convert the calendar date to a new field "day of week." This is a simple example of feature engineering; it is important that both the native data fields and new ones be managed effectively.

- **Checking for bias.** Two types of error are present in data, random and systemic. Random error occurs in all processes reflected in data captured in the process flow. At times, it is insignificant—at others, significant. Teams account for these process uncertainties and errors with confidence intervals and ranges on outputs as appropriate for the decision environment or operational use. The deeper challenge in AI projects is to identify and account for systemic bias. In some instances, this type of bias can substantially impact the usefulness of project outputs. Consider a practical example: measuring body weight. Imagine standing in front of three separate scales, each from a different manufacturer. In turn, you step on each device and record a body weight. Reviewing the results, you note two of the scales produce similar results and one is five pounds heavier. Interested in this difference, you arrange for ten other people to use the scale and notice the same general result. One of the scales reflects body weights multiple pounds heavier than the others. This is a simple form of system error or bias: one of the scales consistently shows higher body weights than the others. Systemic error can stem from a variety of activities and in the national security community this can include the output technical intelligence collectors with automated processing. Teams must check data for these systemic biases.

Systemic bias can be present in any large dataset. It is important to press teams to think about the presence of bias and ways to account for it. The important leader activity is to probe, not necessarily to have all the answers. However, there are several examples that can help leaders frame questions. Not all operational processes are consistent in volume or other parameters over the course of time—some are cyclical or seasonal. Data drawn from these in narrow windows can be subject to bias. In the previous paragraph, the scales are used to illustrate challenges in sensor bias. When developing AI models for other purposes, the team will need to think more deeply about the operational problem and underlying data.

In recent years, models addressing personnel- or citizen-related activities have been especially sensitive to potential bias. Consider a model to evaluate potentially high-performing candidates for hiring in a technology company. The resumes used to build the model were predominately male employees. Therefore, some of the features developed in the model centered on a range of activities mainly engaged in by males. In operation, this type of model might give discounted weight to female candidates who might hold equal potential to male counterparts but do not have some of the indicators present in a typical male resume. This is an example of model bias.

- **Expect data acquisition and exploration to be a major portion of the team's work.** Over the coming years, emerging tools will likely ease some of this burden. But it is unlikely to vanish because data exploration and feature engineering is linked to specific mission tasks, defying attempts to easily render enterprise-wide solutions. So, leaders should expect this activity to be a substantial portion of the overall work. The graphic in Figure 6-2, shared in a 2016 *Forbes* article, illustrates what this has looked like over time based on surveys with data science teams. While some improvements occurred over time, leaders are well-advised to plan for significant time working on data acquisition and exploration, as consistent with these descriptions.

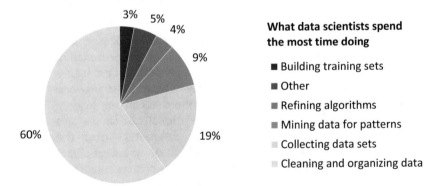

Figure 6-2. Data scientist survey reponses on time allocation in projects

Source: Press, Gil. "Cleaning Big Data: Most Time-Consuming, Least Enjoyable Data Science Task, Survey Says," March 2016, *Forbes*

Technology vendors may advertise notional solutions to the amount of time spent on data preparation; this is an area requiring discernment. Good general advice is to expect significant time acquiring and then preparing data for advanced analytics work or AI model development.

Activity #4: Model Development/ Advanced Analytics

With data in hand and foundational data preparation complete, the team turns to AI model development or advanced analytics. The following paragraphs address AI model development, then aspects of leading performance assessments.

For model development, the team will work iteratively to train, test, and evaluate the potential AI solution. In this context, leaders should expect and inspect certain activities.

- **Clarify the hypothesis regarding the type of model that will perform best.** At the outset, the team should have a clear concept of what they believe the champion model might be for a particular task. The leader should bound this iterative activity to ensure the team is being proactive in identifying the model type that will likely perform best. Leaders should understand the rationale as well as where the model will be deployed in an operational system. For example, a particular government organization ran a large enterprise software to run operational, real-time AI models. The license agreement, however, limited the types of models that could be deployed. Teams must be tuned to these constraints up front or risk wasting time. The target deployment environment may include limitations.

- **Establish baseline model performance with a regression approach or decision tree, where appropriate.** Often teams will be drawn to explore the most sophisticated AI models. We recommend pressing them to first establish how well a foundational model like a logistic or linear regression or a decision tree will perform relative to the status quo in the mission context (these are explained in more detail in the data science chapter for those craving deeper background). Leaders should consider regression models as the workhorse in the space. Any higher-end AI model should be able to create lift beyond these. Otherwise, weigh the value of simplicity over complexity. Recent graduates of data science bootcamps or those with advanced data science-oriented degrees will likely be aligned to the higher-end approaches (e.g., neural nets, deep learning). In reality, teams should establish baseline model performance with a regression or decision tree where appropriate; many of the more complex models rest on these foundational methods.

- **Concentrate on model measures that will define success.** A family of common measures exists for AI models. The team should be clear on which ones are relevant. For example, certain measures are specific to text processing models that would not be used to evaluate a regression model that is scoring workload items. Leaders should be mindful that some measures are relevant to model classes (e.g., graph, text) and others are generally relevant. For the generally relevant measures, probe the team on trade-offs and options that span the following:

  - For binary/supervised problems common measures include:

    - *Precision*: Accuracy of the model on any given call
    - *Recall*: Ability of the model to identify relevant instances
    - *F1*: A mean measure of precision and recall
    - *ROC/AUC*: Receiver operating characteristic, often discussed as performance on an "ROC curve" or Area Under the Curve in understanding performance

  - For continuous measurement problems (e.g., distance or cost), teams might use:

    - Mean Average Error
    - Root Mean Squared Error

Case Example: Cost of Documentation Failures

Failure to appropriately document code and provide a narrative describing the efforts is a potentially fatal flaw that leads to extensive rework, incorrect answers, and an inability to transition work between teams or team members.

For a multi-agency effort, a company was asked to create a solution identifying citizens who should potentially have their passports revoked or a renewal denied. A data scientist working for a company on contract to the government wrote about 2,000 lines of code to address the issue. This model would be run episodically.

The contract changed company hands and the new company was asked to run the model. It would not function and was very poorly documented. The prior company was contacted for transition support. Their staff could not make the code function. The single data scientist who wrote the code had left their firm. Neither the prior company responsible for building the model nor the new transitioning company could understand the code.

The entire effort had to be rebuilt. Complete rework.

Leader implication: Data scientists often view code documentation as a chore and far less exciting than the problem-solving associated with writing the code and sorting out the issues. Leaders must ensure time is allocated and follow-through is present on documentation. This is a very good area to apply the old adage "expect what you inspect."

- **Review the training data approach.** The team has some target models, is prepared to establish baseline model performance, and has agreed on what is important in model performance metrics. Now, they "train a model." To approach this task, leaders should review the data approach. To create a viable model, the team will use a portion of the available historical data to train the model, then use the remainder to test the trained model. This may seem fundamental, but it is crucial for leaders to ensure these two datasets are separated. Note, a three-way split also can be very useful carving the data into training, validation, and testing sets. The data used to train an AI model cannot be used to test its performance. We have observed fundamental mistakes on this elemental task. On a related front, leaders should question the team on how they intend to split and manage the data. Using a three-way split allows the team to train the model with training data, then validate or tune hyperparameters with the validation set. Last, the team will test model performance with the last segment of data. A three-way split is helpful in avoiding what is referred to as "overfitting" the model (linking it too tightly to the training data, which in turn can cause significant underperformance on test or operational data). For each situation, the answer will vary, but the team should have a clear rationale. For example, they may say something like, "We plan to set aside 80 percent of the data for training and will test on the remaining 20 percent."

- **Probe dimension reduction and feature engineering efforts.** Assume for the moment that the team assembled a tabular dataset with 500 columns and 100,000 number of rows (representing events, discrete data collection, etc.) to support the AI model development process. Leaders should investigate what the team is doing to make that data more useful to the various model types being trained and tested. Importantly, more data (features in the columns) is not necessarily better—this can be a common mistake in less experienced teams. One useful task for teams is to consider "dimension reduction." As the name suggests, this process reduces the number of data fields or columns. In this instance, it focuses on the columns or particular features in the table that are less useful. Without a longer explanation, suffice it to say some data dynamics with redundant columns or features can skew results. This is referred to as collinearity or multi-collinearity. A family of tools is available to address dimension reduction and test for undesirable patterns in the data. Feature engineering is the flip side of dimension reduction; its purpose is to create new features through combinations or other processing. Earlier in the chapter, we illustrated this by switching "calendar date" to "day of week." But feature engineering often probes other relationships to create new values (e.g., a ratio of x and y features in the original dataset). Leaders should investigate the team's approach. This is an area to expect clear, concise answers.

- **Inspect test results.** As the team trains a model, they will move to testing activities. This applies the model to a body of data that was set aside for model testing. The team will create some materials that characterize model performance according to the measures agreed upon earlier in the process. Leaders should expect iteration between training and testing. In these sessions, press to understand the team's thinking on factors that might improve performance. Leaders can probe "how do you ensure randomization in the testing as we iterate over time?" The answers should be thoughtful and immediate rather than surprised reactions. Concepts you might hear raised include "seeding" and "shuffling." It is less important to understand those details than to ensure the team is being thoughtful and purposeful.

- **Evaluate documentation.** AI models and associated data pipelines are comprised of software code and should have at least two forms of attending documentation— documentation in the code and a paper or memorandum to explain purpose. While general standards in a loose sense are available to guide code-writing, leaders need to set expectations that code is well organized and, critically, well documented. Many data scientists focus on the creative task of building the data pipeline and tuning the model. In contrast, documenting code can seem an administrative task—this is a horrible vulnerability for the team and for the larger organization. Documentation in code explains the purpose of the different functions as well as their relationships to data and other functions. Software code can include errors in the same way our written language can contain errors in reasoning, grammar, or spelling. Documentation explains what the data scientist intended and clarifies important relationships with respect to the code. In addition to code documentation, it also can be beneficial to require a modeling memorandum that provides a narrative description of the purpose of the model, linkage to a discrete mission task, information about data preparation and organization, and insights around the model implementation and train-test results. Leaders must not assume documentation is occurring, but inspect it to ensure it is being done well.

- **Engage with stakeholders on operational results, accounting for process feedback time.** Having trained and tested a model with historical data, the team will move to evaluate performance with new data. This step will likely precede a full operational deployment. In this step, leaders share the results of the training and testing with the stakeholders, which will likely include operational mission leaders, some working level staff, and programs of record. Then, an evaluation cycle occurs with operational data to ensure performance is roughly in line with the testing performance. This cycle length is dependent on the target process cycle time. This means that, if the model scores an item and the team can know the answer the same day, it had a fast feedback loop. This is not a given—some operational processes will take time before knowing whether the AI model output was correct.

Performance assessments leverage a wider variety of techniques than a strict task for model development but may include using AI models to work through the assessment. The leader's checks for the model development are relevant in a performance assessment, as are some additional items. These tasks may cover multiple capabilities (e.g., various aircraft, weapons, and sensors) in the context of a mission-type assessment (e.g., suppression of enemy air defense) or may focus on a single capability (e.g., the effectiveness of a particular imaging system). These assessments commonly are requested to support a decision on a specific issue or around spending on a portfolio. Consequently, expect a range of dates to be relevant in sharing results. Leaders can enhance team performance by emphasizing and checking on the following:

- **Work to a thesis.** The team should elicit views from operational experts to set an expectation of performance, whether for a portfolio of capabilities or a specific one. People close to the mission bring perspective but are also limited in the range of their observations or technical perspective. The mission-centered views help to center the work of the team. In this process, it is valuable to gain perspective on perceptions of relative performance between capabilities as well as absolute performance. For example, "We use capability x on every operation and without it would be impaired." This is an absolute characterization of a capability regarding mission impact. A relative statement might look like, "We use mortars three times more than cannon artillery for these types of missions. We can seldom use rockets." Where there are existing metrics, those can shape the thesis on broader performance impact.

- **Push for population-based approaches versus sampling where possible.** Classical social science research leverages sampling-based approaches for a range of legitimate reasons. This can take the form of select cases or instances to probe a thesis. In the contemporary data environment, it is often possible to access and analyze the full population of data. For example, the team might deal with a question around the impact of tactical interrogation methods (e.g., what percentage generate leads in the form of new locations and/or names?). One approach is to randomly sample interrogation reports, inspect or process them, and reach a judgement on the percentage that produced new locations/names. The alternative is to access the population of relevant interrogation reports for the mission context (timeframe and geography) and apply AI techniques to answer the question.

- **Create analytic momentum.** The team does not need to know everything before they know anything. Press for emerging insights that support, refine, or change the thesis. Package these preliminary insights in several slides or pages and use them to interact with operational experts and the leadership who make decisions on the portfolio. These interactions will sharpen what is important, clarify what decision-makers need to see, or illuminate flaws in interpretation. The opposite approach waits to interact until the team has fully baked its performance assessment. This brings high potential for problems and rework.

- **Press for the appropriate use of advanced techniques.** Performance assessments illuminate the contributions of one or more capabilities. Insights on those contributions can be buried in text and other reporting. Depending on the task, text, graph, or image processing techniques may increase understanding of the data. The team should have a clear point of view on how advanced techniques fit within the bounds of the task, including the time available. In a number of these tasks, simulation can provide an important input alongside the evaluation of current data. Leaders should look for indications that teams are being appropriately creative in evaluating advanced techniques and planning their integration to produce insights.

Activity #5: Solution Deployment/ Conveying Results

The culmination of an AI project is deploying the solution or sharing the final results to support decision-making (around a performance assessment or experiment).

Once a model that is intended for production is developed, it must be implemented in the context of a larger system; this is often an existing system of record or IT solution. As discussed earlier, an AI team will be a facet of a larger development team. Data scientists must shift gears to support operational deployment—leaders play a key role in guiding this. Leaders should monitor key activities in this transition and plan direct engagement with the development team and the users of the solution.

- **Model and pipeline review with the development team.** Unless the AI team is part of a larger agile development team throughout the process, this review is especially important. The development team has a plan, architecture, and coding preferences. Additionally, the development team must understand the purpose of the model and its performance; this is important to creating shared priority in the implementation. Beyond this high-level overview, the development team will need to understand both the data pipeline (which likely includes feature engineering and modifications to data tables) and the model itself. The development team is responsible for the overall performance of the solution and all processing workflows, so they will need to understand this content well. This is also important for documentation, which reflects the AI team's quality of work.

- **Creating an integration plan.** Production models at scale will normally be integrated into a larger software program. The AI team must be engaged with the larger software development team on integration and testing, both to prepare for test and involvement in the test. Engineering teams will run a variety of test types depending on the system and the software development approach—CICD, waterfall, and so on. Consequently, the AI team must be actively engaged in testing vice naively thinking that model code running in the AI test environment can simply be handed off to the development team.

- **User engagement and orientation.** All AI model implementations should be reviewed with appropriate user groups to overview a novel approach. Some AI solutions are relatively hidden from users, especially as this pertains to workload prioritization and workforce assignment models. Often, the new AI model replaces some existing set of rules or a selection model; the users only deal with the result, even of the existing approach. Other AI solutions include a user interface or changes to a user interface.

With respect to performance assessments, leaders guide the creation of the final results presentation. In the previous activity, one of the emphasis items was building insights incrementally and interacting with a range of stakeholders on these preliminary observations. The results are finalized and presented to a range of decision-makers and stakeholders in this culminating activity.

Returning to the last activity (solution deployment/conveying results), leader emphasis activities regarding performance assessments include the following:

- **Clearly articulating task and context.** As the audience grows beyond the immediate decision-makers behind the assessment, it is critical to ensure the boundaries on the study are clearly defined. Leaders must ensure the team covers the basics on task, geographic, and time boundaries as pertinent. Audiences must clearly understand why the assessment was performed and the intended application of the insights.

- **Communicating key findings with implications.** An excellent document will tell a clear story around the assessment, emphasizing key findings. Contextualizing the findings to operational processes and mission areas is critical. Then, characterize areas in which observations confirm operational theses as well as areas in which the insights run counter to or refine those operational intuitions. Decisional implications should flow from the analytical findings.

- **Characterizing data collection and analysis to underpin findings.** Especially when findings are controversial, the team must be prepared to provide significant detail on the data collection and analysis methods to develop the findings. Operational leaders value operational intuition and feedback from subject matter experts. However, these perceptions are also vulnerable to limits in what any particular expert experiences or sees. Data science techniques, especially when working with population data, can put these expert views and any success stories from individual programs into perspective. Advice: Ensure subject matter experts are brought along through the process but especially ensure they understand the analysis and reasoning on the final results.

- **Providing background on any special techniques and issues influencing findings.** Population-based techniques to analyze bigger datasets can reveal important insights but may rely on less familiar approaches (text processing, clustering, classification, etc.). Teams should be prepared to explain to non-expert stakeholders how they analyzed the data.

Activity #6: Monitor, Adjust AI Model Performance

Leaders must not assume AI models are "fire and forget" in character; build them, deploy them, and leave them is not the reality. Teams will train, validate, and test model performance. Then models are deployed into operation.

Leaders must plan to both monitor model performance and prepare for them to be re-trained episodically. As the operational environment changes, sensors change, and so on, AI model performance will drift. Teams can often create a simple dashboard that will enable monitoring of performance. In other instances, the team will need to periodically pull data from databases relative to performance and assess the model. Either way, this regularized monitoring should be a facet of the expected operational deployment. Leaders should probe with end users and the team the performance limits or thresholds that warrant re-training the model. This re-training is expected. At that point, the team effectively iterates back through Activities #4 and #5 to refresh model performance in the context of changing dynamics in the data.

Leader Emphasis Points and Engagement Areas by Major Process Activity

Table 6-2. Leader Emphasis Issues Across Five Project Functions

Sell	Initiate	Acquire/ Explore	Modeling/Analysis	Integrate/Convey Results
• Connect mission value to cost • Be thoughtful in setting expectations • Anchor anticipated value to relevant benchmark examples • Plan to use existing software and compute infrastructure wherever possible • Engage stakeholders to build support	• Establish baseline performance • Engage end users • Scope the data • Assess the technical environment • Finalize team composition • Finalize the plan	• Gain data access • Explore and modify data • Manage data • Check for bias	Modeling • Clarify the hypothesis regarding the type of model that will perform best • Establish baseline model performance • Concentrate on model measures • Review training data approach • Probe dimension reduction and feature engineering • Inspect test results • Evaluate documentation • Engage with stakeholders on operational results Analysis • Work to a thesis • Push for population-based approaches • Create analytic momentum • Press advanced techniques	Deployed Model • Review model and data pipeline with development team • Creating an integration plan • User engagement and orientation Convey Results • Clearly articulating task and context • Communicating key findings with implications • Characterizing data collection and analysis to underpin findings • Background on any special techniques and issues influencing findings

Table 6-2 also provides a leader framework to evaluate the quality approach employed by teams. Are the teams covering all the essential elements in these activities to avoid the three failure modes: uninspiring results, incorrect results, and projects being too slow?

Leading the People

"A leader is someone whom people will follow to places they would not go alone."

—Joel Barker (Futurist, Author, Filmmaker)

"Leadership is a complex system of relationships between leaders and followers, in a particular context, that provides meaning to its members."

—General (retired) Stan McChrystal, Jeff Eggers, Jason Mangone
***Leaders: Myth and Reality* (Portfolio Penguin; 2018)**

Summary

Leading AI teams means that you are leading practitioners from multiple disciplines including data science, software engineering, computer science, and IT. Data scientists are essential to the development of AI models, but it takes a multi-disciplinary team to deploy and maintain the models in operation at scale. In addition to leadership fundamentals—which are not always executed well—you must lead the talent lifecycle with an understanding of

C. Whitlock and F. Strickland, *Winning the National Security AI Competition*,
https://doi.org/10.1007/978-1-4842-8814-6_7

what data scientists need and value in their development. The demand for data scientists dwarfs the availability of experienced data scientists, thus they have tremendous leverage in deciding where they work and whom they follow. Given the unavoidable attrition, leaders must ensure that AI knowledge is instantiated in reusable code. The government will acquire most large-scale AI capabilities from industry; thus, competency in leading a government-industry partnership is essential.

This chapter begins with five axioms for leading data scientists. We then provide best practices for leading data scientists and the AI team in three areas:

- Foundational practices for excellent leadership of people and teams

- Leading data scientists and the AI team through the talent lifecycle

- Leading AI in the context of a government—industry partnership

We have devoted this book to the art and science of leading AI. Many of the conversations about AI focus on investment, data science, computing, software engineering as well as processes for developing, deploying, and maintaining AI capabilities. All of these are important—the contents of this book address most of these topics. However, the presence or absence of leaders who are prepared to lead AI practitioners enables or inhibits mission impact and business growth using AI more than any other factor.

The boutique data science company, Anaconda, originated the use of the open-source platform, Python, for data science and AI back in 2009. Anaconda surveyed 2,360 data science practitioners worldwide in 2020. They found that over 50 percent intend to switch jobs within the next three years. Depending on the type of organization, anywhere from 29 to 44 percent expect to move within the next year (Figure 7-1).

How long do you plan to stay with your current employer?

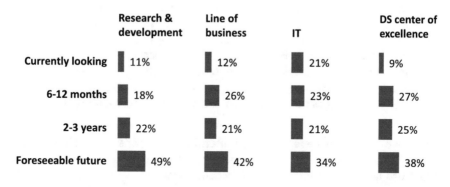

	Research & development	Line of business	IT	DS center of excellence
Currently looking	11%	12%	21%	9%
6-12 months	18%	26%	23%	27%
2-3 years	22%	21%	21%	25%
Foreseeable future	49%	42%	34%	38%

N=1216

IT organizations should take note: fully 44% data professionals situated in your organization plan to seek employment elsewhere within the next year

Figure 7-1. Anaconda survey of 2,360 data scientists

People do not follow institutions; they follow leaders. Institutions are obviously important, and leaders represent their institutions. However, a poorly qualified AI leader in a good institution can cause an institution to fail to recruit, retain, and develop data scientists and AI practitioners. Any government or business executive who is remotely close to AI can attest to the competition for AI talent competition that is illustrated by Anacoda's survey. AI leaders are on the front lines in the competition for data science and AI talent.

Leading people is so important, yet so complex, that you must have a concrete understanding of what leading AI practitioners means. In Chapter 6, we introduced leading data scientists and composing a multi-disciplinary AI team. In this chapter, we examine this further. We provide a set of enduring axioms for leading data scientists, then equip you with a set of best practices for leading the entire AI talent lifecycle, from recruiting to retaining practitioners. Finally, we offer some perspectives on leading data scientists in various government-industry contexts.

Leading Data Scientists: Five Axioms

Relative to other government and vendor career fields in national security, data science is a young career field. This compounds the challenge of recruiting, retaining, and developing data scientists. The 9.11 attack intensified American's interest in joining government and contributing to the national security mission. It is possible that intensity may have lessened somewhat after two decades, especially among technical practitioners who have many choices where to work.

Regardless, once data scientists are "behind the door" in terms of the security requirements for a particular agency and program, they often face challenges with access to data, the availability of the best technology, cultural fit, and other factors. Not every project will feel like a moonshot. Will they work through these challenges and commit to the mission for more than a couple of years? Will they take risks on approaches or be bold in pushing back against overly aggressive thinking? Leaders with sufficient experience in AI are essential to helping practitioners work through these challenges and deliver results.

We have been privileged to lead literally thousands of analytics and AI practitioners over the past three decades. This experience has shown that there are five axioms for leading data scientists:

No Lone Rangers. In Chapters 2 and 6, we introduced that AI is a multi-disciplinary field; meaning you need people with skills in multiple technical disciplines to succeed in an AI project and program. Of these disciplines, it is fair to regard data science as a first among equals. It is the two specialties within data science—data engineer and data scientist—who make data ready for modeling and code the models that produce actionable insights from data. The core AI value chain can be stated as, "No data—no model; no model— no insights."

An effective AI program and project depends on a multi-disciplinary team. Data scientists will not deliver impact at scale on their own. All of the disciplines we discussed are essential. In short, data scientists need others.

Given the role of data science in creating insights from data and the competition for data science talent, we have devoted most of this chapter to leading data scientists. A leader who puts this chapter into practice will find—as we have—that these practices are helpful in leading the entire AI team. We explicitly address the larger team in the section on leading the talent lifecycle.

The heart of data science is complex problem solving using three tools: data, math, and code. You can easily distinguish data scientists from analytics practitioners because the former have advanced math skills and can code algorithms in a programming environment such as Python, R, or Java. Analytics practitioners typically configure and apply existing business intelligence software, such as Tableau, Qlik, or Excel. People who are expert at solving complex problems by coding and applying advanced math algorithms to data are not in abundant supply. A 2012 *Harvard Business Review* article dubbed data scientist "the sexiest job of the 21st Century."

To borrow a phrase from the Department of Defense, the data scientist is a high demand/low density asset. This can and has led to organizations deploying the "lone ranger" data scientist—a data scientist working apart from any other data scientists. We have seen both commercial and government AI centers farm out solo data scientists to organizations who ask for one. For example, a line of business or a government mission center may ask their AI organization, "Send us a data scientist." In some cases, the line of business or government mission center will have the ability to hire individual data scientists.

This may yield good results for a limited time in some special circumstances. However, treating data scientists as lone soldiers creates substantial risks for an organization, such as:

- A mistaken assumption that every data scientist is equally competent across a wide range of techniques, such as the differences between NLP and computer vision (CV).

- A solo data scientist's code is prone to simple keystroke errors or math/logic errors given the absence of peer review in this complex work.

- Innovation and creative problem solving are limited to one person's skills and experience.

- The data scientist grows stagnant over time because they are not benefitting from the development that occurs when working with other data scientists.

- While some technical staff prefer periods of independent work, a solo data scientist is likely to be a retention risk because most crave the sense of being in community with other data scientists.

Domain Knowledge Deficit. In Chapter 2, we summarized the vast array of national security domains where AI applications might improve mission impact by asking you to consider three dimensions: the mission area, the target country or region, and the point in the sense-making—decision-making—action-taking cycle that might be improved by AI. Few professionals in any discipline come with expertise in most or all of these domains. Consider that uniformed members of the armed services spend their entire careers mastering one or two domains. Similarly, intelligence analysts, homeland security investigators, border patrol agents, and other national security leaders are trained and develop expertise over time in one or a select few mission domains. It is no surprise that data scientists—who naturally focus on developing their technical skills—come to the national security space with limited or no domain knowledge.

Given that the goal of AI is improving impact in a mission domain, the need to understand that domain is axiomatic. At the program level, data scientists need mission domain knowledge to provide useful input to the government mission customer on priorities and trade-offs between candidate projects. At the project level, the most important and difficult phase of any AI project is defining a problem suited to AI with available data as well as selecting an appropriate approach. Data scientists cannot perform in this phase without sufficient understanding of the domain.

Speaking to an industry forum in 2019, a senior executive from the Intelligence Community (IC) asserted: "We know what our problems are." The official then listed a number of countries and broad mission areas, such as proliferation of nuclear weapons. In context, the official was making a general assertion that industry and the IC needed to move from problem definition to AI model development and deployment.

The desire for greater model development and deployment is understandable. However, it is naïve to assert that a country or broad mission area is a sufficient definition of a problem suited to AI model development. Getting to a level of problem definition suited to AI model development requires detailed mission domain knowledge.

Cool Problems Attract Talent. Imagine going through medical school and a residency to become a certified cardiac surgeon, and then joining a practice that assigns you the job of conducting electrocardiogram (ECG) stress tests all day long. Cardiovascular disease is the leading cause of death in America, and ECG stress tests are a useful tool for detecting and treating cardiovascular disease. However, your training and passion are for cardiac surgery.

This can be the dilemma of a data scientist. They learn in the classroom how to apply machine learning models, deep learning models, and other complex algorithms to big data. Then, they land in a job where they spend all day for months only cleaning data, or they are assigned an analytics role (e.g., building basic dashboards). Perhaps, worse yet, they are assigned to what is essentially a consulting role working on a strategy related to AI.

All AI work—everything from program strategy through the operations and maintenance of deployed models—is important. However, data scientists train and expect to create and deploy models that create insights from data on an important mission problem. These professionals have exceptionally strong minds for quantitative problem solving. They crave complex problems with, ideally, a slew of data relevant to the problem. Without this type of challenge, they can quickly grow restless, seeking other roles or leaving your organization altogether.

Tremendous Marketability. Anyone who is remotely associated with a team of data scientists is aware of the market opportunities each data scientist has. In Glassdoor's 2022 Best Jobs in America list, data scientist ranks third. As of March 2022, LinkedIn shows nearly 500,000 job postings for data scientists. Why is the market white hot for this discipline?

If you think about the earlier operations cycle, Figure 7-2, this cycle exists in nearly every system in every industry. Farmers execute this cycle in planting and harvesting for optimal crop yields.

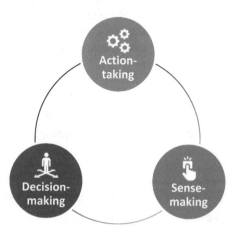

Figure 7-2. Basic operations cycle

Autonomous farm vehicles execute this cycle to safely navigate and perform their tasks. The farm's lighting system executes this cycle to efficiently use power and allocate maintenance resources where most needed. If you let your mind sweep over the world's industries, the number of potential applications is mind-blowing.

AI has the potential to improve this cycle in billions of systems that affect the daily lives of people across the planet. By creating models that produce insights from data, make autonomous decisions, and take autonomous actions, the data scientist is at the heart of this worldwide technological transformation of systems. The leverage that data scientists have in the market is a function of this global demand.

Software Assets. "People are our most important asset" communicates an important truth, but can also devolve into a vacuous buzz phrase, the likes of which were delightfully captured in IBM's Buzzword Bingo ad campaign (2008). We have demonstrated the importance of data scientists in this chapter. However, we encourage you to lead as if the data scientist is only half of your most important asset.

The other half of your most important asset is what the data scientists create. In simple, practical terms, the code they write is a critical asset. If properly equipped and incentivized, your data scientists should be instantiating your organization's intellectual property—data pipelines and models—in code. Doing so has to be part of your organization's work processes and the culture leaders and data scientists create and maintain. As previously demonstrated, expect 10 percent or more of your data scientists will leave your organization each year. You cannot have the data pipelines and models they have created become useless the moment the creators walk out the door.

In one of the major programs we supported, a government agency had a model that identified non-compliance with the law and initiated punitive action against those out of compliance. The model included nearly 2,000 lines of SQL code written by an incumbent, which our company defeated in a contract competition.

As part of the contract transition, our team set up a technical exchange about this model. The data scientist who originally created the model had previously left the incumbent company. There was no documentation of the code, and the code was such that the incumbent could not get it to run.

Leadership: Setting the Foundation

In the early days of our first start-up, Edge Consulting, we gathered everyone monthly for an all-day training and development program, "Sharpening Your Edge." As the senior leaders, we initially did all of the teaching. But we intentionally developed other leaders in the company to join us in teaching hands-on analytics skills, consulting skills, client domain knowledge, team leadership, and other skills key to serving our clients and developing our people. "Sharpening," as it came to be known, was consistently ranked by our people as one the primary reasons they loved Edge Consulting. One of our analytics practitioners put it this way: "I feel like I should pay you tuition once a month for the tremendous value I get out of Sharpening."

During Sharpening, we would often introduce a complex subject by having everyone write their own definition of the subject, then share it with the group. Everyone benefited from the sharing and emerged with a better definition than their original draft. The variance between the individual definitions was often large, even for a term such as "leadership," which was well-known to our practitioners (most of whom had prior military backgrounds). Asking a second order question such as, "What is your leadership style?" would increase the variation among the responses.

Leading. If you are going to lead data scientists effectively, you must have a clear sense of what a leader is and how you are going to lead. Leadership may be the most complex discipline because it focuses on tangible human behaviors as well as related intangible elements such as human will in a wide variety of ever-changing contexts. Leadership can be a nebulous idea, making it even more important for you to lead with a clear understanding of what you are doing and how you are doing it.

We believe that this adaptation of Joel Barker's definition best summarizes what a leader is:

A leader is someone people choose to follow to places they would not or could not go alone.

This definition contains five key concepts and their implications for leaders, summarized in Table 7-1.

Table 7-1. Five Leadership Best Practices

Concept	Implication
Leadership is intensely interpersonal	• Institutions do not lead; people choose to follow other people. • You must lead with attention to behavioral traits—yours and theirs. You must lead with EQ as well as IQ, esteeming others more than yourself. Selfishness, arrogance, and pride are derailers.
People choose to follow or not	• Following your direction is not the same as following your intent. The former stems from your organizational authority. The latter stems from your substantive and relational authority. • You must lead in a way that encourages those you lead to not only follow with their whole heart, but also help you shape the direction because they believe in the desired future you present and in you.
Paint a sufficiently clear picture of the future	• People take courage when the desired future state is worth the cost/effort to bring it about. • You must characterize the desired future state—your "vision"—such that it is tangible enough for them to feel that their path is aligned with the future state.
Encourage the heart	• If the desired future is not a stretch—if the effort required is not that great—if the journey does not require you and them to take courage, then what are you doing? • You must continuously encourage their hearts on the journey. Do not assume that strong technical talent is always matched by an equal amount of confidence. A variety of causes can detract from confidence. Pay attention to women and underrepresented minorities, some of whom can suffer from "imposter syndrome."[1]
Equip the mind	• No one's sword (mind) is sharp enough for the entire campaign. • You must show them the way by continuously sharpening your mind (knowledge and skills) while also promoting the resources that equip them to sharpen themselves.

In terms of *how* you lead data scientists and AI practitioners, we submit that there are two interrelated skills essential to effective leadership: contextual awareness and leading both the head and the heart. As young leaders in the 1980s, we first became aware of these skills through the research of Paul Hersey and Ken Blanchard, research that became known as "Situational Leadership." More recently, General (retired) Stan McChrystal, Jeff Eggers, and Jason Mangone offered a definition of leadership that emphasized the context in which the leader-follower relationship occurs.

---

[1] High achievers—regardless of socio-economic class—can feel deep within that they don't measure up. They generally hold this feeling deep within. Leaders must be aware and engaged, avoiding the assumption that confidence is proportional to confidence in all people.

Like any leader, AI leaders must sharpen their sensing system so that they are continuously refining their understanding of the context. Genuine listening is a core skill, as is the practice of interrogatory leadership (i.e., asking questions that improves the leader's and the followers' thinking). As an AI leader, you cannot listen and ask questions effectively unless you are sufficiently qualified in AI. Data scientists will not necessarily expect you to be an expert practitioner, but they will expect knowledge and experience sufficient for you to have informed discussions with them and to pick up on issues that need attention.

Continuous learning by the AI leader is vital; practitioners are a valuable source of learning. Humility may be the most important character trait in this regard, as the leader cannot learn from followers if the leader views themself as having the right answers to every question. Sensing the context involves both emotional and intellectual intelligence. Drawing upon Hersey's and Blanchard's theory on task and relationship behaviors, Table 7-2 isolates six areas of AI context the leader must continuously sense and seek to understand.

Table 7-2. Six Areas of Context for AI Leadership

Technical		Relational	
Operational	• What is the mission need for AI? How does it align with available data and modeling approaches?	Personal	• What are the individual data scientists' and other AI practitioners' skills, commitment, and needs relative to the task?
Technical	• What is the extant technical architecture? What options are possible?	Interpersonal	• What are the combined team's skills and commitment? What is the relationships among team members—especially those that cross organizational boundaries—relative to the task?
Fiscal	• What resources are available? Are they sufficient to deliver AI results?	Institutional	• How supportive are key leaders to practitioners' development and the project's role in their development?

In terms of how to lead both head and heart, we dare to assert that there is only one correct answer: "It depends." However, we suggest a specific, concrete approach to that general answer.

It is popular today to identify yourself as a servant leader, a leader coach, or a leader who empowers others. Identifying your leadership approach in one way assumes that way works best in every context. Given the almost infinite variety of contexts in which you must lead and the complexity of human behaviors and relationships, approaching leadership in only one way is counterintuitive.

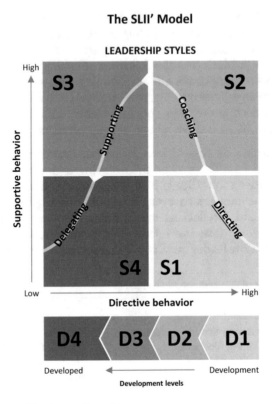

Figure 7-3. Situational leadership II model

We believe leaders must adapt and apply their leadership approach to the technical and relational context. Taking this down to the individual level, we believe you are leading two organs, so to speak: the "head" (knowledge and skills) and the "heart" (courage, confidence, commitment) of the follower. Blanchard's Situational Leadership II (SLII®) model (Figure 7-3) provides a means to diagnose the degree to which individuals are equipped (head) and encouraged (heart) for the task. We believe that leaders can and should apply this diagnosis to individuals and groups. From this diagnosis of the individual's or group's development along with the other contextual factors in Table 7-2, the leader applies the best combination of directive and supportive behaviors to the situation: directing, coaching, supporting, or delegating.

This approach to leadership challenges the false dichotomy between performance and performance capacity (our attention was first brought to this problem through Stephen Covey's thinking). A leader must achieve mission or business results, but this does not imply that the operational outcome is always the singular priority. A leader is always judging whether it is time to pay more attention to the person's or team's welfare, even if that means foregoing some amount of operational outcome. A leader who is singularly fixated on operational outcomes is likely to be like the person who killed the goose that laid golden eggs in a foolish attempt to immediately get more eggs. The wise leader throttles performance and performance capacity based on the situation.

In *Leaders: Myth and Reality,* McChrystal et al. analyze three leadership myths—formulaic, attribution, and results—then offer a framework for leadership based on this definition: "Leadership is a complex system of relationships between leaders and followers, in a particular context, that provides meaning to its members." [2]

In addition to emphasizing the context in which leadership occurs, the book's leadership framework emphasizes the leader's role as an enabler of the system of relationships. The authors strongly imply three of the leader styles in SLII: coaching, supporting, and delegating.

In *My Share of the Task: A Memoir,* McChrystal tells the story of his fascinating Army career, including a detailed account of the historic multi-agency special operations task force he assembled and led in the destruction of terrorist networks in Iraq. Recounting a particularly painful meeting with one of his units after three soldiers were killed by an improvised explosive device (IED)—a fourth solider later died from his wounds—McChrystal declares his personal commitment to the unit's mission and to victory. In that situation, McChrystal demonstrated the need for the fourth SLII style: directing.

Leading Data Scientists and the AI Team Through the Talent Lifecycle

Having laid a solid foundation for leading people, we turn to specific practices for leading data scientists and AI practitioners through the four ongoing activities of the Talent Lifecycle (Figure 7-4). In Chapters 3 and 5, we provided axioms and best practices for leading AI work at the program and project levels, respectively. At the program and project levels, you lead people through leading the work. As you lead delivery of the work, you will also lead people

---

[2] Perhaps biased by our direct observation of McChrystal, who is one of the best leaders we have observed in our careers, we commend this book as one that every leader should read along with "The Leadership Challenge" (Kouzes, Posner).

by recruiting them to your organization, aligning their skills and interests to needs in the market, developing them by equipping their minds and encouraging their hearts, and creating a sense of belonging at the individual, team, and enterprise levels. Here, we cover best practices unique to leading data scientists and AI practitioners in each of those four activities.

Figure 7-4. Talent lifecycle

Belonging. Based on the Anaconda data and the experience of anyone who has led AI organizations, you can safely assume that a substantial portion of your data scientists and AI practitioners are open to leaving your organization at any moment. In large government agencies and large businesses, data scientists will be a tiny fraction of the overall population. It is natural for these organizations to attempt to fit the career needs of data scientists into the talent models and career paths of the majority. Even in small companies, qualified data scientists still have a wide range of opportunities in the market. You can be sure that recruiters are regularly reaching out to them via their LinkedIn and other social media channels. Creating a sense of belonging is crucial to retaining your data science and AI talent.

Retention is an outcome measure and, thus, is not the primary activity you are leading. Creating a sense belonging deep within each individual and in the collective group is what you are leading. People show up and give a day's effort for a job. However, they commit themselves to a purpose and a group of people they believe in and love being a part of. Creating a sense of belonging is your objective; retention is an outcome.

If you worked in tech at the turn of the century, you recall the concerns over the dates in legacy software turning over to the year 2000—the "Y2K" problem. Of the many potential disasters, the U.S. government was concerned that a Y2K glitch might cause the Russian military—with its antiquated missile warning system—to mistakenly conclude that the United States was launching a missile strike against Russia. In 1983, the Soviet military had made such a mistaken assumption and nuclear war was narrowly averted. In response to an order by the President, the government office in which we served put together an analytics system to give Russian and U.S. forces the same missile warning picture during Y2K.

Our government office had the software technology to share data with the Russians. Nevertheless, such an unprecedented operation required much policy and legal review. In a meeting with the general officer who was leading the Russian side of the effort, U.S. officials explained that the tech was ready, but the people-intensive processes took more time. The Russian general remarked, "Get rid of people; get rid of problems." That philosophy may have worked for Stalin, but you will need to do better in leading AI practitioners.

You create a sense of belonging through excellence in recruiting, aligning, and developing activities as well as complementary practices focused on belonging. You begin to create a sense of belonging during the interview process—during which the candidate is also evaluating you and your organization—and you continue developing belonging every single day. Losing a practitioner is like a marital affair—their desire to leave is sown in their mind and heart long before they decide to commit the act of leaving. Once a practitioner decides to solicit and entertain offers, they are more than half-way out the door. Leaders must proactively create belonging in practitioners' hearts and minds before the seeds of leaving take root.

In addition to excellence in the other elements of the talent lifecycle, you create a sense of belonging in your practitioners through vision, shared experiences, and lived values. While some of the practices in Table 7-3 are specific to leaders in industry, government AI leaders can usefully apply many of these.

Table 7-3. Best Practices for Creating a Sense of Belonging

Vision	• AI practitioners expect to be compensated at market value, but most are not simply working for money. Belonging means more.
	• Your organization must have a compelling desired future state for which you rally everyone's best efforts and commitment.
	• Your objective is to impact clients' missions in pursuit of your vision. Financial results are an outcome of impact and running a good business. Growth of the budget is a good analogue for government AI leaders.
	• Always talk with your practitioners about impact and vision, not financial results. For those in industry, we recommend putting the emphasis on mission impact, not company financial results. They care about the former, not the latter. They influence the outcome by delivering on the objective. Talk about what matters to them.
	• Talk about financial results with the leaders who are responsible. Even then, start the conversations with leaders by talking about impact in the market and people development. These are the primary drivers of growing your business.
Shared Experiences	• Shared experiences are the primary means of forming organizational culture and a sense of belonging.
	• Carefully plan and execute a set of rituals and celebrations in your organization, starting with how you onboard practitioners.
	• Virtual work is great, but you need a set of deliberate face-to-face interactions to create a sense of belonging.
Values	• Whatever your organization's values, you, as the leader, must esteem people more than yourself. Think of yourself less and them more.
	• Recognizing the intrinsic value of every person is the heart of leading a more diverse, inclusive, and equitable culture.
	• Your organization is somewhat of an abstraction; you and your leaders are the tangible presentations.
	• People will develop a sense of belonging to leaders who exhibit humility and esteem for all people.

Recruiting. Ample resources are available that can help you create interviews based on what a practitioner can do and conversations about what they want to do. Your practitioners are also a valuable source that you have to engage in refining your interview practices. We focus on two key perspectives regarding whom you need to recruit as well as your relationship with the recruiting team.

Defining roles can lead to arguments over definitions and titles without much practical value. As before, our purpose is to give you practical information rather than establish a canonical definition of AI roles. That said, Figure 7-5 graphically illustrates several key points regarding whom you are recruiting:

- The AI team consists of multiple disciplines; we have defined four of them in Figure 7-5. Often, people in these disciplines work in separate organizations, thus the different colors.

  - People who play well with others help integrate across organizational boundaries.

- Data science consists of two core tasks: data preparation (sometimes called "cleaning," "wrangling," or "transformation") and data modeling. Most data scientists are trained and accustomed to data preparation. However, for large jobs that require industrial-strength operational data pipelines, you must hire dedicated data engineers.

  - Some data scientists become disgruntled if most of their time is spent on data preparation.

- Regardless of whether the output of a model goes into an existing app or an app built for the model, software engineers are normally engaged in the project at some point.

  - User experience (UX) designers are especially helpful in re-thinking and re-designing the end-to-end workflow and the users' physical and digital experience.

- If you need to put numbers of models into production, you will need Machine Learning Ops (ML Ops) and DevSecOps engineers to create and maintain automated deployment pipelines.

  - Once deployed, models require automated oversight to ensure quality output as the data and environment naturally evolve. These skills are, perhaps, the rarest of all.

- IT infrastructure may not be glamorous, but it is an essential part of your AI capability.

  - People who are expert at navigating the long-lead security requirements of national security IT infrastructures are especially valuable.

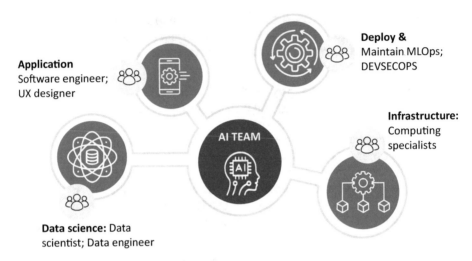

Application
Software engineer;
UX designer

Deploy &
Maintain MLOps;
DEVSECOPS

AI TEAM

Infrastructure:
Computing
specialists

Data science: Data
scientist; Data engineer

Figure 7-5. Multiple disciplines in an AI team

The folly of trying to establish canonical definitions in AI is further established by the many, varied views of practitioners. Some of the best data scientists with whom we have worked do not like to be characterized as data scientists. They view data science as what they do, but they view themselves as mathematicians, physicists, or even full stack developers who happen to be excellent at developing math models.

Both Figure 7-5 and this chapter are designed to help you think about the realities of the multi-disciplinary nature of AI solutions. Focus on the substance; do not chase after the perfect conceptual framework for any part of AI. Doing so is a fool's errand.

If you are in an organization of any size, your data scientists and the other disciplines required for an operational AI capability are, likely, in different organizations. Technical integration is difficult enough; adding multiple organizational boundaries makes integration that much harder. Integration challenges do not merely exist in the technology, but also in people and process. Blended teams require leaders who can effectively lead all of the disciplines. Those leaders must be mindful of the likelihood that multiple organizations mean multiple incentive systems, different cultures, and different processes for developing, deploying, and maintaining a solution. The leader must have the awareness and the levers to affect change across all aspects of integration.

You can simplify the need for integration to an extent—especially for smaller projects—by applying a principle we call "full scope and full scale." Unless your organization explicitly prohibits you from doing so, we suggest you recruit and organize based on this principle:

- **Full scope:** If your business or mission unit is charged with delivering AI models into production, you must hire some capacity across the full scope of disciplines in Figure 7-5. Especially for businesses, you cannot effectively win work, deliver impact to clients, and grow the business if you must always reach across multiple lines of business to build an AI delivery team. Some executives who are incentivized for collaboration across lines of business will argue otherwise. They may be well-intentioned, but they are naïve to what is required to win, deliver, and grow with regard to the many smaller projects you will have in your portfolio.

- **Full scale:** In the event your business competes for an enterprise-scale solution with AI models as a major component, then you can build an integrated team across different lines of business. These enterprise-scale programs are normally of sufficient value that you can get the attention and commitment of multiple lines of business. We would argue that this principle applies in government as the integration across government organizations is no less challenging.

A business of any size will also have the recruiting team in a separate organization, which you, as the AI leader, do not control. You can, nevertheless, have a successful recruiting activity by treating the recruiters as part of your team. Take the time to educate them about your business. Get to know them and their processes. Conduct regular stand-up meetings to sync the recruiters' priorities with your leaders' needs for practitioners. Importantly, make sure that the sunshine that comes with victories and success also shines on your recruiting team. Doing these things will make the recruiters feel and function like members of your team, regardless of how they are organized.

 When our analytics/AI start-up, Edge Consulting, hit a major inflection point in its growth, we hired Candace Paul as a dedicated recruiter. Candace helped us find and hire dozens of highly skilled practitioners for some very difficult work, including deployments to Iraq and Afghanistan.

It grieves us to note that Candice passed away from COVID-19 during 2021. She was a dear friend and valued teammate. We honor her memory here. In doing so, we also express our thanks to the recruiters who have been essential to our success in analytics and AI.

Aligning. Aligning data scientists and other AI practitioners to projects is essential to delivering quality work. You should also think of this activity as a valuable means to develop practitioners and leaders as well as to develop their sense of belonging to your organization. The degree to which they feel a sense of purpose and personal growth on the job, along with the connectivity they feel to their team leader and teammates greatly contributes to their sense of belonging. Deploying "lone ranger" or solo data scientists is a fast path to creating quality and retention problems since the lone practitioner does not have the benefit of peer review and collaboration with other data scientists.

The deployment of solo data scientists can also inhibit the objective of moving useful models into operations. Yes, the insights that customers need is in the model's output—data scientists create the model. However, the insights and the model must be packaged and delivered to the customer, which will increasingly be another machine as we move toward autonomous systems. Data scientists work as part of a capability team that includes application developers, deployment and maintenance specialists, and infrastructure. Deploying solo data scientists, even to a solution development team, assumes away all of the integration challenges we defined previously.

You may choose a different way to organize the multiple disciplines in Figure 7-5. Do not miss the forest for the trees. The main point is that data scientists most effectively deliver AI capabilities into production/operation by working in a multi-disciplinary team. If you deploy data scientists as lone soldiers, you likely discount the impact of these various disciplines working together as a coherent team. You also increase the four risks we outlined in the first axiom.

Whether a government or industry AI leader, do not approach the task of building a cadre of practitioners as an unengaged staffing agency for your data scientists. You must be in control of aligning practitioners and teams of practitioners to work based on multiple factors:

- **Work content:** Technical skills and domain knowledge required

- **Practitioners and team:** Individual and combined team technical skills, domain knowledge, and complementary consulting skills needed for the job; team leadership

- **Development:** Professional growth of the individuals engaged on the team

- **Impact:** Relative importance of the job to the others you have underway and planned

These factors are not static, which is why leaders must continuously evaluate alignment of practitioners to work. You can immediately grasp that practitioners' skills and preferences change over time; sometimes "time" is measured in months. The phases of delivery also create the need to dynamically manage resources allocated to a job. In Chapter 5, we defined a six-phased AI project lifecycle from selling/initiating the project to integrating/conveying results. Leaders must look at how the work content will change over these phases and manage the allocation of practitioners accordingly.

Within most large organizations, some practitioners will naturally evolve to be more analytics practitioner than data scientist. The analytics practitioner has solid descriptive and basic inferential statistics skills as well as being able to configure and apply one or more packaged software products. We noted in Chapter 2 that baseline performance assessments are essential, yet underleveraged. Strong analytics practitioners can excel in this project type. Having analytics practitioners in your business helps you to not only serve these projects, but also to align data scientists to those projects with the most difficult data engineering and math modeling problems.

In the realities of leading an AI organization, you will never have perfect alignment of practitioners to jobs and job phases. For example, you may have data scientists with strong skills and preferences for complex math modeling. But you may be on the front end of a complex job, when most of the work is stakeholder discussions to scope the project, gain required permissions, and access data. Some data scientists will view this as a learning opportunity. Others will view it as a snooze-fest and grow restless. You, as the AI leader, must be hands-on with your people to manage these dynamics. Regular involvement in aligning people to work is the best means for senior leaders to have substantive knowledge of their clients, the work content, and the practitioners that deliver the impact essential to business growth.

Developing. People do not get excited about drinking from or swimming in stagnant pools. Leaders must create a culture and practice of continuous development, starting with your own development. To put this in a wellness context, you will not help them by simply pointing them to physical fitness programs when you are living an unhealthy lifestyle. As we argued in the opening of this book, we do not believe the generalist leader assumption will prove itself in AI. You must be competent in leading the discipline of AI. This book is a starting point, hopefully providing leaders with practical knowledge on the multiple facts of leading AI.

Your development program for AI practitioners needs to cover technical skills and content; domain knowledge; and consultative skills that are complementary to every AI project. Chapter 5 provides a thorough overview of the core AI discipline—data science—which will benefit the technical development of most leaders and analytics practitioners. It will also round out the knowledge of some data scientists. Beyond the technical content in this guide for leaders, there are hundreds of degree and certification programs in data science and related AI disciplines.

Beyond these programs and any AI technical training you deliver within your organization, try to give your data scientists computing resources, data, and problems to solve. incentivizing data scientists to create IP instantiated in code is one powerful way to promote development and increase your organization's enduring assets. Engage your practitioners in hackathons, Kaggle, and similar competitions. These are excellent ways to sharpen your data scientists' skills while also creating useful code and having fun!

In bounding the scope of this book, we decided not to specifically treat the complementary consultative skills herein. We briefly identify what we have found to be the three core consultative skills relevant to any AI delivery:

- The hypothesis-driven approach to complex problem solving helps drive project teams to practical problem and solution hypotheses early in the project lifecycle. Expect your teams to have hypotheses in the first week of a project.

- Commercial deck writing is the best means for writing stand-alone quantitatively based reports for your clients. It is a radical departure both in form and substance from the way government uses PowerPoint. You meet with a customer to discuss their reactions to what they have read, not listen to you brief the content.

- SPIN Selling may not have the best connotative value, but it is an interrogatory approach to systematically isolate what a customer's priority need is. Government officers can usefully deploy SPIN Selling as well as contractors.

Given the availability of technical training resources—and the essential nature of domain knowledge—we focus in this section on helping increase the domain knowledge of your practitioners.

In an interview with Forbes dated 3.23.22, Dr. Jane Panelis, Chief of AI Assurance at the DoD's Joint Artificial Intelligence Center, emphasized the need for domain knowledge in DoD AI:

"The best analytical product is usually a result of leveraging everybody on your team for the skills they bring to the table, respectively; in the DOD, in particular, science without subject-matter expertise is not worth very much."

It would be natural, but misguided, to think that assigning domain subject matter experts (SMEs) to a data science team is the singular path to having domain knowledge on the team. Imagine the data scientist sitting in front of a screen, looking at data that is not well organized or defined. They are simultaneously trying to understand the data, refine candidate hypotheses, and define a suitable problem. If you have engaged in any type of systematic research, you understand that exploratory analysis—the early phase of an AI project—is an intellectual "hit or miss" exercise. The data scientist frames and re-frames questions about the data and hypotheses as they query, plot, and examine the data. An SME can be helpful, but it is impractical for every task to have an SME and data scientist working closely together.

If properly led and equipped, data scientists will learn sufficient domain knowledge. But SMEs are an invaluable source to the data scientists' learning. Table 7-4 summarizes several means for leaders to help data scientists increase domain knowledge. To make any or all of these means practical, AI leaders must lead from the front; you must fully participate in learning yourself. After a team or teams have ingested some domain content, we suggest a synthesis of learning through a facilitated discussion of these questions: 1) What were the salient facts or concepts you learned from the material? 2) What questions or hypotheses were provoked by the material? 3) What additional resources might the team(s) consider in this domain?

Table 7-4. Methods to Build Domain Knowledge

Reading Groups	• Read the same books and articles as a team
Videos	• Watch movies, documentaries, videos; even historical fiction can help
SME Speakers	• Invite SMEs to speak to your teams on an area of domain knowledge
Studies	• Review studies by the General Accounting Office (GAO), government agencies/schoolhouses, non-profit think tanks, and other government or industry groups
Podcasts	• Listen to podcasts on national security topics
Teach	• Have data scientist(s) teach others about salient domain knowledge (teaching something to peers is a powerful way to learn)
Reviews	• Use regularized program/project reviews to teach domain knowledge
Organization	• For large AI organizations, consider organizing your teams by areas of domain knowledge to promote sharing and learning domain knowledge

While Table 7-4 outlines passive means of learning domain knowledge, leaders should also value and expect practitioners to learn domain knowledge in hands-on work. Hackathons, other non-engagement projects, and actual engagements are excellent ways for practitioners to learn domain as they put hands on data in the domain context. In most cases, leaders should structure and integrate the means in Table 7-4 as complements to the domain learning in a project.

Leading in the Government—Industry Context

Virtually all major system developments and modernization programs are delivered by industry. A government-industry partnership is the only way the level of impact envisioned by the NSCAI can be realized. Government agencies cannot hire all of the technical capabilities at the capacity required. That said, the national security community is large and diverse, accounting for well over 50 percent of all discretionary federal spending. There will not be a single model for acquiring and managing data scientists and AI practitioners.

Government officers affect AI implementation through four roles: program executive, program manager, project manager, and practitioner. For large AI programs or major system programs with AI components, a national security agency will always have a program executive and program manager to whom the AI operation reports. Major projects will normally have named government project managers. Although, for many smaller projects, the government project manager is unlikely to be involved in the work on a daily basis.

Government practitioners are less common due to the aforementioned technical capabilities and capacity issue, but there are government AI operations wherein the projects are delivered by government practitioners. However, transformational impacts on U.S. national security through AI depend on hundreds of government-industry partnerships across the national security enterprise. Regardless of the government-industry blend, there is clear government authority over requirements, resources, and performance accountability.

Chris and Frank first met in 1991, shortly after the first war in Iraq. Frank was a government officer in what was then a "black" or covert Navy satellite reconnaissance program, "Program C." Chris had just resigned from the CIA—where he was first an imagery analyst and then an all-source analyst—and joined a large consulting firm under contract to Program C.

The program's culture was one of government-industry partnership in the mission. Everyone knew that government officers were in charge. Everyone knew that contractors were in business. Government officers—starting with the flag officer who was the program executive—did not subscribe to the false dichotomy between mission success and business success. The two parties recognized the interdependencies of their mutual success and a highly collaborative culture flowed out of this recognition.

Some years ago, in response to the concept of government-industry partnership, a senior Intelligence Community executive remarked that, as a C-suite executive in commercial industry, he was well-versed in acquiring various products and services, such as office furniture. A senior CIA program executive with decades of experience in the National Reconnaissance Office (NRO), briefly outlined the difference between a commercial company's capital expenditures and government contracting with industry for a multi-billion-dollar technical intelligence system. The former is a purchase of commodities wherein the buyer-vendor relationship is not exclusively transactional. Acquiring large, complex technical systems requires multi-year collaborative relationships between the government and the vendor.

If the U.S. national security community is to win the AI competition with China while defeating virulent threats from several hostile regimes around the world, there must be large numbers of thriving government-industry partnerships. Since the government is the lead player in this partnership, we use the four roles government officers can play in AI to offer some best practices for leading in the government-industry context.

Program Executive. This government executive leads AI activities. It is common for a government program executive with AI responsibilities to have a broader portfolio such as having responsibilities for business transformation. In recent years, the government has created new roles specific to AI capabilities such as the Chief Data Officer (CDO). When considering all of the levers an executive can pull to affect change, government executives tend to pull on organization and budget frequently.

Creating a potpourri of roles related to AI with vague accountability for delivering capabilities does not drive work forward. The Deputy Secretary of Defense, Honorable "Kath" Hicks, observed this when she considered the incoherent roles and relationships between the department's CIO, CDO, Joint AI Center Director, and Defense Digital Service. She decided to align the latter three under a new Chief Digital and AI Officer.

- **Best practice:** Considering that analytics and AI require multi-disciplinary teams, always align at least the data and modeling capabilities under one leader. Consider giving that leader some full-scope capabilities. Also, ensure that the leader relationships, mechanisms, and incentives across all disciplines (Figure 7-5) are defined such that full-scale AI development and deployment works well. Organizations do not deliver big results—leaders do. However, a fragmented organization with multiple boundaries to cross for an AI capability can make it much harder for AI leaders to move at the speed and scope required.

■ **Note** This practice is not the same as attempting to centralize all AI activity under one organization. Likely, multiple programs will feature AI components. When you have enough work for an AI program, this practice suggests limiting the integration seams by having a single program manager who is responsible for the total capability. We do not suggest the centralization of all AI programs.

Beyond optimizing the organization and leadership, the authority of a program executive is such that they must also attend to several other best practices:

- **AI strategy:** Beyond the visionary direction, the program executive must ensure that the team has the conditions needed to accomplish their goal.

    - Sufficient clarity on priorities (see Chapter 2 for the complexity of this problem) and adequate resources identified and aligned to the priorities

    - The right leaders and incentives in place for results

    - Regular assessments of progress focused primarily on mission impact, deployed capabilities, and implementation of best practices throughout the enterprise

- **Acquisition strategy:** Those with government experience know the stunning amount of unobligated funds the government lurches to spend every August to September. The program executive drives results and the government-industry partnership through an acquisition strategy. Different agencies have differing levels of competency and capacity for managing contracts. Therefore, within your acquisition strategy, consider leveraging external sources such as GSA's FEDSIM group for expertise in acquiring AI solutions on schedule, within budget.

- **Culture:** Those things that shape behavior other than the rules set your organizational culture. Those things include the program executive's language and attitude toward government-industry partnership as well as the tone and expectations you set for your leaders.

- **Highways:** Program executives must clear underbrush and obstacles, creating highways on which major results can be realized at pace. Any single component of the national security enterprise—the Department of the Army, the CIA, Customs and Border Protection, and many others—are large, complex bureaucracies. The NSCAI communicates a sense of urgency for rapid improvement at global scale. As former Secretary of Defense, Bob Gates, describes in his book, *Duty*, moving a large bureaucracy takes extraordinary effort, even during a horrible war.

Program Manager (PM). Relative to AI capabilities, government PMs will be the heads of a dedicated AI organization and components therein as well a major mission system that is developing and/or integrating an AI component, such as an Army air defense artillery system. When either type of PM is acquiring an AI solution (i.e., data and models deployed in some form of software) a corresponding contractor PM typically leads the industry team. When a dedicated AI organization is primarily acquiring data science and related AI services, the role of the industry PM will vary depending on how the services contract is structured. We suggest these best practices:

- **Relationships:** The degree to which there is a government-industry partnership will primarily depend on one factor more than all others combined: the relationship between the government and industry PMs. These two set the tone for relationships at all levels of the partnership. The industry PM must put the mission first and respect the government PM's authority to set priorities and allocate resources. A wise government PM will value the industry PM's expertise and carefully consider their input.

- **Capability:** In dedicated AI organizations, some government PMs choose to direct the contractor staff themselves and actively inhibit any involvement of an industry PM. Candidly, a few industry PMs—even with analytics and AI titles—do not have much substantive value. However, in most cases an involved AI industry executive (PM) brings important value to the program/ project. Some have years of experience leading analytics and AI deliveries, seeing lessons learned across a wide range of projects. They also control levers within the companies to optimize the performance of the industry team and leverage specialized resources, as necessary. Referring to the talent lifecycle (Figure 7-4), government PMs who sideline the AI industry leader are limiting the company's value to recruiting; they incur all the risks outlined earlier in this chapter.

Project Manager. For both program and project managers, we commend to you the axioms and best practices in Chapters 3 and 6, respectively. It is common in some national security contract environments to treat contractor staff as staff augmentation or "butts in seats." Beware trying to directly manage industry staff; instead, leverage their leadership structure. The government acquires solutions development and services with the expectation of quality in delivery. Force the industry vendor to ensure quality is part of the effort with the appropriate oversight of team members daily. If government officers are leading the project with no corresponding industry leadership, we raise the same risks and concerns discussed previously. We have seen this structure work in very select mission environments, but we seriously doubt it can effectively scale throughout the national security enterprise. There simply is not enough capability and capacity to see results anytime soon. We offer three specific areas in which to focus:

- **Hybrid government-industry AI teams.** When mixing practitioners on a team, expectations and roles must be clear. Industry members participate only in the context of a contract. Their respective company makes various types of commitments depending on the contract type. Additionally, contracts have periods of performance and other constraints. Government counterparts operate on a different model. Industry teams may not manage government staff; this can create cultural and performance challenges without careful oversight.

- **Encourage companies to actively develop their staff.** It can seem appealing to simply have companies assign staff to a project and them leave to work. This is a path to two undesirable outcomes. On one hand, the hands-off staff augmentation approach can lead to retention problems. Talented data scientists in a vibrant market stop seeing a career path and find themselves trapped on a single project. Companies play a key role in managing this, but not if the contract culture is staff augmentation. On the other hand, some staff will want to hunker down and stay long-term, building deep mission knowledge of the client the solution. However, they are prone to stagnating. This leads to under-performance over time, creating traps for the government with dependencies on key people that are hard to remediate.

- **Focus on knowledge management and transfer.** As a project leader, ensure solutions are well-documented, user reviews are held with stakeholders, and multiple team members can clearly explain the processing approaches and technological choices. A red flag for any leader is over-dependency on one team member for continuity, knowledge of the solution, or troubleshooting.

Practitioner. If government practitioners are engaged in hands-on development and delivery, then a government project manager is required in almost all cases. Blended teams of government and industry practitioners can be problematic, depending on the contract type. A firm fixed price contract, for example, could be negatively impacted if government practitioners were seen to be the cause of a failure to deliver to the contract terms. It is possible to have industry practitioners delivering one component and government practitioners developing another. This can work in theory, but the substantial differences in the systems and cultures are likely to make this difficult. Ultimately, it is not conducive to scaling and driving results at pace. We caution government leaders to be careful that their government practitioners do not function as the resident cynics.

Leading the Technology

"I could spend an enormous amount of time meeting with technology vendors. I receive dozens of emails per week from these companies."

—Director, Departmental Analytics and AI Center

"…we will "free the data" by removing its current dependencies on IC [Intelligence Community] element applications, systems, and databases…"

—Intelligence Community Information Environment Data Strategy, 2017-2021

"The government lags behind the commercial state of the art in most AI categories, including basic business automation."

—National Security on AI Commission Final Report

© Chris Whitlock, Frank Strickland 2023
C. Whitlock and F. Strickland, *Winning the National Security AI Competition*,
https://doi.org/10.1007/978-1-4842-8814-6_8

Summary

Technology is the muscle-mass of AI solutions, providing the computing infrastructure and software capabilities to use and deploy AI methods. Acquiring and building new technology takes time. New software and hardware are necessary at times, but leaders must decide when these are truly needed and then guide the entire process from advocacy through to approval to operate. Enterprise solutions like Army Vantage, OSD Advana, and Air Force Platform One play important roles, but technology solutions for the vast number of individual systems of record in national security will remain prominent. Over the coming years data must remain a central focus—data access, aggregation, management, security—and will continue to require innovations in technology and processes to provide the fuel for AI work and solutions.

This chapter opens with six axioms, or realities, leaders must grapple with in stating technology requirements or making technology decisions and then proceeds through two sections:

- Technology choices by project type
- Navigating technology issues by leader role

AI is software and technology solutions; image processing, predictive maintenance solutions, event identification, health care diagnostic tools, all these and many more are fundamentally software and hardware to meet mission needs. AI only exists as software and larger technology solutions. All other discussions are general strategy, planning, and so on. If you want AI, teams must write and deploy code, rendered in a programming language (e.g., C, Python, R). If you want autonomous systems, teams build software and technology for the AI functionality, but larger development teams must also craft physical apparatus whether to move over ground, air, or water and interact on its own in the environment.

Data fuels all AI development and operational capability and technologies are required to create data access and enable management. No data, no AI. Data is something we must harness for AI, but we can expect it will always be growing in volume and evolving in complexion. Teams need technology to explore data, perform assessments, and train AI models. Teams need technology to manage data as it evolves and features are added, and so on. Teams need technology to create data pipelines connecting data sources to AI capabilities to render the necessary outputs.

Leaders must make a variety of technology decisions, depending on the role. Foundationally some leaders must choose types of hardware or base computing posture including a cloud versus on-premise posture. Many leaders will make consequential decisions or advocate for access regarding software;

these can carry substantial licensing costs, bring limitations, and open up exciting opportunities.

Our goal in this chapter is to overview the realities around technology, frame some of the big decisions by leader role, and provide some texture on important issues. These technology choices will be in the context of programs and project types as outlined in earlier chapters. These existing programs and new ones are the potential homes for AI-enabled componentry. This will implicitly bring choices on software and technologies to the desks of executives and source selection teams. We revisit those frameworks as useful to illustrate the leader challenge and associated issues.

Technology Axioms

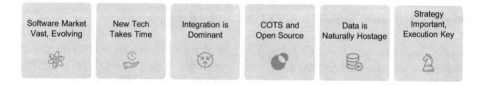

Software Market Vast, Evolving	New Tech Takes Time	Integration is Dominant	COTS and Open Source	Data is Naturally Hostage	Strategy Important, Execution Key

Software Market Vast, Evolving. The technology market is comprised of an enormous amount of commercially available software relevant to AI along with open-source alternatives or complements. Select names may rise to greater prominence in dialogue (e.g., Palantir, Qlik, Salesforce, Python, R), but the reality is a diverse range of potentially relevant solutions. Beyond these commercially available packages, organizations built custom applications and websites using common programming languages and in the course of this work often innovate and share to "open-source" toolkits. To illustrate the magnitude of the market, at the time of writing IBM's software product list included over 1,000 discrete items available.

A private equity firm, First Mark, built the graphic in Figure 8-1, breaking the AI-related market for software into seven major categories. These seven further sub-segment into 93 components, which collectively capture over 800 leading software solutions. Note, these are software packages First Mark considers leaders in the particular portion of the market. The number of technically relevant and viable software is much greater than this.

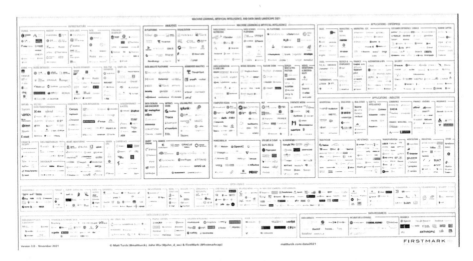

Figure 8-1. Machine learning, artificial intelligence and data landscape—one view

New Technology Takes Time. The government needs new hardware and software for modernization and new solutions. Leaders must be mindful, however, that this process is not typically quick and the effort will likely take months and in some instances a year or more. Whether the goal is to introduce a new class of graphical processing unit or a new piece of COTS software, several major processes are invoked. Sponsors must secure funding by rallying other leaders typically to recognize the value of the purchase and the need. Then the procurement process begins; in some instances a market survey is required to ensure a range of relevant solutions are considered. Any acquisition action takes time to establish a contract with an industry vendor and this can be especially long with competitive acquisitions requiring side-by-side comparison of offerors. Once acquired, the technology must be implemented and an "authority to operate" must be granted, certifying the new capability will be secure and ready. All these processes are obviously navigable, but taken together the process is not inherently fast; it is inherently deliberate and it is useful to plan for months (or over a year) to acquire, implement, and certify new technology.

As an example of how pressure can manifest for an organization, a military organization had immediate access to a cloud environment with necessary software and data to perform a six-month task, but another cloud vendor was trying to persuade this military organization with an immediate need to switch to their cloud service and use the task as an opportunity to demonstrate their capability. The military organization did not have current cloud subscription with this vendor, no infrastructure was provisioned, no contract in place, and certainly no authority to operate. Without doubt all this could be accomplished, but the overall process takes much more time than the military organization had available to perform the AI-related task.

Computing Hardware Issues   AI projects can be supported with a variety of computer hardware and it is good for leaders to be broadly aware of options in the space. The hardware needs for studies projects can be quite different from operational deployments, particularly as more emphasis is directed to edge devices and autonomous solutions.

AI solution performance can be heavily impacted by hardware selection. Teams can draw on conventional central processing unit (CPU)-powered machines or graphical processing units (GPU). CPUs are readily available and relatively inexpensive. They are quite capable of supporting a wide range of analytics and AI tasks. Teams can use select software to distribute processing across multiple CPU machines either in cloud or on-premise environments. In contrast, GPUs were designed for image-intensive processing but lend themselves to intensive AI tasks because of their parallel compute capability. NVIDIA is a well-known provider of GPU-based machines, as an example. GPUs can support high-volume, high-throughput tasks and have been crucial in large-scale training of AI models using imagery and natural language data.

For those developing new operational autonomous systems or edge device capabilities neuro-morphic chip-based processors are emerging and present yet another step forward in capability. This line of innovation is closely linked to facets of AI including deep learning and neural net applications, opening a pathway to much faster processing and the potential for adaptive systems. Chip manufacturers and hardware producers are creating options and research organizations in DoD are exploring applications and opportunities.

The key for leaders is understanding there are options and ensuring consideration relative to mission need and supply chain security, particularly as more specialized hardware is selected. Teams can perform many tasks with conventional CPU hardware. Probe the requirement when a desire for GPU-based solutions emerge. A number of legitimate analytic needs will drive to GPU-based posture, but these are more costly, and leaders should be mindful of matching need to requirement.

Integration is Dominant. We all crave simplicity. One purchase that solves that majority of the problem. The reality in the technology arena is a substantial amount of integration activity needs to occur. This applies to piecing together various components in a cloud environment or stitching together a variety of different software/hardware within a program. All this integration is in addition to either writing software for the core functions or configuring a COTS software.

Certain integrative technologies can be very important in opening up data access. As an example, software like MuleSoft enables developers to render APIs enabling more ready exchange of data between applications. Building APIs is integrative work, but very important for other applications to capitalize fully on what a particular program brings to the enterprise.

COTS and Open Source. Virtually all contemporary COTS analytic software provides options to integrate functions or models rendered in popular open-source data science software like Python or R. This is valuable and leaders should recognize the role of both in the analytics infrastructure. Both Python and R rank among top AI-related software packages students are learning in academic programs and which are showing up in job postings. Python and R constitute, in a sometimes humorous way, warring tribes in data science with practitioners often being more oriented to one than the other. Both packages are very capable and provide important tooling for data scientists in performing AI-related work.

For their part, COTS packages can be very important in addressing substantial enterprise functions related to analytics. Typically, they are backed by robust investment for continuing feature development, have tested capabilities regarding security and common utilities, and may also have consequential R&D in advanced capabilities relative to AI.

Cloud Computing   Materials and conversations regarding cloud are prolific, so it is hard for leaders to miss. That being the case, however, it is worth a few specific comments relative to AI-related work.

The cloud provides a more pliable infrastructure (servers, data storage, software, analytics) on a pay-for-use basis compared to on-premise data centers. Once an organization establishes a cloud account or subscription, it becomes much faster to create new development environments or add resources.

For AI-related activities, the major cloud providers each offer relevant functions. AWS SageMaker, Azure Cognitive Services, Google Cloud Platform Verex AI. Major COTS analytics software is also available on the cloud, such as ArcGIS, Palantir, or SAS Viya. All these are potential accelerators but come with a fee.

Leaders must be savvy about cost drivers in the cloud. As data volumes and streams increase, or the user base increases, cloud costs can rise consequentially. In some program environments this is problematic. Because the cloud is a pay-for-use environment, leaders must be mindful of dynamics that can change the cost profile.

The Intelligence Community, DoD, and generally the Federal government have many options.

Data is Naturally Hostage. Every program is developed to a system concept. These systems move and store data in the context of workflows and users access the applications via specified user interfaces. Without purposeful effort, the data for a specific application is in effect hostage in that application. For example, any particular application might have a user interface written in a particular language (e.g., React) to allow access from a variety of device types. This same application might have core functionality like workflows written in .NET, Java, or Go. Data is then written and read from an application database (e.g., Oracle, PostgreSQL). Data can be made available by APIs to fed into larger aggregation environments.

Data aggregation and access technologies evolved over the past three decades. Data from individual systems of record was aggregated into data marts and data warehouses. These differ in scope but both are founded on SQL technologies for storage and query. Data marts are more narrowly focused and typically smaller. Warehouses often target enterprise-level business or operational reporting functions aggregating inputs from multiple systems. As data variety increased to include streaming data logs, text, and other unstructured datatypes, NoSQL databases emerged in individual systems of record. Data lakes combine inputs from SQL and as well as these burgeoning NoSQL data stores. Each of these levels—system of record, data marts, data warehouses, and data lakes—store data, support queries, but can also present obstacles to effective data discovery and use.

Newer design concepts are emerging in prominence, with some implementation history, to bridge numerous sources across an enterprise to improve discoverability and use. In the current environment, leaders will hear as an example, discussion of data fabrics and data meshes to mechanisms to liberate data. Probe the concepts for a clear linkage to practical implementation approaches because at this writing there are no technologies that cover the range of the data mesh/fabric conceptual requirement.

Leaders must recognize the need to actively liberate data—making it discoverable, accessible, and useable. None of this is without cost, often including substantial network requirements. As a vivid illustration, return to the Aegis Weapon System example in the program chapter. Navy seniors might conceptually want to see Aegis data shared off any particular ship while it is underway. Sharing something closer to the majority of this data, however, requires some combination of substantially enhanced onboard storage, substantial new network connectivity and then some enterprise repository like a data lake in order to make the concept real. Hence the reality; data accessibility requires purposeful steps to liberate the data.

Strategy Important, Execution Key. Organizations require technology and data strategies with compelling visions, but performance changes once new capabilities are deployed. In the technology space, new concepts and new technologies emerge regularly—potentially becoming prominent in strategies and related discussion without thorough discussion. To achieve the fullness of the AI potential, the national security community needs ambitious and visionary thinking, but this must be converted into practical capabilities. In the marketplace, some of the concepts and terms will invariably be overworked. Leaders must recognize this reality and ensure realism in planning, requests for proposals, proposals to the government, and execution.

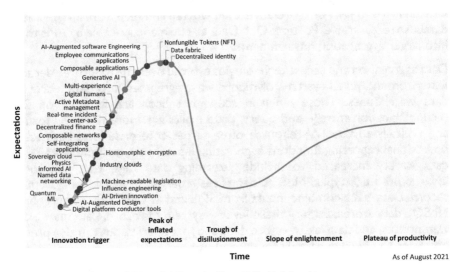

Figure 8-2. Gartner Group Hype cycle for emerging technologies, 2021

The Gartner Group hype cycle illustrates the challenge. In Figure 8-2, a range of technology concepts or capabilities are arrayed on the hype cycle for 2021.

Note that " data fabric" is one of the currently most hyped items. Returning to previous paragraphs, this is a potentially viable concept, but leaders must recognize it as a design concept. An idea, but not one with any single dominate solution and one with a range of interpretation on meaning. Thus defining a requirement for "data fabric" must be developed well beyond the label to maximize the prospect of creating high-performance capability. Deployed capability is ultimately what matters.

Technology Leadership Issues by Project Type

In Chapter 2, we suggested that leaders organize and execute four-types of AI projects (Figure 8-3). The two columns define projects to understand your enterprise's performance and projects to drive improved performance. The former primarily inform decisions to allocate resources to priority needs, while the latter primarily informs operational decisions and actions that drive mission impact. Projects in the rows fall into the categories of studies or operational capabilities. This project-types framework provides one useful structure for analyzing your AI technology needs and choices among the vast array of AI vendors and products.

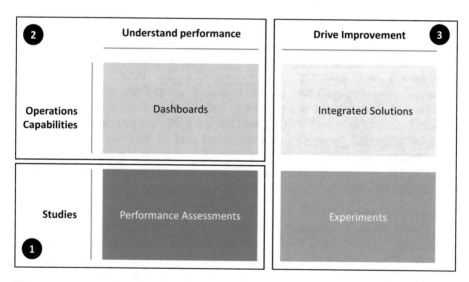

Figure 8-3. Major technology categories by project type

Where technology needs and resources are concerned, leaders will make most of their choices in three contexts (Figure 8-3):

1. Leaders can and should drive studies with available or readily available technologies.

2. Dashboards can effectively operate using widely available COTS and open-source software packages.

3. Driving improvement requires a more robust and technically complex set of tools and processes that are coherent from experimentation to development and testing (dev/test) to production (prod). This coherence is necessary for quality, but also to move at the scale and speed required by the mission imperative of national security. Let's consider each in the three contexts in further detail.

Technology Choices for Performance Assessment Studies

Leaders should use performance assessment studies to regularly test intuitive hypotheses and other questions regarding baseline performance and where AI investment has the biggest potential bang for the buck. Performance assessments are generally one-off projects, the results of which are communicated through some type of report. You need responsive, technically sufficient tools, which in most cases already exist in your enterprise. While performance assessments are designed around a mission problem, the projects are a valuable and generally underleveraged part of your AI technology and data strategies. Nothing informs these strategies better than actually executing analytics and AI on your data, which is exactly what you do in performance assessment studies.

Leaders and teams will execute this type of project multiple times a year—often with more than one assessment running in parallel—and thus the technology must readily flex to meet varying performance assessment demands. Cloud environments can be very friendly for rapidly spinning up and shutting down assessment studies and provide flexibility in activating capabilities already approved for an organization. That said, on-premise data centers and computing environments can also work well in that most have the necessary tools available already. The keys are ensuring ready access to data storage and database software (all three major types: SQL, NoSQL, and graph), and having the security protocols you need for the required data. For performance assessments, open-source languages (e.g., R and Python) with up-to-date versions provide sufficient tools for data preparation, statistical modeling, and the charts and graphs used to communicate performance data. The cycle time required to get new technologies approved on your network generally isn't worth the added benefit to performance assessments given the power of widely available open-source tools.

Leaders responsible for this infrastructure should consider potential compute challenges and ensure a variety of options are available with regard to distributed computing or virtualization along with programming languages. We have found, as an example, it can be valuable in some cases to have "older" programming languages like FORTRAN available because of the capability to perform higher-speed numerical processing. The key is thinking forward to the types of assessments needed by your organization and working to configure the environment flexibly with minimal cost (this tends to bias toward open-source software).

Technology Choices for Performance Dashboards

The second context, performance dashboards, requires greater attention to ongoing infrastructure and data pipelines, as this is an operational capability. Fortunately for leaders and their enterprises, business intelligence (BI) dashboards have been in widespread commercial use for over 20 years. In the early phase of BI technology, enterprise platform leaders IBM, Oracle, and SAP dominated the market. In recent years, Microsoft, Qlik, and Tableau have become the leading players in the space. Two plus decades of commercial competition and open-source development have delivered the operational reliability needed by a capability that is used to measure KPIs on an ongoing basis and inform operational decision-making.

COTS solutions allow the government to benefit immediately from capability developed for similar problems as the COTS applications come with common templates learned from years of experience applying BI to human capital, finance, supply chain, other functional areas. These COTS packages also provide features to resolve many of the data pipeline issues necessary to fuel the dashboard fields. COTS BI software provides relatively simple drag-and-drop features, toggle switches, and other interfaces that ease the creation of data pipelines and visualizations. Consequently, strong analytics practitioners can configure and deploy dashboard software, thus accelerating the pace and scope of impact with less dependency on data scientists.

COTS dashboard software obviously comes at a price, but the tremendous competition in the AI technology market gives the buyer leverage. Tech development and competition over time have commoditized dashboard software with enough competition remaining that buyers can negotiate prices. Each software will have a range of configurations and price options. Use resources such as Gartner's Magic Quad for BI software to research your options and prepare to negotiate with one or more vendors. Most importantly, do the analytical work necessary to clarify your decision problems and KPIs. Apply previous chapters of this book to ensure that decision support is the dog that wags the technology tail.

Additionally, make sure that you check the availability of BI server and user licenses already on your network. It shouldn't surprise you that enterprises buy licenses that then sit unused. Increasingly, enterprise data lakes and analytics environments, such as DoD's Advana capability, provide COTS dashboard and many other software to authorized users. Similarly, your cloud service provider (CSP) will offer a data visualization software, such as Google's Looker. Your enterprise IT shop or AI program manager usually acquires substantial numbers of licenses and pre-negotiated rates for additional user licenses. You will be well served to at least evaluate this option if your enterprise has such a capability.

Alternatively, a team can avoid COTS licensing costs by building dashboards using open-source software, Python Dash, R Shiny, and D3.js (a JavaScript library) being widely used examples. Open-source software also include a number of useful, pre-built data pipeline and dashboard functions, but the team will need to stitch these together to create the solution. The open-source tools require greater programming proficiency than deploying a COTS dashboard package. This means your dashboard developers will need to know the open-source programming languages, which in turn means they are most often data scientists or frontend developers (in the case of D3.js) not analytics practitioners. In addition to its widespread use in the data science community, Python is a robust application development environment. The R software emerged from statistical courses in academe. Consequently, an industrial strength dashboard application is more likely suited to Python or D3.js, but R Shiny may work depending on your infrastructure and the dashboard's performance requirements.

Technology Choices for Driving Improvement

The third context for technology choices by project type combines the normal flow from experimentation to the ultimate objective of deployed operational models in the sense-making, decision-making, action-taking cycle. This context presents a level of technical performance, complexity, and integration well beyond the previous two contexts. Leaders' choices will drive significant operational consequences in multiple technology areas—computing, data, modeling, and UX—as well as the associated engineering processes for developing, testing, deploying, and maintaining AI models. Figure 8-4 summarizes layers of the AI solution stack and helps to highlight the crucial role integration plays in effective AI solution development.

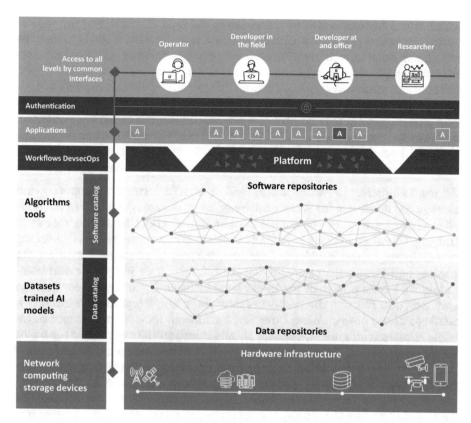

Figure 8-4. AI solution stack, NSCAI report

Exposed, Open APIs   Leaders must make technology choices to meet today's mission needs while also creating the ability to leverage inevitable technology advances for future mission needs. Once the stack is assembled, integrating new technologies comes at some cost in money and time. It is vital that the integration of your stack function more like LEGO blocks than concrete blocks.

Demanding the use of open APIs that are exposed is one means of mitigating this risk. Leaders must have chief engineers/architects with substantial computer/software engineering expertise to analyze and advise on this issue.

Operational AI solutions will vary widely in the type of model and the type of system in which the model operates. Some models have a single sensor or data input, such as face identification on your smartphone. Others purposefully bring together data from several sources or databases to create outputs. Model integration will vary from an existing system ingesting a model's output to model(s) being fully integrated in a sense-making or decision-making system to AI models being one part of a larger autonomous capability, such as an autonomous vehicle. We simply frame the choices in this; further details are provided later in this chapter. (In Appendix A, we provide a more technical discussion of the solution stack with emphasis on AI modeling types.)

At the foundational level of stack, leaders should focus on computing and storage requirements for work envisioned or underway. A variety of AI modeling problems require substantial computational effort to iterate results in training. Cloud computing is helpful in that it allows more responsive scaling of resources to the problem. That said, leaders need to be tuned to the choices and ensure teams are paying attention to their usage of cloud computing. The chief power of the cloud is rapidly spinning up assets for storage and compute, shutting the resources down when no longer needed. In provisioning a cloud environment, however, a team can lock in some unattractive costs relative to the need. Leaders should question the team early regarding their computational requirements. Be mindful of commitments to higher-end processors which may bring ongoing fixed costs, for example larger core virtual machines or graphical processing units. These are helpful for some tasks and unnecessary for others. If the compute environment is an on-premise data center, leaders should pay special attention to the ability to conduct distributed computing across multiple machines and the restrictions that may arise due to competing tasks on the on-premise hardware. In general, take care in assuming on-premise data centers are configured for substantial and dynamic increases in scale at no cost to other work.

Moving up to the data layer, an operational solution will likely require a data pipeline that is very high volume and real-time. Operationally reliable data pipelines can be addressed with a number of COTS data management software; Informatica, Talend, and Pentaho among others. Data pipelines can also be created with a microservices approach using a common programming language such as Java. The focus is ensuring adequate performance relative to the task. To illustrate the challenge, one government agency's data pipeline for populating a large graph database was taking almost 15 days to iterate from a new batch data receipt to posting to the graph. A team rebuilt this complex pipeline using microservices and the time to populate the graph was cut by 66 percent. In the data science community, data engineering is not seen as sexy as math modeling, yet it is often the key to having models that responsively derive insights from data. Leaders must ensure that their data engineers have the right tech.

Training and testing models can create challenges in data access, particularly where edge nodes retain the bulk of data locally. This challenge is often found when operational or tactical units have sensing systems that create larger volumes of data. Leaders must ensure adequate data storage and computational capability are available where they are needed. The team must create a function to gather data especially from the edge. This can draw on a range of emerging technologies—for example, Snowflake, Amazon Snowball, and others—which support capture of large volumes. For tactical systems with limited bandwidth to move data to centralized activities to support training and testing of models, edge data capture devices are a way leaders can ensure access. For an enterprise with substantial edge data requirements, the total technology architecture must therefore deliver coherent data storage and computing between the edge and the enterprise's central nodes, such as headquarters.

The data layer provides one or more data storage technologies and these must match anticipated AI modeling approaches. Fundamentally the choices span SQL, NoSQL, and graph database approaches with the latter rising to greater roles in the past decade. A variety of questions will invoke a variety of modeling approaches. Difficult modeling approaches work best when aligned to a data structure suited to the modeling approach; graph being an obvious example among others. Thus, teams should specify the type(s) of data store technologies based on the anticipated modeling approaches they will use. Leaders should probe not only the near-term but likely evolution of the program and associated data storage design concept, ensuring the alignment of mission problem to the right data to the right modeling approach.

Beyond the variety in modeling approaches driven by the range of users' questions, leaders need to consider how the range of modeling of flexibility in modeling types and features drives computing costs. Operational models are often custom built using common software, such as Python, Java, Spark, among many others. Each of the cloud services providers include significant functionality to create, test, and deploy models. For example, the .NET development environment is very robust and enables creation of a full solution, including data pipelines, enrichment, and processing.

■ **Experiments to Integrated Solutions**   AI solution development will often begin as an experiment or rapid prototype. This project type is valuable to testing new technologies and data science approaches to a problem. Within the national security community, AI experimentation takes place within a system program office as well as in organizations dedicated to experimentation, such as the Defense Advanced Research Projects Agency (DARPA), the Office of Naval Research, and many others.

Setting aside basic scientific research, the majority of AI experimentation needs to have a path whereby useful results make it into operational capabilities. In government AI programs, there can be a chasm between a successful experiment and an operational capability. Leaders must ensure that their integration efforts—both the technologies and processes you choose—are designed and operated to reduce the natural drag and flatten the natural obstacles that occur between experiment results and operational capabilities.

As shown in Figure 8-4, engineering workflows—such as software DevSecOps and machine learning ops (ML Ops)—must be considered an integral part of the technology stack. DevSecOps is the current manifestation of a continuous development—continuous integration software development lifecycle (SLDC), while ML Ops is a relatively new companion process for developing, testing, deploying, and maintaining AI models. Like other layers of the stack, these processes have open-source, COTS, and cloud-based software from which leaders can choose. Just as your central focus is on the mission problem and then the right AI technology, focus this level on an integrated set of engineering processes for delivery of trusted and operationally reliably capabilities, and then align the right technologies to your process. We discuss options further in the program section.

At the top of the solution stack, we find features directly exposed to end users through the application layer. Most of these are created in a custom but standards-based development environment, such as Java or C++. These environments are suitable for massive scale—Facebook's user interface is coded in a JavaScript library, React, for example—and also seek to maintain security features equal to evolving cyber threats. Automated security services—aka "policies as code"—are essential for managing the tension between responsive data access for users and protecting data, including the ability to forensically assess your data environment on a continuous basis.

Technology Leadership Issues by Leader Role

Leaders fill a variety of roles as it pertains to AI-related work and the goal in the remainder of the chapter is to provide some thinking and revisit frameworks to guide technology choices. Over the past several years specifically we observed dynamics in multiple organizations that represent challenges and tensions between various roles with impact to technology selections and use. We can capture these tensions in anonymized comments from interactions with actual leaders in the national security community:

Department/Agency Director: AI must be a top priority and we must leverage this aggressively to create an advantage for our forces.

Major Program Manager in Same Department/Agency: I understand the senior direction or intent, but what am I supposed to do with that? I have existing requirements and problems. There is no new money.

Portfolio Director for Department/Agency: I am tired of hearing about all these small success stories and projects. Can someone give me the big picture and explain what we will do to move the needle on AI?

AI Project Leader in Same Department/Agency: What can we realistically do with the resources we have? We need to show some positive movement, even if it's small.

These tensions are normal and should be expected, but leaders at varying levels can work constructively with these tensions to create progress. Senior leaders in agencies and departments want to see AI have broad and consequential impact. They want confidence every PEO is implementing solutions smartly that feature AI. They want to see increased autonomous systems driven by AI.

As reviewed in Chapter 3, program roles range from individual systems of record (technology or other programs) through senior leader-driven programs at the top of the enterprise. The technology choices and opportunities reasonably vary depending on the role; the following paragraphs sketch out emphasis issues for different program leadership roles.

Overall, program leaders at various levels are well-advised to hold four technology issues central regarding AI solution development:

A. **Perform AI development and specifically AI model development as close to the mission experts as possible.** Domain knowledge and data understanding is crucial and consequently development should be performed close to mission owners and operators.

B. **Focus on data collection and aggregation.** Data access is crucially important to AI acceleration and ultimately AI-enabled operations. Edge data collection, networks, and data aggregation are critical.

C. **Leverage emerging cloud-enabled environments as fully as possible.** In the national security arena on-premise centers continue to hold a significant position, but wherever possible it is advisable to shift activity to cloud-based settings. It is much easier to scale capabilities up and down, provision regularly used software and hardware, and ultimately to manage costs.

D. **Continue to move to DevSecOps and secure, agile development.** This is growing across the national security community as programs shift from waterfall development and major block updates toward a posture more oriented to continuous integration-continuous delivery-continuous deployment. Software factories and shared platforms within the services and agencies as well as joint programs all can contribute.

Technology emphasis issues and illustrations by role follow in subsequent paragraphs. These are addressed in this order:

- Senior department/agency leaders (multiple PEOs)

- PEO leadership (multiple programs)

- Program leadership (multiple projects)

- AI project (assessment or model experiments, development)

- Cross-department AI leaders (potentially multiple departments, PEOs, programs)

Senior Department/Agency Leaders. This role is distinctive in providing oversight for multiple PEOs, driving the annual planning and budgeting process, and understanding and adapting performance for the enterprise. In this regard, select technology issues are very important if the goal is to accelerate AI-related development and deployment. The Air Force, Army, and Navy each have a dozen or more PEOs. The Space Force runs five PEOs. In the Intelligence Community the nomenclature is different but the equivalent organizations number in the dozens. Senior Department/Agency leaders must set conditions and give guidance that moves each of these PEOs forward at rates relative to the importance for enterprise performance in both core mission and business operations. Leaders at this level are uniquely positioned to work re-programming of money between PEOs or programs as well as to advocate for new efforts necessary to fully leverage AI. Three technology emphasis areas are addressed next: data, development process, and tracking/monitoring of AI work.

- **Data capture/aggregation/enhancement/sharing.** In this department/agency-wide context, several technology emphasis areas are especially important. If data is fuel for AI development and operations, senior must ensure each PEO is focused on effective data capture, metadata production, data aggregation, and sharing. It may be tempting to seek one large "data play" and in areas this might be effective. Given that PEOs are organized by functional focus (e.g., Army PEO Ground Combat Systems, PEO Aviation), leaders might reasonably expect opportunities for collaborative AI development and deployment across related systems. What is each PEO executing to improve edge device data capture, address network connections especially for tactical systems, and data aggregation and sharing across the programs in a PEO? Especially as it pertains to tactical systems, substantial data is potentially hostage in locations with limited communications bandwidth and with limited data capture options at the edge. This data is potentially crucial in developing AI solutions. Communications capabilities requirements, especially for autonomous systems powered by AI, may be substantial. Is the current plan going to deliver necessary change on the necessary timelines?

- **Cross-PEO infrastructure and process.** Initiatives spanning multiple PEOs are creating important capabilities within the national security community for military services and agencies. Service/agency leaders can create tremendous value with shared development infrastructure (within PEOs or between PEOs) and ensuring a shift to DevSecOps (Development-Security-Operations) as an integrated, agile development process. As an illustration, the USAF Platform One and Kessel Run initiatives create substantial infrastructure and process support for combat and combat support initiatives. As written on the Kessel Run website, the program "builds, tests, delivers, operates and maintains cloud-based infrastructure and warfighting software applications for use by Airmen worldwide and delivers them on time, as needed and with efficiency and cost-effectiveness above other acquisition methods or practices in the Air Force and Department of Defense." Meanwhile, the USAF Platform One initiative creates a cloud-based DevSecOps environment. The two initiatives are collaborating and merging capabilities to provide capability pertinent to multiple Air Force and DoD programs. For its part, the Navy Project Overmatch is an aggressive effort to bring networks, hardware, software and software factories to a posture able to support AI-enabled operations at much faster speeds overall. While the focus is enabling AI, the applicability of this effort is broad. Project Overmatch is clear the program will not create AI models, but rather enable this work by data science teams close to the mission across the Navy.

- **Tracking and monitoring AI progress.** Technology deployment to enable effective monitoring of AI development and deployment is clearly within the span of department/agency leaders. Leaders will set priorities, issue policy, and carry the budget process forward. But in the absence of tracking and monitoring, it is impossible to understand the AI progress as the work will be inherently decentralized across all PEOs, major programs, and programs of record. Many organizations handle problems like this with episodic data calls or reviews. While these data calls plainly can work, they often lack the structure inherent in an approach designed to fuel dashboard indicators for an enterprise and are frustrating to organizational participants. For a challenge like this, a web application can provide a means for both data collection and then display and even analysis. From a technology perspective, many dashboard implementations leveraging COTS software make direct connections to existing databases to either directly display data or to perform calculations then display. Tracking AI-related deployments across a large enterprise will require gathering data not readily available in databases. This data will be input by various programs and projects across the organization. In this respect, a custom application may make more immediate sense than implementing one of the major COTS business intelligence or dashboard solutions. Either way, the leader must recognize the need and then probe staff on the best option to gather and visualize data providing insight to the progress on implementing AI.

Program Executive Office-specific Technology Concerns. Across DoD and the national security community, there are a finite number of PEOs or equivalent organizations. Each of these is responsible for acquisition oversight, planning, and coordination around a family of related programs. In the chapter addressing programs, the Navy's Integrated Weapon System PEO illustrates the challenge. Numerous other PEOs are tackling similar issues with some addressing enterprise business issues and others more combat or combat support system development. AI-enabled solutions in the purview of a particular PEO may perform best when bringing together data from various programs and projects.

- **Integrative data collection/aggregation/ enhancement.** Arguably one of the most important technology questions for PEOs centers on integrative capabilities across their related programs. While AI is built around a single sensor or data stream input, it often requires data from multiple data streams or systems. To experiment with models and ultimately deploy AI models, data must be collected, aggregated, and appropriately enhanced with metadata. This capability may not exist adequately within any of the given programs within the PEO. If so, either via reprioritization, reprogramming or additional funds these integrative activities must be addressed to enable data access. This may require a data lake, edge data collection, and network enhancement or episodic bulk downloads to effectively assemble the data. While enterprise-wide solutions may help, we might logically expect to see functionally related programs create these integrative capabilities. As an example, the Navy faced challenges with respect to financial management and auditability. Analysis of the situation indicated more ready access to information across multiple software capabilities and databases was crucial. Consequently, the Navy Financial Management community working with a PEO decided on an API-driven approach to raising data accessibility and opportunities for integration. The Enterprise Integration Program implemented a COTS solution to render multi-tiered APIs to create a Central Data Exchange.

- **Identifying solution paths for new models.** Especially where AI models must bridge multiple sensor or system inputs, a crucial question will center on where to deploy the new model. Models may be deployed within existing programs, but the difficulty is this may require construction of new data pipelines and functionality to enable the models. Leaders should not underestimate this challenge. In some environments, an inference or model engine might usefully be a new system of record with associated architecture, data pipelines, model engine, and workflow connections to existing programs. Whatever the solution path, PEO leaders must ensure new functionality is both conceptualized and appropriate technologies are selected to render them operational.

Program Leadership. For the vast majority of programs, AI will be an important facet but only a facet. As with autonomous-driving vehicles, AI is a part, not the whole. Program leaders will have broad concerns beyond AI functionality but must ensure those elements are well-conceived and supported in the architecture. Fundamentally, program leaders must ensure the selected technologies will enable accurate outputs, adequate speed, and maintainability. Speed and accuracy can be related as it pertains to the hardware and software combinations chosen for a given architecture.

- **Runtime environment.** Leaders should probe teams on the model deployment environment to be used in the operation (runtime capabilities). These will continue to evolve but as an example available approaches recently and currently include PyTorch, TensorFlow, and Open Neural Network Exchange (ONNX) as examples. Each of these (and other similar capabilities) integrate tightly with technology to run AI models and enable optimal hardware performance. Teams will make design decisions about these model environments, the larger software architecture, and the hardware integration. Certain selections can preclude or disadvantage options. Leaders should probe teams on design combinations with attention to ease of integrating various model types and ensemble modeling techniques. As mentioned earlier, throughput times on operational processing can require spinning up multiple nodes in a distributed computing environment and depending on licensing arrangements this can substantially impact cost. Major COTS software solutions can include model engines, inference engines or the like. In the design, it is important for leaders to probe these capabilities and think toward future years as data sources may increase, hardware changes, and or model types need to adapt for accuracy.

- **AI development environment.** Program leaders must ensure AI teams can access adequate development environments for testing and training models, including careful attention to data access. Not all AI models training and testing requires large-scale compute. In fact, for a range of mission problems the datasets may be smaller and quite manageable computationally. For others, the training and testing can be computationally demanding. Cloud environments can be leveraged for that or the program can create its own cloud subscription or instance (i.e., this will be further described later in this chapter and illustrated in what the Navy Jupiter program is to parent Advana program). The leader challenge is to ensure the team is thinking ahead on likely training-testing demands along with data access constraints and making reasonable technology choices.

- **COTS versus custom build.** One of the most fundamental choices will be configuring a major COTS software package (or integrate one or more) and building a custom application to implement the AI-enabled solution. Large enterprise software packages increasingly include AI-related functionality. Typically, these provide a range of other capability that is mission-relevant whether in supply chain, data management, human capital, finance, and so on. They also typically bring integrative capabilities to allow open-source software programming for AI models (e.g., the ability to plug-in Python models). Common trade-offs are cost, speed to operations, degree of customization given mission need. Whatever the case relative to a particular initiative, this is one of the more consequential choices.

- **Cloud versus on-premise environment.** A number of core combat and combat support mission areas may present challenges for the cloud in operations, while the cloud may be crucial in developing the software. The choice on deployment environment must account for security concerns, operating environment, and distinctive or unique mission demands (e.g., unique hardware for deployed systems). In any event, the cloud environments offer important functions that potentially accelerate AI deployment, but as with COTS these services come with cost. For the program leader, the up-front choice on how to leverage cloud versus on-premise resources is important.

AI Project Leader Technology Issues. This is particularly pertinent for project leaders addressing either performance assessments or AI experiments as the technology choices for operational deployments will likely be made by the larger development team. For leaders tackling an individual performance assessment or experiment, the crucial issue is whether to advocate for some specific change in the available environment for the project, knowing these changes or additions can take substantial time. For example, in the hardware arena broad options are available to support AI-related work: conventional central processing units, graphical processing units, emerging neuromorphic chip-based units, and super computers in varying types. Some experiments may explicitly focus on hardware not available in the current environment. For the project leader this immediately raises an execution question: do you take data to some other environment with the target hardware (and maybe software combo) or add the gear to the current? As a general note, government cloud environments in the national security community can speed access to some of these capabilities and should be high on a leader's list of options.

Cross-Department/Agency Leader Issues. At the DoD, Office of the Director of National Intelligence (ODNI), and Department of Homeland Security (DHS) levels, it is possible to form cross-department/agency AI-related programs. DoD is most aggressive to date both in the form of the Advana platform and environment along with the JAIC and its Joint Common Foundation effort (both further detailed later in this chapter). Without question, programs at this level can be beneficial; however, the challenges are not inconsequential particularly when in core military and intelligence mission areas, as any development crosses major organizational boundaries and is inherently far from mission experts. Early in the AI cycle centralized activities may make sense at this level only to find over time that each department/ agency is better suited to address needs closer to the mission experts. Adaptation on this front might be expected. That being said, some early cross-department initiatives demonstrated clear value-add and are driving significant progress.

DoD description of Advana

Technology choices and investments at this level should reflect the high-level dynamics of crossing major organizational boundaries and being potentially far removed from mission experts. Some functional areas will lend to these cross-department platforms, while others will be inherently more challenging and require a substantial amount of other work especially in data collection, aggregation, and enhancement. Leaders can usefully focus on the critical difference in providing a platform and environment on the one hand and trying to perform AI solution development on the other.

Technology environments to enable performance assessments and enterprise dashboards at this level are high-pay-off. Teams evaluating specific capabilities need environments to bring data and perform a range of analytic functions to create assessment outputs. Similarly, a wide range of enterprise business functions (human capital, finance, facilities), as well as summary reporting of operational activities and readiness need wide exposure for Defense, Homeland, and Intelligence senior leaders. Data lakes with robust analytic capabilities and software to build dashboards are enormously valuable at this level. On the other hand, AI model development at this level should be carefully considered and focus on filling gaps in service or agency capabilities, mindful of the potential distance from mission and data experts. Because AI development ideally occurs as close to the mission owners and experts as possible, model development especially for core combat and combat support missions can be less desirable at this cross-department level.

Practically speaking, the relative challenges at this level are illustrated in contrasting the OSD-sponsored Advana effort with the Joint AI Center initiative to work command and control solutions and other core defense mission areas. Advana is an analytics environment created to serve DoD. Based in an Amazon Web Services environment, the Advana program provides an array of software and readily available data sources to support AI-related work. Initially conceptualized in the Comptroller's office focused initially on supporting the DoD audit, Advana expanded the range of data sources and the variety of software over time to provide a robust capability especially pertaining to performance assessment, dashboards, and even some AI-related experimentation. Teams can form data pipelines, configure data storage, perform complex processing and choose from a variety of visualization tools. Advana's early successes arguably stem in large measure from bringing together a variety of high-relevance data sources via API accesses into a data lake to support analytics. The program runs in a cloud-based environment which is inherently scalable; making it relatively easy to spool up new analytics teams and efforts. From a technology perspective, the program is disciplined with respect to adding new software and this is an important case for others. Data and data source variety is tremendously important. From a technology perspective, with minimum essential software in place, data source variety becomes crucially important in driving the value of the Advana program to DoD. Every new piece of software brings along a potential funding, acquisition, implementation, authority to operate, and operations and maintenance tail. New data brought into the environment adhering to the security protocols is a relative light lift but very high value.

The Advana architecture is illustrated in Figure 8-5.

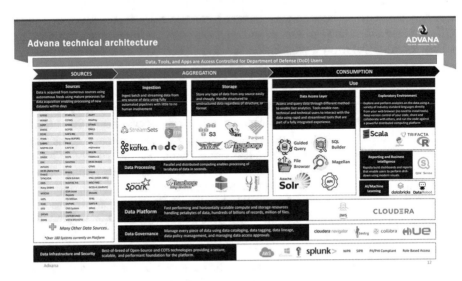

Figure 8-5. Advana technical architecture, July 2021

The Advana environment provides a substantial body of technology for each of the AI project types. In the core of the architecture graphic, note the "data processing" component. Advana is based on the AWS cloud capability and Elastic Compute provides the base processing. In AWS, this allows teams to configure different processor types as virtual machines. For experiments, this provides some latitude in available processor types and will support a range of options for an operational capability underlying an application. In the same area, Apache Spark, Hadoop MapReduce, and Cloudera provide great range with respect to distributing compute jobs across multiple compute nodes and clusters. In each functional block of the architecture, a leader will find solid options for a team working AI-related projects. In the upper right are the programming languages most common for data science work. In the upper middle, all the basic tooling to ingest, store, and manage access to data sources. On the far left is a thumbnail of the data sources, which continue to grow as the program matures.

For leaders working a performance assessment and dashboarding tasks across the Office of Secretary of Defense or Joint Staff, Advana is a logical first consideration as an environment to perform work. From a technology perspective, it is best to leverage what is in Advana now, before thinking first about trying to add new software to the environment. The program welcomes new data sources and as the architecture indicates a variety of tools are available to support ingest, storage, and access.

For cross-department leaders, Advana is a great illustration of two technology selection principles:

- **Focus on data collection/aggregate/sharing.** Robust tooling in Advana and the early program successes on aggregating make it a logical home for other OSD- and joint staff-related efforts in particular.

- **COTS and open-source for basic AI work.** The Advana program nicely covers all the basics. The COTS Qlik Sense software allows for dashboard creation, leveraging point-and-click graphical user interfaces. At the same time, the array of common open-source tools for data exploration and performance assessment address all the common needs for teams.

DevSec Ops product stack

Container management technologies	API gateways	Programming languages	Databases
• Kubernetes	• Kong	• C/C++	• SQL Server
• VMWare Tanzu	• Azure API	• C#/.NET	• MySQL
• PKS	• AWS API	• .NET Core	• PostgreSQL
• OKD	• Axway	• Java	• MongoDB
• Docker EE (K8S only)	• 3 Scale	• PHP	• SQLite
	• Apigee	• Python	• Redis
	• ISTIO (service mesh)	• Groovy	• Elasticsearch
Container packagers		• Ruby	• Oracle
• Helm	• Artifacts	• R	• etcd
• Kubernetes Operators	• Artifactory	• Rust	• Hadoop/HDInsight
	• Nexus	• Scala	• Cloudera
	• Maven	• Perl	• Oracle Big Data
	• Archiva	• GO	• Solr
	• S3 bucket	• Node.JS	• Neo4J
		• Swift	• Memcached
			• Cassandra
			• MariaDB
			• CouchDB
			• InfluxDB (time)

Figure 8-6. Overview of software in JAIC joint common foundation

Transitioning from Advana, another cross-service/agency effort is manifest in the JAIC Joint Common Foundation (JCF) effort, which seeks authority to operate late in 2022 with classified data. As an organization, the JAIC seeks to perform or support AI experimentation and AI model deployment including efforts in core combat and combat support mission areas such as joint all-domain command and control or joint fires. To support this aspiration, JOIC is building the JCF. The JCF also is a cloud-based environment that aspires to serve multiple DoD programs as a place to bring their data and explore AI capabilities.

For cross-department/agency leaders, an important technology question is how many of these environments are truly required and how do they meaningfully differentiate as we seek to accelerate AI deployments? Figure 8-6 illustrates the software packages available in the JCF, which would align to the functional type decomposition in the Advana architecture (meaning data processing, ingest, storage, access, exploration, visualization, etc.). Many of these capabilities are quite similar to those in Advana or other options like USAF Platform One. At some level, this should not surprise leaders because the major technical building blocks are not infinite, while the array of discrete software packages in the market is vast.

Two technology considerations and a service-oriented issue represent emphasis issues for cross-department/agency leaders:

- **Creating new cloud environments versus tenancy on existing environments.** The Navy Jupiter program is a fantastic example of this basic choice. The Navy needed to address financial as well as other enterprise reporting issues. The service could have created a new cloud environment, aggregated data, and built dashboards. Instead, Jupiter is a tenant in the Advana environment allowing the service to move much more rapidly to the desired capability. In the cloud environments standing up the initial capabilities and accounts are the longer-timeline activities. Once established, it is a shorter path to establish tenant relationships. This "make versus leverage" decision is a key technology choice for senior leaders at this level.

- **Platform versus service.** The Intelligence Community created CS2 to deliver AWS commercial cloud capabilities across the IC. It is another thing altogether to create an organization to build AI solutions. Navy Project Overmatch, as an example, is focused on laying down a computing, software, and network foundation expecting the AI models and projects will be executed by a wide range of organizations on the platform. It is an entirely different posture to aspire to provide a platform and build models from a centralized position.

Summary View of Technology Issues by Role. The aspiration of this chapter is to highlight the major issues leaders should probe in shaping plans or in influencing development. With existing systems, a number of gaps will be present and present needs for new programs or re-prioritization or even re-programming decisions. Because the AI pay-off may be uncertain, finding ways to leverage performance assessments and experiments on existing technology environments helps to mitigate investment risks while progressing toward a more AI-enabled future.

Table 8-1 summarizes the major technology emphasis issues addressed in this section.

Table 8-1. Technology Emphasis Issues by Leader Role

Department/Agency-Level Leaders	PEO Leaders	Program Leader	AI Project Leader	Cross-Department/Agency Leaders
• Data Capture/ Aggregation/ Enhancement/Sharing	• Integrative Data Collection/Aggregation/ Sharing	• Runtime Environments	• Ability to leverage current environment with no change	• Creating New Cloud Environment versus Establishing Tenancy on Existing
• Infrastructure and Process	• Identifying Solution Paths for New Models	• AI Model Training Environments	• Lead time is new HW or SW	• Platform versus Service
• Tracking and Monitoring		• COTS versus Custom Build	• Ability to use a cloud environment beyond the organization	
		• Cloud versus On-Premise Computing Environment		

About aiLeaders

We believe that national security begins with making sense of data about the world. We believe that collaboration between humans and AI solutions can give America a competitive advantage over adversaries. And we believe that winning in the AI era requires leaders who are equipped to drive practical results in AI programs and projects. Equipping those leaders is our focus.

aiLeaders is a boutique advisory firm created to provide leaders the objective, expert consulting and coaching their organizations need to compete and win with AI. The founders of aiLeaders, Chris Whitlock and Frank Strickland, have over five decades combined of practical experience leading analytics and AI in the private and public sectors. They are uniquely experienced and incentivized to help your organization develop the leaders and create the strategies to compete and win using advanced analytics and AI.

Index

Printed in the United States
by Baker & Taylor Publisher Services